IN PURSUIT OF PROFESSIONAL GOALS

In Pursuit of Professional Goals

Selected Addresses and Articles by

George R. Catlett and Norman O. Olson

1960 - 1972

Library of Congress
Catalog Card No. 72-96308

This book contains addresses and articles by two of the leaders of the firm of Arthur Andersen & Co. A list of the volumes prepared in this manner follows:

Title	Author
Behind the Figures	Arthur Andersen
A Search for Fairness in Financial Reporting to the Public	Leonard Spacek
Footsteps Toward Professionalism	Joseph S. Glickauf
In Pursuit of Professional Goals	George R. Catlett and Norman O. Olson

Foreword

FOR MANY YEARS George R. Catlett and Norman O. Olson have been closely associated in their work in the firm in the Chicago and St. Louis offices and more recently as Chairman and Vice Chairman of the firm's Committee on Accounting Principles and Auditing Procedures. The publication of some of their addresses and articles together in this book is most appropriate.

The accounting profession in the last ten years has been going through a very trying and disconcerting period when many serious problems have arisen. Accounting principles, auditing procedures, reporting practices, and ethical rules have been under attack from many sources. Questions involving scope of practice, independence, and conflicts of interest have arisen. Under these circumstances, Messrs. Catlett and Olson have in their addresses and articles recommended a course of action for the profession that could represent real progress established on a solid foundation.

Their general theme has been that the public is entitled to the very best in financial information at all times, that soundly conceived objectives are essential, and that no profession can serve the public interest adequately if its service is simply rendered on the basis of minimum legal or technical requirements. Also, outmoded customs cannot be effectively superseded merely by a consensus approach.

Accounting principles should be based on those concepts that best serve investors and all other users of financial statements. Auditing procedures should be carefully determined and executed in a competent and independent manner. Ethical rules should be for the benefit of the public rather than for the protection of auditors. Only by having a clear vision of what is actually needed and the best way to accomplish it can the accounting profession assume its proper role in our society.

Our firm has for many years been dedicated to the establishment of the highest possible standards in accounting and auditing, for the profession as well as for our own practice. Messrs. Catlett and Olson, along with all of the personnel of the firm, have been doing their part toward accomplishing this mission.

The attainment of excellence in all aspects of service should be the major goal of every profession. Since this and other professional objectives necessarily have elements of idealism, it is to be expected that the pursuit of goals will continue indefinitely. The accounting profession, however, should not get buried in the details of its daily work and thus lose sight of its ideals.

PAUL D. WILLIAMS

George R. Catlett

About George R. Catlett

Mr. Catlett grew up in Fairmount, Illinois. He received his B.S. and M.S. degrees from the University of Illinois and was employed by the Chicago office of Arthur Andersen & Co. in 1940. He was in procurement work for the Army Ordnance Corps from 1942 to 1946, becoming a major.

After military service, he became a manager in 1946 and a partner in 1952. He was in the St. Louis office from 1953 to 1958. He then returned to the Chicago office, and in 1962 became Chairman of the Committee on Accounting Principles and Auditing Procedures, a position he still holds.

Mr. Catlett was a member of the Accounting Principles Board of the American Institute of Certified Public Accountants from 1965 to 1971, and was vice chairman during the last three years. He has also been a member of the Council and several committees of the Institute.

He has been president of the Illinois Society of Certified Public Accountants, the Alumni Association of the College of Commerce and Business Administration of the University of Illinois, the Board of Directors of the University of Illinois Athletic Association, and the Chicago Chapter of the American Ordnance Association. He is also a member of the American Accounting Association, the National Association of Accountants, and various civic and charitable organizations.

He was selected by the Society of Accounting Students, University of Hartford, to receive its 1972 National Merit Award for distinguished service and accomplishment in the accounting profession.

He is the author of several articles in accounting magazines and is co-author (with Mr. Olson) of "Accounting for Goodwill," published by the AICPA as Accounting Research Study No. 10.

Norman O. Olson

About Norman O. Olson

Mr. Olson is a native of St. James, Minnesota. He received his B.A. degree from St. Olaf College, majoring in economics and history. After serving three and one-half years as a naval officer during the Second World War he attended the University of Minnesota and earned his M.A. degree in 1948 in the fields of accounting and economics.

He was employed by the Chicago office of Arthur Andersen & Co. in 1948, was made a manager and transferred to the St. Louis office in 1953, and became a partner in 1958. In 1962 he returned to Chicago, where he is Vice Chairman of the Committee on Accounting Principles and Auditing Procedures.

Mr. Olson is a member of the Illinois Society of Certified Public Accountants and the American Institute of Certified Public Accountants. He is chairman of the AICPA Committee on Accounting for Companies in the Development Stage and a former member of the AICPA Committee on Auditing Procedure. He has also served as a member and chairman of the Illinois Board of Examiners in Accountancy.

He is involved in many civic and charitable activities. He is a member of the Board of Trustees of Lutheran General and Deaconess Hospitals in Park Ridge, Illinois, and served as Chairman of that Board for several years. He is also a member of the Executive Board of the Norwegian-American Historical Association and a past president of the National Alumni Association of St. Olaf College.

He has written several articles for accounting magazines and is co-author (with Mr. Catlett) of "Accounting for Goodwill," published by the AICPA as Accounting Research Study No. 10.

Contents

Selected Addresses and Articles by
George R. Catlett and Norman O. Olson

Relation of acceptance to accounting principles

Adapted from an article in *The Journal of Accountancy*, March 1960—Catlett

General acceptance is not necessarily the best test of the soundness of accounting principles.

"GENERALLY ACCEPTED accounting principles" is a term that is an integral part of the standard form of auditors' opinion relating to financial statements. This term is referred to frequently throughout accounting literature and is also incorporated in many legal documents. The two modifying words, generally accepted, have had a significant effect on the development and meaning of accounting principles.

Accounting Terminology Bulletin Number 1 (issued in 1953 by the American Institute of Certified Public Accountants Committee on Terminology as a review and resume of bulletins previously issued) sets forth various definitions of the word, principle. In this connection, the Bulletin states as follows:

> This third definition ["A general law or rule adopted or professed as a guide to action; a settled ground or basis of conduct or practice"] comes nearest to describing what most accountants, especially practicing public accountants, mean by the word *principle.* Initially, accounting postulates are derived from experience and reason; after postulates so derived have proved useful, they become accepted as principles of accounting. When this acceptance is sufficiently widespread, they become a part of the "generally accepted accounting principles" which constitute for accountants the canons of their art. It is not convenient, either in conversation or in writing on accounting subjects, to add "(meaning number three)" each time the word *principle* is used, though that essentially is understood.

As indicated in the above definition, general acceptance has been considered to be the basis on which accounting principles rest.

The term, accounting principles, as used by accountants covers not only the underlying and basic concepts and standards but also the conventions, practices, and procedures followed. The exceptions and comments included in auditors' opinions with respect to the appropriateness of the accounting principles applied in the preparation of financial statements and the consistent application thereof refer to practices and procedures as well as to basic concepts.

Until about 1933, auditors' opinions were directed primarily at the fair presentation of financial statements. At that time a need for some standard against which to judge financial statements became evident, and public accountants adopted the practice of referring to "accepted principles of accounting" in expressing their opinions on financial statements. A few years later this term became "generally accepted accounting principles."

This particular terminology was adopted in order to achieve some uniformity in the determination and application of accounting principles, and to obtain a wider support of some of the practices sponsored by the American Institute of Certified Public Accountants, the Securities and Exchange Commission, and the New York Stock Exchange.

If accounting principles are dependent upon acceptance, the first question is—acceptance by whom? Considering the literature that is available on this subject, one would assume that an answer could readily be found. However, this is not the case.

In attempting to determine what constitutes general acceptance, a wide variety of viewpoints can be found, some of which are as follows:

1. Actual usage in business and industry is required because accounting principles must be accepted by business managements and not be imposed upon them.
2. Accountants in public practice have a responsibility to be discharged in this area, and acceptance by them is a necessary prerequisite.
3. Pronouncements of the American Institute of CPAs are said to be the most authoritative statements and, therefore, are the best evidence of acceptance. A similar view is held by some with respect to the pronouncements of the American Accounting Association.
4. The entire accounting profession (accountants in public accounting, industry, education, and government) must be involved in any general acceptance.
5. General acceptance results only from authoritative support by those best qualified to render accounting judgments.
6. General acceptance may, in some instances, result from laws and governmental regulations applying to business organizations.

The actual use of accounting principles in business and industry as a necessary indication of general acceptance can be supported on a logical basis. However, history indicates that managements of business organizations have not always followed sound accounting practices, that managements are sometimes under pressure to show the most favorable financial position and operating results under the alternative accounting practices available to them, and that there is a tendency at times for inadequate practices to be followed and thus to become accepted by custom. Therefore, actual usage in business and industry may indicate acceptance, but such usage does not necessarily assure soundness.

Public accountants have an important responsibility to discharge when they give opinions relating to financial statements. Acceptance of accounting principles by this group would appear to be essential. However, acceptance by public accountants alone would not seem sufficient to constitute general acceptance.

Acceptance by whom?

Some accountants contend that pronouncements of the American Institute become generally accepted, and may be so considered, because of the eminent position of this organization in the accounting profession. Such pronouncements may lead to general acceptance by the profession, but there is no reason to assume that the opinions of the individuals on an Institute committee would necessarily be conclusive from the standpoint of the profession as a whole. The supplemental notes to the Accounting Research Bulletins issued by the Institute's Committee on Accounting Procedure have specifically stated that "the authority of the bulletins rests upon the general acceptability of opinions so reached."

The pronouncements of the committees of the Institute and the AAA have not been in agreement in all respects. Also, these committees have covered different areas of principles and practices, and neither one has covered some areas where current problems exist. The 1957 revision of Accounting and Reporting Standards for Corporate Financial Statements, published by the Committee on Accounting Concepts and Standards of the AAA, makes no reference to "general acceptance" of the recommendations.

Recognition by members of the accounting profession as evidence of acceptance may have some merit. The accounting profession, however, consists not only of members of the Institute and the AAA, but it also includes all public accountants and all accountants in business, education, and government. The Controllers Institute of America,* the National Association of Accountants, and other organizations have qualified accountants as members. Some accountants do not belong to any organization. Therefore no one group is in a position to speak with authority for the entire accounting profession.

The viewpoint that the best evidence of acceptance is authoritative support of those most qualified to render accounting judgments (whoever they may be) sounds impressive, but this test would be very difficult to explain or to apply in actual practice.

Laws and governmental regulation relating to accounting principles may attain general acceptance because no practical alternatives may be available to business. Fortunately this has not been a major factor up to the present time, and the accounting profession should make every effort to avoid any further trend in this direction.

The only conclusion that can reasonably be reached is that there is no clear understanding as to the identity of those by whom accounting principles must be generally accepted.

Acceptance to what extent?

Even if it could be decided to whom accounting principles must be acceptable, how can it be determined when there is general acceptance? Since general acceptance does not necessarily represent a majority, what is a minimum acceptance and how does anyone know when it exists? In some industries widely varying practices are followed and changes in practices are occurring; under these circumstances the financial statements present completely different results. Thus, there may be two or more different practices relating to the same kind of transactions which are considered to be generally accepted and are so described in the various auditors' opinions. Determination as to when a new practice becomes acceptable and an old practice ceases to be acceptable is very difficult for the individual accountant and it presents a serious problem even for the large public accounting firms.

A governmental body, such as the Securities and Exchange Commission, may pre-

*Now the Financial Executives Institute.

scribe an accounting requirement which, by the nature of its influence on both business and the accounting profession, may become generally accepted. However, the SEC has usually followed the lead of the accounting profession (particularly the American Institute), and it may continue to do so if the profession demonstrates the necessary leadership in meeting the accounting problems of our rapidly changing times. A most unsatisfactory situation would exist if governmental organizations such as the SEC were the only ones who could obtain general acceptance of the changes that are needed.

Generally, acceptance can easily be judged when practically all of the business community and the accounting profession are following a particular accounting practice; but during periods of transition and change it becomes quite difficult for the accountant to know which of the alternative practices are generally accepted and which are not. There is no measuring device available.

Financial statements on which accountants in public practice express their opinions are being used more widely than ever before by stockholders, management, creditors, customers, investors, labor organizations, and governmental bodies. Therefore progress and improvement in accounting principles on a sound and logical basis is necessary. Otherwise the accounting profession will not be living up to its responsibilities and will certainly retrogress.

How does "generally accepted" affect progress and improvement? Assuming that some important improvements are necessary and possible (and it would be very unfortunate to assume otherwise), let us consider the question once asked by a new junior in an accounting firm: "If financial statements of a corporation should be prepared in accordance with generally accepted accounting principles, how can the corporation ever improve its financial reporting to meet changing conditions and new requirements when it is limited to the accounting principles and practices that are generally accepted?" This question might also be asked by experienced businessmen and accountants, and it is not easy to answer.

Improvements in accounting

There has been considerable discussion in the accounting profession with respect to such subjects as providing for depreciation in excess of that on historical cost to reflect changes in price levels and recording long-term lease obligations in balance sheets. Without going into the pros and cons of the arguments on these subjects, assume for purposes of illustration only that they do have merit and should be done. Financial statements incorporating practices such as these are not acceptable to most public accountants or to the SEC, and the principal reason given for this position is that the proposed practices are not generally accepted. How, then, can progress ever be made? Has such a strong artificial barrier been established that no significant changes can be made, since the first few cases can never be in accordance with generally accepted accounting principles?

Most accountants would prefer that the profession rather than the SEC take the lead in improving accounting principles and practices. One of the first hurdles any company faces when possible accounting improvements are suggested by management is that the public accountant must take exception in his opinion relating to the financial statements because the practice is not generally accepted. The managements of most publicly held companies do not want this type of exception in the auditors' opinion, since it probably would be misunderstood by many stockholders and others. Managements frequently are frustrated when they want to be progressive and make improvements that seem obviously desirable to them, since the public accountants cannot give an unqualified opinion (even when they agree with the management) because the proposed practice cannot be said to be "generally accepted."

Evolutionary process

The evolutionary process relating to new developments in accounting principles and related practices can be stated briefly. This process tends to follow a course that might be divided into five general phases. Assuming significant amounts are involved, these phases are as follows:

Phase 1—where no general acceptance exists in business or in the accounting profession of either the basic principle or the related practice. An example of this is price-level depreciation. If such depreciation in excess of that on historical cost is provided by a company, disclosure is required in the financial statements, and the public accountants take exception in their opinion to the fact that this practice is not in conformity with generally accepted accounting principles even though they approve of it.

Phase 2—where general acceptance of the basic principle exists, but the related practice is not in accordance with the principle. An example of this is the recording of long-term lease obligations and reflecting them as liabilities in the balance sheet under the principle of recording all liabilities. Most companies do not record such lease obligations and public accountants do not generally recommend this practice, although a few companies, with the approval of their public accountants, have done so. The degree of disclosure in financial statements with respect to information relating to long-term leases varies considerably.

Phase 3—where general acceptance of the basic principle exists, but there are several alternative practices, some of which fall short of the principle. An example of this exists with respect to provisions for pension plan costs under the principle of providing for all costs. There is no majority practice. Many public accountants give unqualified opinions on almost any of the alternative practices, but a few take exception if reasonable provisions are not made.

Phase 4—where general acceptance of the basic principle exists, but there are related alternative practices, one of which is the majority practice. An example of such a majority practice occurs in the capitalization of intangible drilling costs on productive wells in the oil industry under the principle of matching costs and revenues. The minority practice is the charging of such costs to expense as incurred. Some public accountants give unqualified opinions on either of the alternative practices, and others take exception in their opinions if the costs are charged to expense as incurred.

Phase 5—where general acceptance of the basic principle exists, and there is recognition of that principle in practice, with no significant alternative practices. Under these circumstances, most public accountants take exception in their opinions if a contrary practice is followed.

These transitional phases have occurred and are occurring, usually over a period of many years, but new accounting principles and practices may not go through all five phases. It is recognized that an evolutionary type of transition usually cannot be accomplished quickly and that a period of experimentation may be necessary, but some of the transitional hurdles may represent roadblocks that favor the status quo, and those companies and accountants who seek improvements tend to be penalized for their efforts. Furthermore, the present-day responsibility of public accountants to meet the accelerated pace of business developments may not permit leisurely transition periods of ten to fifteen years or longer.

Alternative practices

Accountants generally recognize that accounting principles are not scientific laws and must constantly be adjusted to meet changing conditions in order to be of maximum usefulness to all groups in our society who rely on financial statements. Uniformity in the application of accounting principles makes financial statements more useful.

However, a wide variety of alternative accounting practices exists today. Diversities of practices under similar conditions, with significant effects on the resulting financial statements, may meet the test of flexibility, but they do not develop confidence in such statements by the persons who use them.

Instances could be cited where three different practices, with widely varying effects on the financial statements, are followed under similar circumstances in the same industry. The criterion of general acceptance has eliminated some alternative practices, but it has also been used as an excuse to justify other alternative practices that did not previously exist.

Provision for costs under pension plans might be taken as an example. Pension plans with fixed retirement benefits have been in existence for many years, and they have become quite common in the last five to ten years. Under a fair interpretation of sound accounting principles, the cost of such plans should be accrued as an employment cost on some reasonable basis over the period that employees under the plan are working. However, the actual practices followed vary from "pay-as-you-go" to a full provision for all current-service and past-service costs over the employment period. In many instances the differences are quite significant. Accounting Research Bulletin Number 47, issued by the American Institute's Committee on Accounting Procedure in 1956 (and still effective), stated that "the Committee believes that opinion as to the accounting for pension costs has not yet crystallized sufficiently to make it possible at this time to assure agreement on any one method, and that differences in accounting for pension costs are likely to continue for a time." Enough companies are following each of many different practices so that most of them are considered to be generally accepted, and unqualified opinions are being given by many public accountants on financial statements prepared under this wide diversity of practices.

Generally accepted vs. sound

"Comparability" and "uniformity" are terms that are sometimes referred to in a derogatory manner by accountants as connoting an undesirable rigidity and an attempt to put them in strait jackets. Those persons who argue against comparable financial statements and uniform accounting principles are failing to recognize the real issues. If investors, creditors, and others are confused and misled by invalid comparisons and misstated results under the guise of general acceptance, the accounting profession is certain to be called upon sometime to justify its course of action in the court of public opinion.

Public accountants, under the guidance of the American Institute, have chosen to refer in their opinions on financial statements to "generally accepted accounting principles" rather than to "sound accounting principles." The main arguments sometimes advanced in favor of "generally accepted" are: (1) general acceptance results in more uniformity; (2) when a practice becomes generally accepted, it must be sound; and (3) when soundness, rather than acceptability, is the criterion, the only assurance of the reasonableness of the results is the judgment and reputation of individual accountants or firms, and their conclusions cannot be challenged on an objective basis.

These arguments do not have the merit that they did twenty years ago. Public accountants during the intervening period have assumed increased responsibilities as a profession and have achieved greater competence. They must stand behind their judgment and their opinions, and there is no reason at all why their conclusions cannot be challenged. Also it is a well-known fact that general acceptance has not always reflected soundness in the past, and this same lack of soundness exists in some areas at the present time.

When public accountants give opinions that financial statements "present fairly . . .

in conformity with . . . accounting principles," should the principal requirement be that the practices followed are generally accepted, or that sound practices have been followed with the result that statements fairly present the financial information under the circumstances? In my opinion, a fair presentation is the real test. Generally accepted accounting principles should be compatible with a fair presentation, but there has been a strong tendency to let "acceptance" cloud the issues in actual practice.

Some accountants in public practice have taken the position that their responsibility under the standard form of opinion is to determine that financial statements "present fairly . . . in conformity with" accounting principles and practices that have some degree of acceptance. With this viewpoint, they are thus protected and are not required to decide whether the financial position and results of operations are really presented on a sound basis in a particular case. This view, of course, is deplorable when considered in terms of the responsibility assumed by public accountants.

If the accounting profession is to attain the responsibility and recognition in our society that it is seeking, the principal emphasis with respect to accounting principles should be changed from general acceptance to a determination and defense of sound accounting principles. Acceptance would usually follow as a matter of course.

Conclusion

The development and use of sound accounting principles should be the most important objective of the accounting profession. The problem becomes one of determining the best way to accomplish this objective.

The criterion of "generally accepted" as related to accounting principles has achieved uniformity in some important areas and has served to retard the attainment of desirable uniformity in other important areas. Alternative practices have flourished. The principles that have been generally accepted have not always proved to be sound and have not always resulted in a fair presentation in the financial statements. The test of general acceptance has hindered progress as much as it has encouraged progress. There is no common understanding concerning "by whom" there should be general acceptance or "to what extent" it should exist. No group of accountants has been in a position to judge the degree of acceptance. As a result of all of this, the conclusion might well be reached that a new approach would be more effective.

Accounting is generally recognized to be more of an art than a science, and it must serve a useful purpose. Enough flexibility to meet changing conditions and varying circumstances is required, and too much rigidity would not be practicable. On the other hand, wide diversities in the principles and practices followed in preparing financial statements under similar situations undermine the confidence in such statements by the millions of stockholders and investors, as well as by the large number of creditors, labor organizations, governmental bodies, and others who use the statements. A proper balance must be achieved between the necessary flexibility and a desirable degree of uniformity and comparability.

"Sound accounting principles" should, in my opinion, be the focal point around which the accounting profession builds its future. Our current accounting problems should be studied and solved on the basis of merit, after careful consideration of the cumulative experience of the business world and the accounting profession. Accountants in public practice should not hide behind the hazy veil of "general acceptance." The accounting profession should meet its responsibility in as direct a manner as possible and be held accountable for the results.

The new Accounting Principles Board of the American Institute has an unusual opportunity to assume leadership on behalf of the accounting profession in the determination of sound accounting principles in a way that was never accomplished by the Committee on Accounting Procedure. One of the reasons it has been necessary to rely on "general acceptance" is that the accounting profession has never effectively assumed the responsibility of determining sound accounting principles on an overall basis. The task of the Board will be extremely difficult and will require considerable study and effort. However, a series of basic objectives and concepts could be developed and promulgated, so that a body of accounting literature on this subject would progressively be made available. The future of the accounting profession may be more dependent upon the success of the Board's activities in this area than is generally realized.

The Board will not be in a position to dictate sound accounting principles, but there is every reason to believe that the results of a well-conceived and executed program would meet with considerable success and acceptance, not only in the accounting profession but also in business practice. Our complex corporate system, with widening stock ownership and increasing conflicting interests, may be faced with more and more governmental control of its accounting unless the accounting profession assumes the leadership that is required.

Factors that influence accounting principles

Adapted from an article in *The Journal of Accountancy*, October 1960—Catlett

Sound accounting principles could represent a framework of professional standards that would become generally accepted because of merit and not because of custom.

ACCOUNTING HAS BEEN created and developed to accomplish various desired objectives and, therefore, it is not based on fundamental laws or absolute precepts. Accounting has evolved over many years through trial and error, and it should be continually advanced and improved on a basis that is responsive to the requirements of the various groups in our society who use the end product—the financial statements.

The accounting profession has a tendency to overemphasize precedent and to view its problems in retrospect. History is an interesting record of human experiences, but analysis and discussion of the past are helpful only to the extent that they are of assistance in performing a more useful service. Therefore, a continuous reappraisal of accounting principles in the light of both past experience and current circumstances is necessary.

Considerable emphasis has been placed on the "general acceptance" of accounting principles. The viewpoint that this is not necessarily the best test of such principles was discussed previously in another article.[1]

Changes in economic and social conditions have had some effect on accounting principles and their application, but in this area the accounting profession has too often looked backward rather than forward. The improvements in accounting principles and practices during the last twenty-five years have lagged behind the developments in scientific research, production, marketing and distribution methods, and management techniques in this era of atomic power, electronic computers, jet airplanes, and wonder drugs. Accounting principles and practice have not kept pace during this

1. "Relation of Acceptance to Accounting Principles," *The Journal of Accountancy*, March 1960. (Beginning on page 1 of this book.)

period with the needs of our democratic, free enterprise system.

The suggestion has sometimes been made that the term, accounting principles, is misleading and creates the wrong impression, because it indicates a precision that is not actually possible. This term could be changed, but there does not seem to be a better alternative, and any substitute that would convey the idea that there is less than an authoritative basis for accounting might not serve the desired purpose. Admittedly some confusion exists with respect to terminology, but the real challenge to our profession is not a revision of words or the clarification of definitions but the development of underlying postulates and concepts to provide a proper basis for the determination of appropriate accounting principles and practices.

What are some of the factors, in addition to general acceptance, that have had an important influence on accounting principles? These factors might be classified under the general headings of conservatism, consistency, disclosure and governmental regulation.

Conservatism

Conservatism results in resolving doubts in favor of understating assets and current income and overstating liabilities and current expenses. This is a philosophy or attitude and not an accounting postulate or principle. Conservatism has generally been considered by the accounting profession to be a prime virtue, and it has had some very subtle and far-reaching effects on accounting. It is inherent in such accounting principles and practices as valuing inventories at the lower of cost or market, anticipating losses but not anticipating gains, carrying property at original cost less depreciation or depletion when fair value may be considerably higher, and reflecting investments in unconsolidated subsidiaries at cost when underlying book value is greater.

Conservatism is only relative, since what may be conservative to one person may be nonconservative to someone else. For example, what is conservative to a creditor may be misrepresentation to a selling stockholder. CPAs have generally concluded, as a result of experience, that in case of doubt it is preferable to lean in the direction of caution, even though this cannot always be supported from a purely logical or theoretical standpoint.

Accounting for business activities many years ago was naturally conservative since it was essentially on a cash basis or was primarily for completed ventures. As the need has grown for the financial measurement of numerous transactions in various stages of completion, the problems have increased tremendously, but some of the obsolete accounting characteristics have been retained.

In the case of family-owned companies, the managements may be interested in a philosophy of ultraconservatism that results in keeping net assets and net profits as low as possible for various reasons, including those related to income and inheritance taxes. Creditors, such as banks and insurance companies, have generally preferred conservative financial statements with emphasis on liquidating values. This situation still exists to some extent, but there has been a trend away from overconservatism with the advent of professional managements, widespread and constantly changing stock ownership, and a general shift in the interest of creditors to earning power and away from liquidating values.

Conservatism has not only influenced accounting principles, but it has also been one of the reasons for the wide variety of alternative accounting practices that are all considered to be "generally accepted." An analysis of such practices will indicate that many of them reflect different degrees of conservatism. This is illustrated by the following examples of practices that generally result in a more conservative balance sheet and tend to result in a more conservative current income statement:

1. The LIFO method of inventory costing as compared with the FIFO method.
2. The charging of research and development costs to expense as incurred as compared with capitalizing such costs.
3. A full accrual of pension plan costs as compared with a partial or minimum accrual.
4. The completed-contract method for construction companies as compared with the percentage-of-completion method.
5. Recording in the accounts the accelerated depreciation allowed for Federal income tax purposes as compared with the recording of straight-line depreciation.

Company managements frequently select from the alternative practices available to them on the basis of the degree of conservatism they prefer, rather than on the basis of the principles involved or the practices that might best reflect the actual facts.

One fact that is sometimes overlooked is that conservative accounting may result in a nonconservative income statement at a later time. Costs and expenses that are applicable to future operations and are incurred for the purpose of producing income in subsequent years are in many instances charged off currently because of a conservative point of view or because there may be no conclusive indication that they will be recovered. Thus, costs may not be matched with revenues that are produced as a result of such costs. The argument is sometimes made that a corresponding group of costs may be incurred and charged off in later years, which may approximate the amortization charge that would have resulted had such costs been capitalized in prior years. The deferment of costs where appropriate should not be disregarded merely because a continuation of the unsound practice may offset the erroneous effect in future periods.

Operating loss carry-forward credits for Federal income tax purposes are not ordinarily recorded as assets, primarily because there is no assurance that the credit will be realized later on. The credit when actually realized is usually added to income of that year rather than what would seem to be the preferable approach of taking it directly to earned surplus as a retroactive adjustment of the prior years in which the losses occurred. As a result, the net income of a current year may be greatly inflated as a result of losses in prior years. In such a case, a conservative practice relating to the balance sheet may result in a much higher degree of nonconservatism in the income statement.

One of the principal arguments used against the accounting recognition of the change in the purchasing power of the dollar is that this would result in an upward restatement of assets, which is unthinkable because of the fiasco in the 1920's involving appraisal write-ups. On the other hand, the lack of recognition of increased costs due to price-level changes related to property and other assets has, in my opinion, resulted in overstated profits, which is certainly not conservative.

A proper degree of caution and prudence in accounting is desirable and necessary, since an uncontrolled lack of conservatism could be disastrous. However, conservative accounting practices may in some instances misrepresent the facts as much as nonconservative practices.

Consistency

The standard form of auditor's opinion states that the accounting principles have been "applied on a basis consistent with that of the preceding year." Consistency is important if comparisons of financial statements are to be made from year to year and if trends are to have any significance. Material changes in the application of accounting principles may be made by a business from time to time, and the fact that such changes are made is generally disclosed, as well as the effect of the changes if it is practicable to determine it.

Some accountants take the position that the choice among various alternative practices is not as important as the consistent application of the practices selected. However, this seems to result in the viewpoint (whether it is fully realized or not) that it is all right to be wrong, as long as you are consistently wrong. The distinction between alternative practices may not always be as clear-cut as "right" and "wrong," but not all of such practices present the facts in an equally satisfactory manner.

The accounting profession might well consider Ralph Waldo Emerson's statement, "A foolish consistency is the hobgoblin of little minds, adored by little statesmen and philosophers and divines."

Consistency is a desirable attribute in accounting and the preparation of financial statements, but it does not represent a principle, and it should not be used as an excuse to justify the continuance of unsound practices.

Disclosure

Financial statements and the related footnotes should disclose any significant information necessary for a proper understanding and evaluation of the financial position and results of operations of an enterprise. In other words, there should not be a failure to disclose any material facts required to make the financial statements not misleading.

The concept of adequate disclosure of significant data is, of course, commendable. However, in some instances this has resulted in many complicated footnotes that are technically correct, but not particularly informative or understandable to the average reader.

Disclosure has been used to some extent by accountants as a defensive and protective measure. In some cases, unsound accounting practices have been justified on the basis of disclosure. In other cases, footnote coverage of significant facts has been considered to be a substitute for appropriate adjustment of the accounts. The line of reasoning that about any practice with some acceptance can be followed as long as its use is disclosed was expressed in 1932 as follows:

> "The more practicable alternative would be to leave every corporation free to choose its own methods of accounting within the very broad limits to which reference has been made, but require disclosure of the methods employed and consistency in their application from year to year."[2]

The above philosophy is still being followed to a considerable extent by the accounting profession.

Many of the accounting problems in actual practice arise from questions involving the timing of the recognition of income and costs between accounting periods. Various possible alternatives may have a significant effect on net income for individual periods, and the mere disclosure of the practices selected is of questionable value. With the wide publicity given earnings per share, and the use of financial information by an increasing number of stockholders and others who are not well informed on accounting matters, additional emphasis is required in the direction of simplified financial statements prepared on the basis of sound accounting principles. It should not be necessary to read and understand the fine print of voluminous footnotes or technical parenthet-

2. Quoted from a letter dated September 22, 1932, written by the American Institute's Special Committee on Cooperation with Stock Exchanges to the Committee on Stock List, New York Stock Exchange.

ical comments before knowing whether the figures in the financial statements are reliable and really mean what the reader has a right to assume they mean.

Disclosure is a necessary phase of financial reporting, but it should not be used as a crutch to lean on or as a justification for alternative practices.

Governmental regulation

Governmental regulation, both by laws and by administrative action, has had a significant influence on accounting principles. Such regulation can be classified in two general categories; levying of taxes and safeguarding the public interest.

The Federal income tax statutes and regulations have had an effect on many accounting practices. Some company managements prefer to keep their accounts on the same basis for both financial accounting and tax purposes for the sake of simplicity, or they may believe that the use of a different method in their accounts might jeopardize what they consider to be a favorable basis for tax purposes. Many are influenced to such an extent by high tax rates (presently more than 50 percent for many companies) that this overshadows other aspects of accounting.

While in some respects the accounting for the determination of Federal income taxes may not be in accordance with sound accounting principles, the accounting required for tax purposes may be desirable for raising revenues, for encouraging the development of natural resources and selected industries, for assisting small business, and for many other reasons. However, the accounting profession must recognize that income tax statutes and regulations are not intended to establish and do not necessarily reflect sound accounting principles for financial reporting purposes.

Governmental regulation with respect to safeguarding the public interest has concerned itself primarily with such matters as the rates and prices to be charged customers, as in the case of public utilities; the management of the public's funds by banks, savings and loan associations, trust companies, insurance companies, etc.; the information to be given to the public in connection with the sale of securities; and the formation of corporations and certain corporate activities. My comments are not directed to the need or desirability of these responsibilities that have been assumed by the Federal and state governments. Such regulation has been established by representatives elected by the citizens of our country and exists for specific purposes. It is appropriate that the responsible agencies should require various reports and other data needed by them in the administration of the applicable laws.

The accounting profession should, of course, cooperate fully with the Federal and state regulatory agencies in the performance of their duties, but it should, at the same time, make every effort to narrow the gap between accounting principles prescribed by them and sound accounting principles. This, of course, will take time. In the meantime, those accounting practices that are prescribed for regulatory purposes should not be controlling in the determination and use of sound accounting principles for other purposes merely because they are prescribed by a governmental agency.

Conflicting interest in our society

Federal and state statutes are enacted for social, economic or political purposes. Such laws establish the facts to be accounted for and may affect the results of the application of accounting principles, but laws do not necessarily establish or determine proper accounting principles. Furthermore, it will be most unfortunate if accounting principles and practices for financial accounting and reporting purposes are ever legislated for business generally by our political representatives or by agencies created by them, as is presently being done in the case of insurance companies. If the accounting profession determines and follows sound accounting principles as a free and democratic group, it will have a much better chance of retaining the right to determine such principles.

Financial statements, with respect to which CPAs give opinions, are read by various types of users, such as stockholders, managements, creditors, employees, governmental agencies, customers and potential investors. Each of these groups has, in varying degrees, conflicting interests which are much more significant today than they were twenty-five years ago. At one time the stock ownership and management of many companies were closely related and the family-type business was common, even among relatively large companies. A trend has been occurring toward professional management (with relatively small stock ownership) and toward wide dispersion of stock ownership to more than thirteen million persons.

Significance of varied interests

An increasing amount of money is being borrowed to finance business, with debtors and creditors having more of an impersonal relationship. Labor organizations have grown much stronger and claim to have a direct interest in the financial reports of companies with which they bargain. Governmental bodies in the field of regulation have increased their authority. Many millions of potential investors are being urged to invest in American business. An interesting aspect of this problem is the fact that many persons have more than one interest; as an example, employees are often customers and may also be stockholders.

The accounting profession has the responsibility for developing accounting principles that are useful and fair to the various groups with conflicting interests and that can be defended when challenged. Otherwise, if a lack of confidence exists, the natural course of action is for such groups to turn to the government for help. This trend is occurring in many other areas, and decisive action is required by the accounting profession to prevent such a further trend from occurring in the field of financial accounting for business.

Importance of uniformity

With conflicting interests such as those that now exist, it is not an easy task to establish accounting principles that meet the tests of maximum usefulness and fairness. A proper balance must be achieved, and this can be accomplished only by a clear and objective analysis of the problems involved and by the use of careful consideration and judgment. While financial statements and related data may take several forms or include various degrees of detailed information for different purposes, it is essential that the basic accounting principles be the same for all enterprises organized for profit and for all industries. However, the application of such principles would vary, depending upon the circumstances.

Determination of accounting principles

Influences which have little to do with accounting principles have played a dominant role in determining the practices followed. The existing philosophy in this regard is based on a self-perpetuating circle of logic that accounting principles are accepted because they are sound and they are sound because they are accepted. This results in "the tail wagging the dog," since many accounting practices are justified merely on the basis of acceptance (custom), which is given more weight than the fairness of the financial presentations that result from their application.

The question exists as to whether it is possible and practicable to determine objective standards against which to evaluate sound accounting principles. In my opinion, such objective standards can be developed. Actually, the major problem facing the profession is not whether this can be done, but how and when the objective can be accomplished.

Sound accounting principles are not scientific laws or absolute rules, and they do not represent perfection. "Sound" is used in the sense of well-founded, reliable, logical and fair. Accounting is not a science and, therefore, cannot be treated as one. Whether the term "accounting principles" is preceded by "generally accepted," by "sound" or by nothing is not particularly important. What is important is that the accounting principles *be* sound. If sound accounting principles are determined, they will probably become generally accepted.

Up to the present time, there has never been a really adequate basis or foundation for accounting principles. The conclusions expressed in accounting literature and committee bulletins have been merely those of individuals expressing their own viewpoints that reflect their personal experiences. Accounting practices have evolved over a period of many years, and authors have developed accounting postulates and principles as a rationalization to support what was already occurring.

The report of the American Institute's Special Committee on Research Program dated September 1958, included the following statement:

> "The broad problem of financial accounting should be visualized as requiring attention at four levels: first, postulates; second, principles; third, rules or other guides for the application of principles in specific situations; and fourth, research."

The postulates are the antecedent conditions or essential prerequisites to accounting principles. The principles must meet the tests of the postulates, and the practices must be supported by the principles. This framework of accounting standards and guides must be developed in that order. Then the accounting profession for the first time could have "sound accounting principles."

There would still be considerable room for judgment by individual accountants in applying these accounting principles in specific cases. However, CPAs would have the responsibility of properly relating the accounting practices followed by companies to the professional standards established. Primary attention could then be given to the "fair presentation" of business facts, and CPAs would not need to be distracted by arguments as to degrees of acceptance or whether conservatism, consistency, and disclosure are more important than principles.

All phases of business are rapidly becoming more international in scope. The world is getting smaller and national boundaries have less significance. Each country has its own laws, customs and conditions, but accounting principles are not entirely nationalistic in nature. "General acceptance" has almost no meaning or significance on an international basis at the present time. "Sound accounting principles" would be a term and a general concept that could be understood by accountants everywhere, and it would serve as a basis for developing a common understanding and solution of their mutual problems.

Responsibility of the profession

CPAs must make up their minds as to whether or not they want to be members of a truly independent and strong profession which will discharge properly its public responsibility. If the profession has the will and determination to assert leadership and take a positive stand, then it will succeed; otherwise, failure, in the long run, is almost inevitable. The profession, in my opinion, has not exerted decisive leadership in the field of accounting principles, particularly in the last twenty-five years. Sufficient recognition has not been given to the necessity of fairness, as previously discussed, and to the fact that accounting principles have not kept pace with other developments in our economic system.

The American Institute is the only nongovernmental organization with any chance of determining sound accounting principles and having them generally recognized as authoritative. For this reason, the Institute has an important responsibility. The Institute's Accounting Principles Board, with its assigned mission and with its research staff and project advisory committees, has an outstanding opportunity to be of service to the accounting profession and the business world generally.

A question may exist as to whether managements of companies and governmental agencies, such as the Securities and Exchange Commission, would accept a determination of sound accounting principles by the American Institute. Also, would such action be considered too presumptive and thus fail from lack of general recognition?

A thorough and well-conceived program conducted on an objective basis should result in conclusions that would be recognized and accepted. If the principles are properly determined and documented by sound reasoning, they will be difficult to disprove or ignore. Some company managements and trade associations would complain about the Institute imposing a "strait jacket" without the authority to do so. However, they would find it most difficult to argue effectively against sound accounting principles objectively determined.

General acceptance of bulletins

An example of how industry has followed a pronouncement reflecting the application of sound accounting principles occurred after Accounting Research Bulletin No. 44 (Revised) was issued by the American Institute's Committee on Accounting Procedure in July 1958. Prior to that time, many companies were deducting accelerated depreciation for income tax purposes and using straight-line depreciation in their accounts, but some of these companies were providing for the deferred tax and some were not. If this Bulletin, which properly recommended deferred-tax accounting, had not been issued, the two alternative practices with widely varying results would have been followed indefinitely, and CPAs would have continued to give opinions that both practices were "generally accepted." There was criticism of this Bulletin from some company managements, but within about a year, it was being followed by almost all companies with the exception of some public utilities, which were exempted under certain conditions. The conclusions in this Bulletin, but for the exception relating to public utilities in some situations, are sound and cannot be challenged effectively.

So long as a wide variety of alternative accounting practices is available as being "generally accepted," companies will use them. The attitude of many managements is that they are not interested in pioneering in the area of accounting principles, and they do not want to do anything that has what they consider to be an adverse effect on their financial statements unless other companies are following similar practices. Therefore, some independent organization must take the lead, since recommended improvements must precede general acceptance.

Neither the American Institute nor any of its committees has chosen to take unilateral action with respect to accounting principles. They have preferred to rely upon the subsequent general acceptance of their pronouncements on specific problems. However, accounting controversies cannot be satisfactorily settled on an item-by-item basis without the proper relationship being established to well-conceived objectives and sound standards, since such problems continue to recur in different forms faster than they can be solved. Under such circumstances, the pronouncements offered as solutions merely become a series of disconnected and unsupported personal preferences of the committee members.

CPAs have a serious and important public responsibility, and the American Institute, which represents them, should be able, after considering the viewpoints of all affected parties, to arrive at appropriate and fair conclusions with respect to accounting principles and to defend such principles. It is recognized that CPAs cannot compel their clients to follow the accounting principles they espouse. On the other hand, clients cannot insist that CPAs give opinions that financial statements "fairly present" the financial position and results of operations unless the CPAs actually have such opinions.

Conclusion

Accounting principles and practices have been influenced considerably, not only by the concept of general acceptance, but also by the factors of conservatism, consistency, disclosure, and governmental regulation. Sufficient recognition has not been given to changes in economic and social conditions or to the purposes which accounting should serve. Thus, what has been "generally accepted" in the past will not meet the tests of the future. CPAs must look forward.

A new trail in the development of accounting principles can be blazed. With sufficient effort and determination, an objective approach is almost certain to be successful, if the interests of all segments of our society are given adequate consideration. Sound accounting principles could represent a framework of professional standards that would become generally accepted because of merit and not because of custom. The risk involved in a positive and constructive course of action is far less than in not assuming the necessary leadership.

Research and development costs in published financial statements

Before the National Association of Accountants Conference on Research and Development, Boston, Massachusetts, February 8, 1963—Catlett

Accounting for research and development costs requires the establishment of objectives in financial reporting and the determination of appropriate criteria.

ACCOUNTING FOR RESEARCH and development costs represents one of the most difficult subjects facing us today. With the technological explosion of recent years, and with increased emphasis on the need to develop new products, research is an integral part of the operations of many companies.

In preparing my comments I did some investigation of this subject, and found that a great deal has been written but little progress has been made in solving the problem. I was reminded of the fact that if you steal from one author it is plagiarism, but if you steal from ten authors it is research.

Most of the discussion at this conference has related to the control of, and the internal accounting for, research and development from the viewpoint of management. Therefore I thought that it might be worthwhile to look at research and development from the standpoint of overall corporate policies as well as the annual report to stockholders, the prospectus for potential investors, the evaluation of the performance of management and the success of a company. My comments relate primarily to company-sponsored rather than government-sponsored research.

Significance of research and development

The significance of research and development today is quite evident. The annual cost of such activities in the United States amounts to many billions of dollars, and is a very important factor in the operations of many companies.

The Financial Analysts Federation, which is made up of the societies of financial and investment analysts in various cities, publishes an annual report, which includes comments on several industries. It has commented on R & D in various reports, and the following statement on the electronic industry was included in its last yearly analysis:

> "Information with respect to research and development is one of the most essential features of the annual report of an electronics company. Most of the reports were very inadequate. We grant that competitive factors are involved and are perhaps even more of a problem than in the sales breakdown, but would observe that seven companies reported in enough detail to warrant a rating . . . well above the average. Satisfactory information includes the amount spent on research and product development, the areas into which research is directed, the organization of research and development activities, how these functions are defined, details regarding government research contracts, the extent to which research outlays are capitalized, and similar matters."

It was also stated that none of the annual reports were completely satisfactory as to R & D, but two were noteworthy, and five were above average. One annual report was commended for including research outlays in the "Highlights" and the ten-year summary.

Although R & D has been receiving attention by managements from an internal standpoint, there has not been sufficient consideration given to it by industry and by the accounting profession from the standpoint of published financial statements and the soundness of the underlying accounting.

This is an area of accounting where alternatives exist. In many cases, companies have the option of (1) charging the costs to expense as incurred, or (2) capitalizing the costs as an asset and amortizing such costs over an arbitrary period of time. Almost no meaningful criteria exist for when the various alternatives should be followed, and little can be said in favor of the accounting being affected very much by the facts.

Accounting research

Most of the research done on accounting for R & D has had little influence on current practices. This subject should be given a very high priority on the agenda of the Accounting Principles Board. A question may exist as to whether this subject can be successfully segregated from other ones dealing with the wide range of intangible assets.

The accounting profession has long made the mistake of trying to deal with individual problems without first establishing a framework within which the problems can be solved in a coordinated and logical manner. I hope that the Accounting Principles Board can see the need to develop some basic premises and to consider what the objectives of financial statements really are. Only in this way can any real progress be made.

Disclosure in financial statements

The disclosure of data relating to R & D in financial statements and in other information in stockholders' reports and prospectuses varies from limited information in a few cases to almost no information in a majority of cases. There are, of course, reasons or excuses for this situation; some of them may have merit, and some of them do not. These reasons are generally considered to be along the following lines:

1. Not customary to disclose such data.
2. Not desirable for competitive reasons.
3. Not required by the Securities and Exchange Commission or the stock exchanges.
4. Not required by independent public accountants.
5. Might be misleading.

You could well ask yourselves whether or not these reasons can be logically supported.

Many examples could be cited of companies and industries in the past that were reluctant to publish information of all sorts, because of competition, government regulation, labor relations, and a host of other such alleged factors. In almost every case the fears were not warranted, and subsequent developments proved this to be the case. As you probably know, there was a time when many companies did not publish sales figures, and their income statements started off with gross profit or profit from operations. This practice is still followed in some countries. Managements at one time thought that the disclosure of sales would be ruinous, but the reporting of sales is commonplace today. Publicly held companies are under increasing pressure for disclosure of important financial information.

There has been a gradual trend toward the inclusion of R & D costs on a separate line in published income statements. In such cases captions such as "research, design and development costs" are generally used. Some companies have combination captions such as "advertising, selling, administrative and research expenses" or "product development, selling and administrative expenses." Most companies still have R & D buried in cost of sales, G & A expenses, or some other general caption, with no indication of where it is or how much it is.

A few companies have R & D set out separately in stockholders' reports in such places as a ten-year summary or an historical "Highlights" page. There are also charts and graphs showing R & D costs in a few cases.

Mr. Jack M. Whitney, a member of the Securities and Exchange Commission, gave a speech last Tuesday which was reported in *The Wall Street Journal* of February 6, 1963, in part as follows:

"He said the SEC's special stock market study, on which the commission will report to Congress in April, will focus on disclosure problems and 'produce a lot of food for thought and action.'

"Without saying what specific areas the report will cover, Mr. Whitney expressed personal displeasure that companies don't have to disclose more details on research and development programs. His apparent concern is that such programs attract some investors who hope the research will pay off in future profit but don't really understand what the research involves."

This whole area of disclosure is one that should be seriously reexamined by many companies. Disclosure is particularly important so long as alternative accounting practices exist.

Accounting for R & D

There have been two general methods of accounting for R & D costs. The practice in many cases has been to charge off the costs at the time they are incurred. The other practice, which has been followed in a relatively few cases, has been to defer certain of these costs to the future with an attempt to match them with the related benefits. A third method, which has been used in isolated cases, has been to accrue the cost prior to its incurrence.

From the standpoint of accounting principles, what has been the logical basis for expensing all R & D as incurred? Conservatism has probably been the most important factor. Conservatism results in resolving doubts in favor of understating assets and current income and overstating liabilities and current expenses. Conservatism has generally been considered by the accounting profession to be a prime virtue, and it has had some very subtle and far-reaching effects on accounting. However, conservatism is only relative, since what may be conservative to one person may be unconservative to someone else. What is conservative to a creditor may be misrepresentation to a selling stockholder. Accountants have generally concluded that in case of doubt it is preferable to lean in the direction of caution, even though this cannot always be supported from a theoretical standpoint.

The second factor that has encouraged the expensing of R & D costs as incurred is consistency. Consistency is featured in the standard form of auditor's opinion, which states that the accounting principles have been "applied on a basis consistent with that of the preceding year." Consistency is important if comparisons of financial statements are to be made from year to year and if trends are to have any significance. Consistency is a desirable attribute in accounting and the preparation of financial statements, but it should not be used as an excuse to justify the use or continuance of practices that can be improved upon.

The third factor resulting in the current expensing of R & D is custom. Companies have a tendency to follow the same general accounting practices as other companies.

There are two accounting concepts that are now generally recognized and relate to the accounting for R & D costs. First, costs should be matched with the related revenues and, second, costs should not be deferred to future periods unless there is a reasonable expectation that they will be recovered. There is a difficulty, however, of determining whether the costs, if deferred, can be related to and recovered through future operations.

My experience has indicated to me that the accounting profession slipped off the track some place along the line and has been approaching the problem of accounting for intangible assets from the wrong direction. With all of the emphasis on trying to match costs and revenues through various arbitrary techniques of capitalizing and amortizing costs, everyone seems to have lost sight of the question of whether huge amounts of deferred intangibles are really assets.

There is also the problem of the responsibility and accountability by management for the costs incurred. When costs are charged to expense, is the management performance and accountability for results of operations obscured? It may be argued that a company spending approximately the same amount for research and development each year will get the same annual charge regardless of the method followed in accounting for the costs. This, of course, is generally true, but it does not follow in all cases, and there is no assurance in any given situation that it will continue. The management of a company could improve profits by reducing research and development expenditures (with possible future adverse effects), and the stockholders might easily be misled, at least temporarily.

From an accounting standpoint, there is little difference between the cost of outside research for a company (such as that done under contract by a university or a professional research organization) and research by the company's own staff. It is desirable that costs of special projects, such as the development of a particular product, be segregated to the extent practicable. When a company purchases a patent or the results of research from someone else, such costs are more likely to be capitalized and amortized than the company's own research costs. This probably occurs because of the more direct expectation of related future sales and profits that prompted the purchase.

The mere fact that a particular research project is not productive does not mean that it has no future value. A company with a broad range of products may find that it must incur R & D costs on five products to get one or two good ones, or that a certain level of continuing research is required to maintain the desired degree of product development. It can logically be argued that all of these costs are the costs of the marketable products that result. One of the reasons that the pharmaceutical industry was vulnerable to criticism by a congressional committee a few years ago for alleged excessive profits on products sold was that the costs of research and development related to those products (which undoubtedly were significant) were not directly reflected as costs of those products. Studies of that industry show a marked relationship between the expenditures for research and development and sales volume, but such expenditures are generally not related to the specific products from an accounting standpoint.

There may be situations where a relatively fixed level of R & D activity on a long-range basis is vital to maintain a company's competitive standing in its industry. For a variety of reasons some of this research and development effort may be accelerated or delayed for a time, with the result that the costs incurred for this purpose may fluctuate from year to year. In some circumstances it might be appropriate (although it has seldom been done) to provide for such costs by a charge against income each year, based upon the year's pro rata portion of estimated long-range costs, irrespective of the actual costs incurred during the particular year. In the years when the costs incurred for R & D are less than the allocable portion based upon the long-range estimate, a reserve would be built up to absorb the excess of incurred costs in future years over the portion allocable to those years. In some years the opposite situation might occur with incurred costs exceeding the allocable costs, and a deferred charge would result. This approach is based upon the viewpoint that each dollar of sales is using up a certain amount of past research and development, and that a proper matching of costs and revenues requires a provision for the replacement of this expiring asset. This approach has some of the earmarks of normalization but in any event it warrants further study.

I know of one company that made an investigation of the results of its R & D efforts, and the management was convinced that over a period of several years, because of profit trends, there was a definite tendency to do the least R & D work in the years it was needed the most, and vice versa.

Most companies, for income tax purposes, prefer to deduct R & D costs as incurred. However it may be accounted for in a different manner in the corporate accounts. If there is a material difference between the amount charged against income in the accounts and the amount deducted for income tax purposes, proper tax allocation accounting should be followed.

Evaluation of research output

It has been estimated that over 90% of the R & D work done by most companies is devoted to solving technical problems that can yield known commercial applications; the balance of 10% might be classified as fundamental research. The evaluation of the results of this work is obviously an important matter in companies where expenditures in this regard are relatively substantial. The development of new products and processes and the improvements of existing ones, as well as the reduction of costs, are all-important, both to the growth and to the long-term survival of a business.

Management must evaluate the R & D efforts of its company, since it is responsible for the costs incurred and the results achieved. No purpose is served by merely saying that there are no effective ways to measure the accomplishments.

As we all know, the incurrence of costs does not necessarily produce results commensurate with the amounts expended. The only measurement of R & D success, or lack of it, that is meaningful at present is its reflection in subsequent changes in sales and profits, but these are also affected by many other factors. Most companies do not disclose sales or profits by product lines in published data (although the day may well come when they will), and some products may be going up while others are going down. If R & D costs are not set out separately, profitability might temporarily change in inverse proportion to the amount of such costs without the reader of financial statements knowing it.

Conclusion

In conclusion, I would like to emphasize that more meaningful published financial statements are going to be necessary because of the increasing use to which such statements are being put. Improvements in this regard, particularly in difficult areas such as the accounting for research and development costs, can be achieved only if we establish proper objectives and have the will to accomplish the desired results. Progressive corporate managements recognize their responsibility to report to stockholders and other interested parties in a useful manner.

The accounting profession also has a responsibility to establish better criteria and standards, both for the accounting and for disclosure. The mere fact that this represents a difficult problem does not mean that it cannot be solved.

Progress involves not only what companies do, but how they report on what they do. New approaches and better techniques are needed. Improved reporting is one way that our free enterprise system can demonstrate its effectiveness.

Effect of income taxes on financial accounting and reporting

Before the Conference of Accountants at the University of Tulsa (Oklahoma), April 17, 1963—Catlett

Federal income taxes have had a significant impact on financial accounting and reporting. However, the objectives of taxation are different from those for financial accounting, and these objectives should not be confused.

I APPRECIATE the opportunity of being here today and discussing with you the effect of income taxes on financial accounting and reporting.

With Federal income tax rates for corporations at 52%, or even if these rates are reduced by a few percentage points, the tax aspects of most business transactions are certain to have a far-reaching effect, not only on management decisions but also on the manner of accounting for transactions resulting from such decisions.

There has been considerable discussion for many years of whether income taxes should be computed on the basis of sound accounting principles and practices as determined by the accounting profession. While the Congress and the Treasury Department have undoubtedly given some consideration to "generally accepted accounting principles," they have also given considerable attention to other aspects of the computation of taxable income.

Basis of taxation

The Federal income tax laws and regulations are designed for the purpose of raising revenues, but it must be recognized that many social, political, economic, and incentive factors have an effect on the taxation process. This situation is almost certain to exist in a free enterprise, democratic society such as ours, and I am not suggesting that it should be otherwise.

There have been numerous instances in which the accounting profession has made concentrated efforts to persuade the Congress and the Internal Revenue Service to base tax laws and regulations on sound accounting principles. An example of this was the inclusion in the 1954 Internal Revenue Code, after many years of discussion, of the provisions which permitted taxpayers on the accrual basis, at their election, to defer the reporting of prepaid income until the periods in which it was earned, and to deduct reasonable additions to reserves for various types of estimated expenses. However, as you undoubtedly recall, these provisions were repealed within a short time on a retroactive basis.

Another example involving the application of accounting principles is the recent Schlude case in which it was decided by a five-to-four decision of the U. S. Supreme Court that the Commissioner of Internal Revenue was justified in including in the gross income of a dance studio the negotiable notes or amounts already due and payable under contract, regardless of whether the services to be given in return for such notes or payments due had been performed. The American Institute of Certified Public Accountants filed a brief as amicus curiae in this case, in which it was argued that the income should be recognized when the related services were performed. The dissenting opinion written by Justice Stewart, and concurred in by Justices Douglas, Harlan and Goldberg, stated in part as follows: "The most elementary principles of accounting require that advances be considered reportable income only in the year they are earned by the taxpayer's rendition of the services for which the payments were made. The government's theories would force upon an accrual-basis taxpayer a cash basis for advance payments in disregard of the Federal statute that explicitly authorizes income tax returns to be based upon sound accrual accounting methods. It seems to me that this decision, the third of a trilogy of cases purportedly decided on their own peculiar facts, in truth completes the mutilation of a basic element of the accrual method of reporting income—a method that has been explicitly approved by Congress for almost half a century."

These two examples represent areas in which the Congress, the courts, and the Treasury Department are putting the system of taxation on a questionable basis. Expediency has sometimes overruled logic and common sense in the administration and interpretation of statutory provisions, and occasionally in the statutes themselves. In order to obtain the maximum tax revenues or to reduce the loss of tax revenues to a minimum, expediency has sometimes been allowed to result in the levy of taxes at the earliest possible time, without regard to whether the amounts received represent earned income, and the disallowance of deductions that do not represent legal liabilities of a fixed and measurable nature, even though, to a businessman, such amounts would clearly represent liabilities under the accrual method of accounting.

There are other matters, such as the dividend-received credit for corporations, the nontaxability of interest from municipal bonds, accelerated depreciation, investment credit, and percentage depletion, in which the Congress has taken action on the basis of decisions relating to national policy. These matters represent areas in which there is a clear distinction between the computation of taxable income and the determination of profit for financial statements.

Effect of taxation on accounting practices

Federal income taxes have had a significant impact on all phases of accounting and financial reporting. Certain methods allowed for income tax purposes have almost immediately become generally accepted practices for corporate accounting purposes. One example of this is LIFO, which became a popular inventory pricing method after it was allowed for tax purposes. Without such allowance it is doubtful that this practice would have received very much attention. An important factor in the "general acceptance" of LIFO for accounting purposes has been the fact that it must be recorded in the accounts in order to be allowed for tax purposes.

The recognition of some sort of price-level depreciation for tax purposes has been proposed by many accountants, because much of the depreciable property in this country was acquired when the purchasing power of the dollar was less than it is today. A recognition of this increased depreciation, in terms of the loss of purchasing power or the increased replacement costs, has been proposed to Congressional committees for many years. However, most business managements are not willing to reflect this economic fact in their financial statements unless it is recognized for income tax purposes.

It appears, therefore, that there has been a tendency for income tax laws and regulations to have a direct influence on accepted principles of accounting or on their application. This arises, at least in part, because general acceptance, as such, does not necessarily represent a sound basis for accounting standards. The term "generally accepted accounting principles" was developed in the 1930's to fill a void that became evident during the depression and at the inception of the Securities and Exchange Commission.

Deferred taxes

One of the big arguments among accountants is the one relating to deferred-tax accounting. If a company records income or expenses on the same basis for both book and tax purposes, then there is no deferment or prepayment of taxes. However, there seems to be an increasing number of items for which the recognition of income or the amortization of costs is reflected in a different accounting period for book purposes than for tax purposes. The question is whether the tax effect of the difference in timing should be recognized in the accounts.

Those accountants who argue against any tax deferment contend that the taxes payable for a particular period represent the current tax cost to the company, and this is the only cost that should be recognized for the period regardless of any differences that may exist between book and tax accounting. However, the accounting profession has gradually adopted the position that the tax effect of many of these differences must be recognized in order to obtain a proper matching of costs and revenues. While we do not have time today to discuss all of the ramifications of deferred-tax accounting, I would like to discuss briefly a few examples.

Many companies that sell on an installment basis reflect the profit from the transaction in their accounts in the year of sale, but pay the income taxes on such profits as the installments are collected. However, under these conditions it is necessary in the year of sale to provide for the taxes to be payable in future years, in order to relate the profit on the sale with the related tax cost.

The area that has affected almost all companies and has caused the greatest amount of discussion in the accounting profession involves depreciable property. This problem began with the five-year amortization under certificates of necessity during World War II, and continued with the accelerated depreciation provisions of the Internal Revenue Code in more recent years. This general problem was compounded further in 1962 with the tax regulations on the depreciation guidelines and enactment of the investment credit. Some companies have recognized the five-year amortization or the accelerated depreciation for both book and tax purposes, with the result that there has been no tax deferment. The question then becomes one of whether the depreciation in the accounts is reasonable under the circumstances. On the other hand, many companies, under these conditions, have taken only straight-line depreciation in the accounts, so that taxes otherwise payable on book income have been deferred to future periods. Most companies have recognized these deferred taxes.

There has been great confusion in the public utility industry because various Federal and state regulatory agencies have issued orders in all directions on the subject of accelerated depreciation. Some agencies require deferred-tax accounting, some agencies make it optional, and some agencies require that the tax benefit flow through to income currently.

The regulations on depreciation guidelines have presented some additional problems. Of the companies that are following the guideline lives, some are recognizing the same lives in their accounts and some are not. Many accountants believe that companies should book depreciation on the guideline basis if it is used for tax purposes, not only to indicate that the lives are being used on the basis of good faith, but also to recognize that the shorter lives are actually realistic. An important factor to consider in connection with the guideline depreciation is that the reserve ratio tests and other aspects of the guideline regulations may result in companies accelerating the replacement of equipment and other property so that the useful lives actually are shorter than they have been previously.

The railroads are an example of a big industry where the guideline lives are substantially shorter than those previously used, and where the longer lives are still being used for book purposes. The Accounting Principles Board of the American Institute of CPAs issued an Opinion that under these circumstances provisions should be made for deferred taxes. The railroads, under the regulations of the Interstate Commerce Commission, are not providing for the deferred taxes, with the result that millions of dollars of deferred-tax benefits are flowing through to current income. One railroad, which I will not name but which is typical of that industry for 1962, published its annual earnings of $22,300,000 as compared to $12,600,000 for 1961, or an increase of about 77%. If the effect of the "flow-through" of the tax benefits from guideline depreciation were eliminated and deferred on a proper basis, the increase in net income would be almost completely eliminated.

The investment credit has created what has probably been the biggest public controversy that the accounting profession has ever had. You are probably aware of the articles on this subject that have appeared in publications such as *The Wall Street Journal* and *Barron's* (the financial weekly) as well as in syndicated newspaper columns and elsewhere. *Business Week* published a much-discussed article under the heading, "A Matter of Principle Splits CPAs."

The controversy related to the practice to be followed by companies in their accounts in reflecting the tax benefit of the investment credit. The disagreement revolved around the question of whether the investment credit should be amortized over the life of the related property, should be reflected in net income as a reduction of the income tax provision, or should be split, with 52% being deferred and 48% flowing through to net income. The Accounting Principles Board issued an opinion, based on the support of two-thirds of its members, that the credit should be amortized over the life of the related property. The situation was confused further when the SEC subsequently announced that it would accept either full amortization or the 52-48% split for industrial companies, and either of these methods or 100% flow-through for public utilities where the practice is sanctioned by the applicable regulatory authority. The public controversy has subsided to some extent, but the effects are still with us.

In the case of the investment credit, a tax statute had a significant impact, not only on the accounting profession but also on the financial and business community, and I might add that the extent of the controversy far exceeded the importance of the item being discussed.

Other areas of differences

There are various other areas where differences exist in the timing of charges to income as between the accounts and the tax returns. Some of the more common of these are:

1. Research and development costs in manufacturing companies.
2. Exploration costs in natural resource companies.
3. Intangible development costs in the oil and gas industry.

While some companies expense these costs as incurred for both book and tax purposes, other companies capitalize them in the accounts even though they are expensed for tax purposes. These items should be capitalized net of the related current tax benefits and amortized on a net basis in order to match the costs with such benefits.

Percentage depletion allowable for tax purposes in the case of natural resource companies may exceed cost depletion in the accounts, but it does not usually present a shift of charges between periods and, thus, no tax-deferment accounting is necessary to obtain a matching of costs and revenues.

With respect to the accounting for intangible development costs, there has been a gradual transition. Originally, most companies expensed IDC as incurred because it was an income tax deduction. There has been a trend for many years toward capitalization, and today most of the publicly held companies in the oil and gas industry capitalize these costs. The practice of deferring the tax benefit from the deduction of IDC for tax purposes over the period the costs are amortized for book purposes is now being followed by a few of the companies, including two of the largest.

Under the accrual method of accounting and under the accounting principle of providing for future costs and losses when they relate to current periods and can reasonably be foreseen, companies establish various accrual and reserve accounts, the provisions for which are not currently deductible for tax purposes. If it is reasonable to assume that a company will have taxable income in the future against which these accruals and reserves can be deducted when they are used for the purpose intended, then such provisions should be made net of the future tax benefit.

Effect of taxes on business decisions

There have been a great number of business mergers in this country since World War II. This has been the result of many factors, such as the desire for diversification and estate tax problems of family owned companies, but it has been facilitated by tax-free merger provisions of the Internal Revenue Code and the pooling-of-interest concept of accounting, which permits companies to merge through an exchange of stock without recognizing any acquired goodwill. Many company managements do not believe that the amortization of goodwill through the income statement represents proper accounting (and they may well be correct in this view). The nondeductibility of acquired goodwill for tax purposes (except when the business might be disposed of) has had an effect on many business decisions.

Carry-forward of operating losses for tax purposes

Income statements and earnings per share can sometimes be very misleading when they reflect the tax effect of operating losses carried forward. It is the customary practice to reduce or eliminate current tax provisions in income statements when operating losses are available to be carried forward for tax purposes. Thus, income may be approximately doubled, or at least increased significantly, because of losses in previous years. In my opinion, the tax effect of the operating loss should be credited to earned surplus and allocated to the year that had the loss in a restatement of prior-year income statements. This is a subject that requires further study and consideration by the accounting profession.

Taxes can unduly influence business decisions

As we all know, the tax effect of any significant transaction must be considered by a company management prior to consummating the transaction. This, of course, is necessary; but there are instances in which decisions may be based too much on the tax effect, and as a result a management may not take a course of action that is best for the business in the long run.

A company president recently told me that LIFO had been influencing his decisions too much. His company is in a business in which the prices of both the raw materials and finished goods move rather rapidly. What he had in mind was that the company had lost a great deal more money on items purchased and sold in trying to manipulate the LIFO base for maximum tax advantage than it had ever made from the resulting tax savings. Although taxes are an important factor in business transactions, they should not have more influence on management decisions than is warranted by the circumstances.

Conclusion

In conclusion, I would like to recommend the following points for your consideration:

1. Tax laws and regulations should not attempt to prescribe accounting for financial purposes.
2. Tax laws and regulations should follow sound accounting principles insofar as practicable.
3. Congressional policies relating to social and economic matters may properly be reflected in tax legislation, but they should not be confused or intermingled with matters of accounting principle.
4. Corporate managements should not let alleged convenience, economy, and expediency lull them into following unsound tax practices for financial accounting purposes. Dual sets of records may prove to be the most economical and the soundest approach to the differences between book and tax accounting.
5. Deferred-tax accounting (which may also take the form of prepaid tax accounting) is essential to a fair presentation of financial position and results of operations when significant differences between periods exist in the timing of income and cost recognition for purposes of the tax return and the accounts.
6. The accounting profession must determine sound accounting principles, and these should be established irrespective of the tax laws and regulations.

Taxes are inevitable and their influence is irresistible, but we can and should learn to keep them in their proper perspective.

Accounting research

Before the Faculty Research Seminar, College of Business Administration, Arizona State University, Tempe, Arizona, March 11, 1964—Catlett

Creative and logical thinking, properly recorded and carefully documented, will serve as a basis for informed discussion and will inevitably lead to progress.

THERE ARE THREE AREAS I would like to discuss with you today:

1. The need for improved research in the field of financial accounting and reporting.
2. The research that is being done.
3. The research that should be done.

I would like to begin this discussion by stating that the need for research in financial accounting and reporting is greater today than it has ever been. The research being done is not sufficiently effective, and it is not, in general, meeting the need. When the research that has been done in the accounting field is compared to that done in scientific, medical and other fields, the deficiency in the accounting field is appalling. The blame for this can be shared by business, government, academic institutions and the accounting profession.

Need for research

The first question is whether we have problems that require research in order to reach adequate solutions.

Mr. G. L. Phillippe, Chairman of the Board of General Electric Company, gave an outstanding address to the American Institute of CPAs' Annual Meeting in Minneapolis last fall. His general theme was that the development of sound accounting principles and practices is very important both to corporate management and to the accounting profession. He said:

"Neither the accounting profession nor corporate management would stand to gain by allowing the initiative to pass to others on the development of sound accounting principles. This, I repeat, could happen if we don't face up to the needed decisions.

"But it is not only for the benefit of

either corporate management or the accounting profession that action is needed.

"In my judgment, the public as a whole has a stake in the development of sound accounting principles. There is a great and growing need for improved public understanding of, and information on, financial matters. In an economic democracy — 'people's capitalism' or whatever words you choose to hang on it — improved public understanding is essential."

The fact can hardly be disputed that there are very major problems in accounting today that are crying for solutions. The tragedy has been the relative slowness with which the accounting profession and the business community have reacted to doing something about these problems.

While there may well be some disagreement concerning what kind of research would be most productive, it seems obvious to me that good research is needed very much.

For some reason or other, much research on accounting matters has tended to be done on a highly theoretical and impracticable basis, and it has had very little impact on our daily lives. If a need exists, surely some way can be found to make research more effective.

Research being done

The American Institute of Certified Public Accountants inaugurated an elaborate research program in 1959 at an annual cost of about $150,000. This has been done in part by permanent staff members and in part by university professors engaged for specific projects. This has been of limited success and has not yet been very effective. The whole program is currently being reviewed so that improvements can be made. A few firms, including our firm, have done some fairly effective applied research with spasmodic efforts toward basic research.

There has been some feeling, among university people at least, that in the business field basic research should be done at universities and applied research should be done by business organizations. This segregation has never worked out in practice.

Accounting research has, for the most part, not produced the needed results, because such research has not been based on a proper foundation, has not been done with the proper perspective, has not been responsive to the needs of our society, and has not involved sufficient time and effort by qualified individuals.

One of the first steps frequently taken in accounting research is to think in terms of opinion polls and questionnaires. Our firm receives many of these. The second step is usually a summarization of present practices, a tabulation of existing customs. The third step involves a liberal selection of quotations from such authors as Littleton, Paton, Finney, Montgomery, May and Gilman. Then, as a fourth step, the opinion of the writer is given. About all this accomplishes is a rehash of data and viewpoints already known. The lack of new and creative thought is appalling.

Much of the so-called accounting research has been a piecemeal approach that has not been related to the needs of present-day business. It is obvious that most of our accounting concepts and principles (to the extent they have been identified in accounting literature) have been arrived at by a "reverse" logic; in other words, the wide variety of practices being followed are tabulated and the assumptions and principles (upon which the practices are supposed to be based) are then established and supported. This is all backwards, and is somewhat similar to building a house before drawing the plans.

I have read quite a few documents that purported to represent research in accounting. If the same quality of research had been done in other areas, we would still be pushing a plow and living in tents.

Research that should be done

Research should be done by qualified people who are willing to spend sufficient time and effort to do it properly. This cannot be done in a person's spare time.

Most public accountants do not have time to do very much research work. Even in the larger public accounting firms, it is frequently difficult to accomplish creative research with men who have full-time jobs on other matters.

In our firm, we have found that it is necessary to budget and allocate a fairly substantial amount of time and money each year for the purpose of research and the determination of the policies we should adopt with respect to accounting principles. One of the first hurdles to get over is to find out what the problems are. We have established procedures whereby we have a continuous flow of actual cases between all of our offices and the Home Office. This enables us to be constantly in touch with most of the important problems that are encountered in our practice.

The faculty and graduate students of universities and colleges can make a definite contribution to accounting research if they will approach each problem in a critical fashion and not assume that what they have been taught or what they are teaching is necessarily preferable. This may even involve a professor questioning what he has written in his own books.

A tremendous need exists for basic and fundamental accounting research. In many other fields of study, universities have taken the lead in basic research and have produced numerous ideas and discoveries that have been used in business and in the scientific, engineering and medical professions. In accounting, this situation has not existed to any significant degree.

My own experience with research indicates that it is a highly personal activity. It cannot be done by groups and committees. Also, the emphasis should be on what ought to be done rather than what is being done. The great emphasis on reading what has already been written, on summarizing current practices, and on trying to obtain a consensus solution, all tend to dilute and misdirect the efforts of the researcher.

Accountants seem to be trained to look backward rather than forward—to start with outmoded premises rather than establishing new premises—to become preoccupied with bookkeeping techniques rather than determining whether the results are best.

Conclusion

A few general suggestions for accounting research might be the following:

1. Less emphasis should be placed on existing customs.
2. The compilation of statistics and opinions does not constitute effective research.
3. The real problems need to be determined.
4. Original thinking is necessary.
5. Research cannot be done without knowing the business aspects of the problems and the circumstances in the business community.
6. There is a need to be responsive to social changes and the needs of our society.
7. The development of complete, detailed, and sound reasoning for the conclusions reached is the most important aspect of research. "Why" is more important than "how."
8. Last, and perhaps most important, the basic objectives of accounting need to be established if meaningful research is to be done.

The pronouncements of many committees have merely been the personal opinions of the committee members without any background and support for the conclusions stated. Carefully documented reasoning is far more influential than unsupported opinions. Sound and logical thinking properly recorded will serve as a basis for informed discussion and will inevitably lead to progress.

Accounting research can play an important role in solving our many problems, and I am confident that ways and means can be found to make research more effective.

Controversy over uniformity of accounting principles

Adapted from an article in *The Journal of Accountancy*, December 1964—Catlett

The procrastination and indecision that have characterized the controversy over uniformity must be eliminated. The opportunity exists for the accounting profession to regulate itself on a successful basis. The question is not whether progress is being made but whether the progress is sufficient.

THE ACCOUNTING PROFESSION has become involved in an extensive controversy over the necessity for more uniformity of the accounting principles underlying corporate financial statements.* Actually, there is substantial agreement on certain points, although there has been a tendency to overlook this fact. Confusion and misunderstanding have resulted from a lack of clarification of the points of disagreement, some of which are quite important.

Agreement

A careful review of the principal articles and speeches that have dealt with both sides of this controversy indicates agreement on several aspects of the problem of achieving more uniformity of accounting principles, despite the fact that there are serious questions concerning the best methods of implementation.

The areas of agreement are, in general, as follows:

1. Improvement is needed.
2. Basic accounting principles and concepts should be more clearly defined, and they must be developed within the economic, social, legal, and political structure of our society.
3. There will always be limitations on what can be expected of financial statements.
4. Accounting should not be based on rigid rules or standard manuals for all business.

* A distinction is sometimes made between uniformity of accounting principles and comparability of financial statements. However, these phrases are complementary in nature; and, insofar as this controversy is concerned, they relate to the same problem. The significant matters of concern are the accounting principles and practices which have a material effect on the financial statements.

5. Accounting, to remain useful, must be responsive to necessary changes.
6. The immediate objective is to narrow the areas of difference and to eliminate undesirable alternative practices.
7. Research, study, and discussion are important prerequisites in reaching sound conclusions.
8. Cooperation by means of discussion and exchange of views with representatives of industry, stock exchanges, governmental regulatory agencies, academic groups, and other interested parties is necessary.
9. General regulation of corporate accounting by the Securities and Exchange Commission or any other governmental agency is not desirable, and should not be necessary if the accounting profession and company managements can make satisfactory progress.
10. The management of a company has the primary responsibility for the company's accounting policies and for the preparation of its financial statements, and there is no intention that CPAs should infringe upon the management's proper prerogatives in this regard.
11. In reporting on financial statements, CPAs have a responsibility to state clearly any explanations, qualifications, or disagreements which may be deemed to be appropriate.
12. The accounting profession has a serious educational responsibility, both within the profession and within the business community.
13. The use of judgment and the maintenance of personal integrity will always be important characteristics of the accounting profession.

As indicated by the above list, there are wide areas of agreement which can be used as a basis for improvements in the future.

The report of the Institute's Special Committee on Research Program (1958), which preceded the establishment of the Accounting Principles Board, discussed accounting principles and the necessity of narrowing "the areas of difference and inconsistency in practice." The report recommended that "reliance should be placed on persuasion rather than on compulsion," and that the Institute "should take definite steps to lead in the thinking on unsettled and controversial issues."

Since this report has generally been considered to represent a desirable approach to the problem at the present time, the current controversy is concerned more with how and when the objectives should be achieved than with the objectives to be eventually attained.

Disagreement

The areas of disagreement are identifiable, but they are not easily segregated; and they are very subtle in nature. The controversy tends to revolve around the following factors: (1) urgency; (2) disclosure and consistency; (3) persuasion; (4) extent of uniformity; (5) professional judgment; and (6) management prerogatives.

Urgency—The urgency of narrowing the areas of difference and eliminating some of the more undesirable alternative practices depends upon an individual's evaluation of the present situation and his view of the need for improvement. The question is not whether progress is being made but whether the progress is sufficient.

In the 1930's, committees of the American Institute, in cooperation with the New York Stock Exchange and the newly created Securities and Exchange Commission, made considerable progress in the improvement of accounting practices, financial statements, and auditors' reports. The concept of "generally accepted accounting principles," which contemplated adequate disclosure of the practices followed and consistent application of those selected, was developed to fill a void that had previously existed. The impetus provided by the financial crisis and the threat of the authority of the SEC, as well as the leadership provided by prominent accountants of that period, resulted in improvements.

The rate of progress slowed during World War II and has not been effectively reestablished since that time. Accounting is similar to many other man-made service devices, in that achievements of the 1930's are inadequate to deal with the challenges of the 1960's.

Basic changes of far-reaching significance have been taking place in our free enterprise system in a relatively short period of time. A trend has been developing toward wide dispersion of stock ownership in publicly held companies that have professional management with relatively small stock ownership. Today there are about eighteen million stockholders in publicly held companies, and one out of every six adults owns stock in such companies.

Financial statements are being used much more extensively by stockholders, managements, creditors, employees, customers, potential investors, governmental agencies and others. Each of these groups has, in varying degrees, conflicting interests, which are of greater significance today than they were thirty years ago. Thus, the accountability of management for its performance and the methods by which it communicates the results of this performance have become increasingly important.

To some extent, accounting will always be evolving to meet the needs of our society. Unfortunately, reliance on evolution is frequently used as an excuse for not taking any significant action as a profession. Also, changes in some accounting practices in recent years have been in the direction of deterioration rather than improvement. Evolution and usage do not guarantee progress. To assume that unsound practices will be eliminated automatically is to ignore history.

The statement is sometimes made that evolution in accounting should proceed in somewhat the same manner as evolution in common law. This analogy is not a good one because common law is determined by independent judges (without clients) and juries in a court system—with testimony, cross-examination, filing of briefs, written decisions, and a public record. There is nothing comparable to this in the field of accounting.

Urgency does exist, and this should provide an incentive for improvements rather than being a major point of dispute.

Disclosure and consistency—Disclosure of significant information and the consistent application of accounting principles have been considered essential elements of financial reporting for many years. This subject is related to the "uniformity" problem because, as more emphasis is put on disclosure and consistency, less emphasis is put on uniformity. Those accountants who downgrade the need for more uniformity consider financial reporting adequate if there is disclosure of the alternative practice selected and if such practice is consistently followed. They conclude that CPAs have no right or responsibility to go beyond the determination of whether an accounting practice is one that has some acceptance in usage.

The opposite viewpoint is that disclosure and consistency are desirable for reporting purposes, but they are not a satisfactory substitute for more uniform accounting principles. The readers of financial statements should not have to attempt (usually unsuccessfully) to adjust them to a comparable basis by using footnote information, which is frequently confusing and technical.

Consistency is sometimes considered to be more important than the selection of the practices followed because the operating results over a long period of time will be the same. This view is based on the belief that the only problem results from periodic cut-offs for purposes of published financial statements, and since these periods are too short to be very accurate, readers of financial statements should not pay very much attention to the reported annual financial position and operating results.

The fact is that a great many people do use annual financial statements and must rely on them for important purposes. Every effort should be made to have statements that are as accurate and comparable as practicable. No useful purpose is served by merely contending that consistency is more important than the practice itself or that a year is such a short time that there is no real necessity of trying to report on a better basis.

The deficiencies and inadequacies of accounting and the fact that financial statements do not serve all purposes as well as some readers would like are not reasons for avoiding an effort to have accounting serve as many useful purposes as possible.

Disclosure and consistency, while desirable and necessary characteristics of financial reporting, have unfortunately been used in this controversy as a "smoke screen" for concealing the real problem of establishing sound accounting principles.

Persuasion—The report of the Institute's Special Committee on Research Program (which is referred to above) indicates that reliance should be placed on persuasion rather than on compulsion. Much publicity has been given to this viewpoint by those accountants who favor gradual evolution and who argue for education and persuasion rather than what has been alleged as force and compulsion.

Insofar as American Institute members are concerned, the auditing and reporting standards and the Code of Professional Ethics could all be described as a form of compulsion. Laws for the common good require enforcement, but no one considers that a free country should not have laws. Likewise, a profession must have standards. To describe the adoption and enforcement of such standards as an unwarranted intrusion upon the rights of the members is to argue against even having a profession. The question is—to what extent are standards required?

As far as clients are concerned, any qualification or threat of qualification (relating to accounting principles) in a CPA's opinion on financial statements can be considered as compulsion, because of the effect of such a qualification. When Accounting Research Bulletin No. 44 (revised) on the subject of declining-balance depreciation was issued in 1958, the members of the Institute generally supported the Bulletin. Many companies, facing an opinion qualification by their auditors, changed their accounting practice to conform to the Bulletin. Otherwise, the undesirable alternative practice would have continued indefinitely and probably would have become the predominant practice. This action for more uniformity in 1958 was desirable.

The arguments against compulsion have some of the same characteristics as the viewpoint of the automobile driver who demands his "freedom" to drive one hundred miles per hour on a crowded highway, even though it may have a detrimental effect on other members of our society. The degree of "persuasion" or "compulsion" that an accountant prefers in improving accounting principles is almost directly related to the degree of uniformity of accounting principles he considers to be desirable.

Extent of uniformity—One of the major unresolved questions relates to the extent of uniformity that is desirable.

The advocates of "flexibility" and "experimentation" contend that complete comparability of financial statements is undesirable and unattainable and should not even be held out as a possibility. The opposite viewpoint is that more comparability should be achieved in important areas where alternative practices (some of them supported with very little logical reasoning) have a significant effect on financial statements. In any event, the possibility of more comparability should not be rejected simply because it can never be completely achieved.

Some accountants argue that accounting principles are already sufficiently uniform, and that the problem relates primarily to the application of such principles as reflected in practices and methods. Regardless of the terminology used, there are numerous differences in important accounting practices between companies, and it is misleading to indicate that these differences involve methods only, and not principles.

The view is sometimes expressed that uniform accounting principles would prevent changes in accounting to meet new conditions and to facilitate improved practices. This same allegation can be made against the present concept of general acceptance, since new concepts cannot easily be adopted because they do not meet the test of being "generally accepted." Actually, uniform principles determined on a sound basis would facilitate changes; the need for improvement would be more readily apparent and the principles to be adjusted would be more easily identified.

The usefulness of financial statements depends to a great extent upon their comparability. This is one of the reasons that accounting is done in terms of dollars as a common denominator. Many of the decisions by investors, managements, creditors and other users of financial statements are based on comparisons and analyses of trends and ratios of one entity with another, one period with another, or one entity with predetermined bench marks. Insofar as investors are concerned, however, the need for uniformity in accounting principles in the preparation of financial statements between companies is similar to the need for consistency in the application of accounting principles by one company.

Uniformity in approach to accounting relates to those matters that are unique to particular industries as well as to those that are common to many industries. Basic principles should apply to all companies.

The exact circumstances, conditions, and management attitudes and objectives are never identical in two companies. This does not mean that similar principles should not be applied in evaluating the results of management stewardship. Examples of this would be: while many factors affect the obsolescence of inventories, the principles requiring that the cost of obsolete inventories be written down to market value should be the same; and while many factors affect income taxes, the principles relating to tax allocation should be the same.

Dissimilar facts would not be forced into an inflexible mold to produce an illusion of comparability. Rather, the facts, whatever they may be, should be reflected in the financial statements on the basis of uniform principles so that the financial information would be expressed in comparable terms, enabling comparisons to be made in a meaningful manner.

Professional judgment—The argument that the elimination of undesirable alternative practices will result in a rule book that will eliminate the exercise of professional judgment is ridiculous. The fact is that very little professional judgment is needed to evaluate accounting practices if all that is involved is looking around to see what methods are being followed by other companies and are considered to be acceptable as reflected in their published reports. No judgment is involved when CPAs accept any one of various alternative practices selected on the basis of what is available today at the "bargain counter."

Considerable determination and ability, on the other hand, is required on the part of the profession to establish proper objectives and sound criteria for the establishment of uniform accounting principles. Professional judgment is required to apply those principles in the wide variety of existing circumstances and conditions.

In considering the use of judgment, there are two areas of decision-making with respect to the selection or evaluation of the accounting principles and practices of a particular company.

The first area of decision-making is concerned with the application of judgment to the facts to arrive at a reasonable result. In many respects, the facts determine the accounting; the accounting does not determine the facts. Thus, judgment must be applied to arrive at the most appropriate accounting under the circumstances. Those who oppose "comparability" allege that the proponents want to apply uniform methods without regard to judgment or without recognition of the differences in facts in each case. This allegation is erroneous, because the use of judgment and a proper interpretation of the facts are always necessary. Also, different individuals in exercising their professional judgment may not arrive at exactly the same conclusion under a given set of facts. An illustration of this would be research and development costs for manufacturing companies; one satisfactory practice that would adequately deal with the wide variety of circumstances could probably never be determined. This does not, however, lessen the need for uniform criteria to serve as guidelines in the application of judgment.

The second area of decision-making, which should be substantially narrowed, relates to the selection of accounting practices from among the available alternatives. Such decisions involve not only the facts but also what is permitted by CPAs, what has been customary in the past, and what the minimum requirements may be insofar as governmental agencies and stock exchanges are concerned. The application of judgment to particular conditions is obviously involved in any significant accounting decision, and no two situations are exactly alike. However, the selection of some practices may be made more on the basis of permissiveness and the desired effect than on an evaluation of what best presents the facts. A few examples of areas where this may occur are:

1. Accounting for a merger of two companies in situations where any one of the following practices is considered acceptable: (a) a pooling of interest (with no goodwill recognized); (b) a purchase without subsequent amortization of goodwill; or (c) a purchase with subsequent amortization of goodwill.
2. Recognition or nonrecognition of equity in undistributed earnings of subsidiaries in both the income statement and the balance sheet. While there may be reasons for nonrecognition of this equity in the case of some foreign subsidiaries, both practices (cost basis and equity basis for the investment) are considered equally acceptable, even for subsidiaries in the United States.
3. Accounting for costs of pension plans, which covers a wide spectrum of practices all the way from "pay-as-you-go" to a full accrual basis (current-service cost plus amortization of past-service cost).
4. Accounting for construction contracts on the percentage-of-completion basis or the completed-contract basis.
5. Inclusion or exclusion of relatively large nonoperating and nonrecurring gains and losses in net income and "earnings per share."*

* Editor's Note: Items 1, 2, 3 and 5 subsequently covered by APB Opinions 8, 9, 16, 17 and 18 issued from 1966 to 1971. Item 4 was included in an exposure draft of an APB Omnibus Opinion and was later deleted.

All of the above matters are more than questions of bookkeeping methods, since they also involve accounting principles. The effect of these alternative practices can be very significant, and to contend that all these variations are the result of different circumstances cannot be supported. These are examples (and many more could be cited) of areas where more uniform principles, supported by improved criteria, are needed as a guide in the exercise of professional judgment.

CPAs will find as time goes on that it would be a great advantage to the profession and to them individually to give up some of their unrestricted freedom, in order to permit the development of principles and criteria. The level of performance of the entire profession would thus be raised. This does not involve pressure or directives to force professional accountants to think alike, to follow rigid rules dictated by an authoritative body, or to act against their own best judgment; it does involve having recognized criteria so that there will be a true profession. Accounting standards are fully as important as auditing and ethical standards.

Management prerogatives—Those accountants who favor more uniformity of accounting principles and comparability of financial statements are sometimes charged with displaying a lack of knowledge of the nature of business, and a yearning for simple answers to complex accounting problems. This view is self-serving, since it should be quite evident that those persons who favor more uniformity are as knowledgeable as those who do not.

The opponents of uniformity contend that management has a responsibility to adopt those accounting practices that in their judgment best fit the circumstances and risks of their particular company and type of business. They also point out that these judgments will not result in exactly the same decisions as those reached by other managements faced with different circumstances, risks, and attitudes. Management does have this responsibility, and it is unlikely that anyone really contends otherwise. However, sound and uniform principles and criteria are needed for the use of management in making these determinations and for the use of CPAs in evaluating such decisions. To the extent that management can select from various alternative practices (sometimes under pressures for short-term benefits) more on the basis of what is available than what best fits the circumstances, the narrowing of differences arising from such alternatives is desirable.

If management loses any of its prerogatives with respect to the improvement of accounting principles and practices, it will be by default and not from having prerogatives taken away by the American Institute of Certified Public Accountants or any other organization.

SEC position

The possibility has existed since the Securities and Exchange Commission was established that unless the accounting profession does a better job of developing uniform accounting principles on a sound basis, the SEC might take over this responsibility. The imminence or remoteness of this eventuality is unknown, but it continually creeps into this controversy.

The SEC, since its inception, has generally followed the philosophy of placing primary responsibility on the accounting profession for the determination of appropriate accounting principles. While this subject has been mentioned in several speeches given in recent years by commissioners and staff members, the most concise statement of the Commission's current position is set forth in Accounting Series Release No. 96 (January 1963). This Release points out that the Commission for many years has favored the development of uniform standards and practices on major accounting questions. It recognizes that there may be sincere differences of opinion with respect to the proper principles of accounting to be followed in a given situation. This Release also indicates that disclosure in the auditor's report and in footnotes to the financial statements is accepted in lieu of conformity with the Commission's views only if such disclosure is adequate and the points involved are such that there is substantial authoritative support for the accounting practice followed. Also, such disclosure is acceptable only if the position of the Securities and Exchange Commission has not been expressed previously in rules, regulations or other official releases.

The fact remains, however, that the SEC is responsible for safeguarding the public interest. It does have a statutory responsibility to the public, and the day could come when the conclusion would be reached by the SEC that the accounting profession is not doing an adequate job of establishing the necessary principles.

Another fact is that there is a steadily growing demand for more comparable financial statements. This demand will not be satisfied by a continuing controversy over what should be done about the situation. In the end, someone will lead in achieving this objective. The SEC is giving the accounting profession and the business community a chance to do what is necessary. This opportunity may not last indefinitely.

Viewpoint of businessmen

Most businessmen want sound, fair and uniform principles of accounting. Most of them do not want government regulation or inflexible rules, but they do deplore the necessity of having their financial position and operating results compared with other companies that appear to be using more favorable accounting practices. During the investment credit fiasco, businessmen probably were more interested in having all companies on the same basis than in which of the alternatives was followed. This situation is similar to a football game in which the players are not as concerned with whether a touchdown counts six points or ten points as whether it counts the same for both teams.

Gerald L. Phillippe, Chairman of the Board of General Electric Company, in his address at the American Institute's 1963 Annual Meeting (subsequently published in *The Journal*),[1] emphasized that "it is vital to all concerned that the accounting community come to a position all its members can support and do so before others take the lead." He not only stated that a "ring of authority is needed from the accounting profession," but added that the present "lack of leadership has many deleterious consequences."

Willis Gale, former Chairman of the Board of Commonwealth Edison Company, discussed in an address various alternative accounting practices and indicated that the business community faces a serious situation in this respect. He said that businessmen "need the help of an accountant with a little backbone." He pointed out that many managements "observe the varying practices of other companies and see no reason why accounting policies should not be tailored to suit what they regard as their own particular objectives." He then made the following observation:

> "Fundamentally, I think the cause of the trouble is a laxity in the professional standards and independence of the accountants. I believe that business would readily conform to fair standards if principles were established on a sound basis and adhered to by all members of the profession."[2]

Responsibility of CPAs

Much of the present controversy has involved the reasoning of various individuals without adequate consideration being given to the original assumptions and premises

1. "Top Management's Stake in Financial Reporting," *JofA*, Dec. '63, pp. 37-38.

2. Address at the University of Chicago Graduate School of Business, December 4, 1963.

upon which this reasoning has been based. The disagreement really has arisen from a basic difference in viewpoint concerning the responsibility of CPAs to the public in the field of accounting principles. Some accountants apparently consider that the responsibility of CPAs is being adequately carried out under present conditions and that the controversy is a tempest in a teapot or a "false crisis precipitated by false prophets." In the opinion of the author, CPAs must proceed more aggressively to establish uniform accounting principles, on an appropriate basis, that will serve as base points for purposes of reporting to the public. Otherwise CPAs will not be carrying out the responsibility that has been given to them in our society and that the public has a right to expect from them.

Some organization in the business community that has sufficient authority and standing must assume active leadership in the development of accounting principles. The American Institute is in the best position to do this. Some members state that the Institute has no inherent or legal authority to dictate accounting principles to industry or to arrogate unto itself the sole authority for the development of accounting principles. The Institute cannot and should not dictate to industry, but it can establish principles and standards for its members. The Institute, as the only national organization of CPAs, can take the lead on behalf of its members in assisting them in carrying out their responsibility to the public. A void in leadership exists now, and all segments of our society would accept the Institute's leadership if it were discharged in a responsible, intelligent and forthright manner.

The Accounting Principles Board, during its first five years of existence, has not lived up to the original hopes and expectations of many Institute members. A period of trial and error may have been inevitable. The prolonged controversy over uniformity of accounting principles may have been unavoidable. However, the APB can accomplish a great deal if it will adopt a constructive program to accomplish positive results in a more expeditious manner. This program should be approached on the basis of (1) thorough research, coordinated on a better basis with predetermined objectives, (2) improved cooperation with other interested groups and organizations, (3) more effective study, analysis and discussion of problems, (4) a better understanding of the objectives and purposes to be accomplished, (5) the isolation of areas of agreement and disagreement, and (6) a sincere desire to accomplish improvements. This program also requires a clear description of the purpose of accounting and financial statements, an adequate definition of "generally accepted accounting principles," the identification of sound principles, and the establishment of usable criteria. Such a program undoubtedly would receive the support of a vast majority of the Institute members.

Some of the problems facing the APB may resemble a chasm, but it must be remembered that a chasm cannot be crossed in halfhearted steps; a leap forward may be necessary.

Conclusion

CPAs must stop worrying about who is right and get on with the job of determining what is right. They must avoid stressing symptoms and consider the causes. They must stop being concerned with prerogatives and emphasize responsibilities. They must have conviction and not merely opinions.

CPAs need a rededication to independence in reporting so that they can carry out their responsibility to the public under our free enterprise system without being unduly influenced by their clients or abdicating their responsibility to governmental agencies. The procrastination and indecision that have characterized the controversy over uniformity must be eliminated. The opportunity exists for the accounting profession to regulate itself on a successful basis. The integrity, competence, and future of the profession are at stake.

Comparability in accounting—a strait jacket or an opportunity?

Before the Rockford, Illinois, Chapter of the National Association of Accountants, September 21, 1965—Olson

The achievement of comparability in financial statements involves the establishment of uniform accounting standards and sound criteria that the accountant can apply to particular situations as he performs the difficult task of judging and assessing the facts.

MR. CHAIRMAN, MEMBERS of the Rockford Chapter of the National Association of Accountants, it is a pleasure to have this opportunity to address you this evening. I am especially pleased to be here on this special occasion for your Chapter, and I want to add my congratulations to all of you for your Chapter's achievements in the Stevenson trophy competition last year.

Let me say at the outset that whatever I may indicate in the way of criticism of accounting this evening stems from a conviction that the accounting profession occupies a very important place in the maintenance of our free enterprise system, as important as that of any other profession, organization or institution. Accounting provides the information on the profits and financial affairs of business which, in the long run, may decide how our country's capital and resources are used. The soundness of the information that accounting provides may affect the soundness of the decisions of individual business managements. Information provided by accounting is used by investors and creditors, and thus becomes a factor in determining the market price of a company's stock, the interest rates it pays on borrowings, and its credit capacity.

Action versus evolution

As in all professions, improvements in accounting and financial reporting will come only with painstaking effort and research. Since we are a public service institution, specific efforts in this regard are expected of us. There are those who say that ours is a good profession comprised of good people; so it is. They also imply, however, that growth and improvement will be automatic and that improvements will be achieved in lasting fashion through evolution, rather than through deliberate actions to institute the improvements that so many people believe are needed.

Whether or not you and I are the progeny of our tree-climbing, banana-eating friends is not the subject of my discussion. Nor will I speculate on whether a million years from now the strange creatures that inhabit this earth will deny that they were ever descended from man. But I do want to say that in the area of accounting, as in all other human endeavors that have created our system of civilization, the spirit and ingenuity of people must be brought to bear in determined effort toward improvement, rather than waiting for the evolution and change resulting from some natural laws. Furthermore, there is a serious possibility that evolutionary changes in accounting might be more retrogressive than progressive.

Let us also discard the complacent philosophy that says things aren't too bad, that the American investor is as well or perhaps better informed than his counterpart in other countries. This is a philosophy that, in substance, excuses inaction and failure to do something about a situation on the basis that we have to take the good with the bad in this world and that this is the way the Lord intended it to be. The service that our profession provides should be as excellent as it is humanly possible to make it.

One of my Swedish friends likes to tell me, a Norwegian, a story about the creation. When the angels had finished making the world, they presented it to the Lord. He complimented them on the outstanding job they had done and said He was particularly impressed with the balance that had been achieved in everything; the beautiful had been balanced with the ugly, the desirable with the undesirable, the good with the bad, the pain with the comfort. The Lord said He had only one complaint. He asked the angels, "But didn't you make Norway too beautiful?" The angels replied, "Don't worry about that Lord, wait until you see the Norwegians."

But even we Norwegians have a responsibility to improve ourselves.

So much for my motives. This is our profession; let's not be afraid to examine our performance critically and strive for the excellence that the public ultimately demands from all the professions that serve it.

Alternative accounting practices

It is not within the scope of our discussion here to analyze in any depth the improvements that should be sought in accounting. I do want to talk briefly this evening about the issue of comparability in accounting and its relationship to sound financial reporting.

Alternative acceptable accounting practices exist and are available in identical situations. In recent years the principal controversies regarding accounting principles have revolved around the question of these alternative practices, which produce differences in reported financial results when no differences may exist in the economic facts. You are familiar with many of them. Let me mention just a few.

One company may use an accelerated method of depreciation, such as the double declining-balance method. Another might use the straight-line method. One company may record its equity in undistributed earnings of investments; another might not. One company may use the LIFO method of determining the cost of inventories; another company might use the FIFO method. A wide variety of practices exists in connection with the accounting for the costs of pension plans.

In the area of business acquisitions and mergers, alternative accounting procedures produce almost unbelievably different results. Let us assume that the Rockford Company buys the Chicago Company, that the net assets of the Chicago Company are $500,000, and the Rockford Company issues common stock worth $1,000,000 on the market for the capital stock of the Chicago Company. Under the so-called pooling-of-interests method of accounting, the Chicago assets would be recorded at $500,000 on the books of the Rockford Company; under the purchase or acquisition method, these same assets would be recorded at $1,000,000. In the majority of such stock transactions, either method would be acceptable, even though under one method the balance sheet would show $500,000 more assets than under the other, and, depending upon whether costs in excess of book values are amortized (another alternative), a larger net profit could be reported under one method than the other.

Since both the purchase and pooling-of-interests methods are considered generally acceptable, both methods are being used. Can we truthfully say that both methods are right?

Attempts to eliminate these differences in accounting and to achieve uniformity have been characterized by some as efforts to put strait jackets on business, as attempts to eliminate the need for judgment on the part of public accountants, as a move toward a dictatorship by CPAs, usurping the responsibilities of management—all destructive of our basic concepts of freedom in business enterprise.

Would comparability be the strait jacket that many have professed to fear? Or would comparability in the financial reporting of the various business enterprises that you people represent provide even greater opportunities for the free movement of capital and for improving the system of free choice which should characterize all our business life? In examining these questions, let us take a brief look at the uses of financial statements.

Financial statements provide information concerning business enterprises. I think we would all agree that this information is of significance only if it can be used. Therefore, the soundness of individual accounting practices must be judged in terms of the usefulness of the information provided by financial statements as a result of those particular practices.

Whom do financial statements serve?

Over the course of the latter half of the nineteenth century and the early twentieth century, two developments had a profound impact on accounting and financial statements. These developments affected the kind of financial information that was needed and influenced the manner in which the information was used.

The first development was the introduction of the limited liability or corporate form of organization for conducting business. General legislation providing for limited liability companies was enacted in England during the latter half of the nineteenth century—surprisingly recent. Under the sole proprietorship or partnership form of doing business the owners could generally keep such records and follow such accounting practices as suited their particular needs.

Under the limited liability or corporate form of conducting business, however, the legal capital of the business enterprise became an important concept, and rules were introduced against its reduction as a protection for the creditors, since, under this form of doing business, the creditors could no longer look to the owners or partners of the business, but only to the corporation itself.

The second development in this period was the emergence of corporations with large numbers of widely held ownership shares that were continuously traded. This development, together with certain other changes, resulted in business management becoming an agency often distinct and apart from the owners of a business.

In 1897 only 37 industrial stocks were listed on the New York Exchange; at the end of 1963 this list had expanded to more than 1,500 industrial stocks. The number of stocks listed on other exchanges has also expanded greatly, as has the number of companies whose securities are traded but not listed. The number of stockholders in American business corporations is now approximately 18,000,000, more than twice the number of stockholders just nine years ago in 1956.

The need for public financial information about business

This dispersion of business ownership into numerous shares freely traded by large numbers of stockholders has created a need for the publication of financial information about business enterprises, information that formerly had been largely regarded as private.

In today's world, the primary purpose of accounting in the public sphere of business is to supply information that investors can use to make informed decisions with respect to buying and selling ownership interests in the business, that creditors can use to make decisions concerning the terms under which they will extend credit to the enterprise, and that others can use for appropriate purposes. Also, whether we like it or not, there is a broad legitimate public interest in financial information about business today, beyond that of stockholders and creditors, including the interests of government, labor unions, consumers and others.

Importance of information about profits

While other goals are ascribed to business as a positive social force contributing in various ways to the happiness and welfare of our society, the achievement of profits as a return to owners for the risks they assume is the primary goal. It is natural, therefore, that the quality of a business and of its management is judged primarily on the basis of their success in achieving profits.

It is to be expected, then, that information about profits will ordinarily constitute the most important and useful financial data concerning a business entity. Such information relates to the central purpose of business activity, and is of significance to all who have rights and interests in a business. The organization of the major portion of business enterprise today is the corporate form, whose ownership interests, shares of stock, are continuously traded. This has created a demand for reliable information concerning profits, on an annual basis and for periods shorter than a year as well.

Regardless of the quality of the investor's judgment and the many factors that mold his opinions on stock values, it is the appraisal of the prospects for future profits (earning power) that primarily governs the price at which the shares of stock in a business are traded and indicates how much the business is worth. Future profits provide the basis for both dividends and investment growth.

It appears, then, that the statement of profit and loss (or statement of income) is probably the key financial statement. I look at the purpose of the statement of income as being to provide a record of the past profits of a business, upon which some judgments about the future can be made.

Business decisions involve the power of choice

Let us assume that there are 1,000 business enterprises in this country, all of whose shares are traded publicly. Let us assume also that only one of these 1,000 business enterprises prepares and publishes financial statements, and that none of the other businesses provides any information concerning its profits and resources to the public.

Under these conditions, how useful would the financial information furnished by the one company be? Would it be useful to the investor in making decisions about which stock to buy or sell, and at what price? Would it be useful to the creditor, who is trying to assess relative risks of various lending opportunities?

I think we would agree that such financial information concerning only one of the 1,000 companies would have very little, if any, usefulness. We would say to this company, "Fine, you have made $1,000,000 this year, but maybe all of these other 999 companies do a better job than you do. Maybe their earnings per share are higher. Maybe their earnings in relation to tangible resources are better. We don't know whether your performance is good or bad."

I believe that this illustrates the crux of the matter. Decisions in our free enterprise system involve the process of choice. When it comes to investors, this involves the process of choosing to buy or sell the shares of one business enterprise from among the shares of numerous businesses. This goes for creditors, too, who have various lending opportunities. Thus, the financial information that a business discloses about itself will be useful only if the information provides a basis for comparing that business with others.

Furthermore, this process of choice is forward-looking. When we make decisions of any kind we may well look to experience and to the past in the process, but our decision is significant only with respect to the future. To the extent that we, as accountants, provide historical information upon which decisions are made in business, that data should be presented in a manner that makes it most useful to a reader in assessing the future—the future which, someone has said, is all we should be concerned with, since that is where we shall spend the rest of our lives.

The arguments over comparability

As fundamental as the issue would appear to be from this example, why should there be any resistance to achieving the ultimate in comparability in financial statements? Even some of those who have been general proponents of the elimination of alternatives in accounting practice and supporters of greater comparability have done so with the hedge that complete comparability is perhaps not desirable. Why? A writer in *The Journal of Accountancy* several months ago in discussing this question was careful to use the term "useful comparability," implying that there was a "useless" variety. Let us consider and evaluate some of the arguments that we hear.

Management rights and prerogatives

Those of us who have favored more comparability in financial statements among companies are sometimes charged with displaying a lack of knowledge of the nature of business, and a yearning for simple answers to complex accounting problems. The opponents of greater comparability contend that management has a responsibility to adopt those accounting practices that in its judgment best fit the circumstances and risks of its particular company.

Management does have this responsibility and no one really contends otherwise. However, if management is to make these difficult determinations, and if CPAs are to successfully and intelligently evaluate such determinations and decisions, sound and uniform accounting principles and criteria are needed so that management and CPAs can discharge those responsibilities. Management, in selecting from various alternative practices, sometimes yields to the pressure for short-term benefits rather than making the decision on the basis of what best fits the circumstances. This is undesirable from the standpoint of the company as well as the public.

Consider the case of the accounting for the investment credit. As you know, the standards of our profession now permit either the deferral of the investment tax credit, recognizing it as a credit to earnings over the life of the property, or the so-called "flow-through" method, recognizing the credit in income immediately in the year in which it is received. Without going into the pros and cons of which is the better method, it is certainly hard to conceive how different circumstances could affect the accounting for this item.

For the most part, the decisions of whether to defer or to take immediate benefit from the investment credit are not being made on the basis of what best "fits the circumstances," but are being made on the basis of what others are doing. This illustrates that it is the availability of alternatives that has stripped management of its prerogative to use judgment to assess the facts, and has made it a prisoner of poor accounting principles.

So, far from stripping management of its prerogatives, uniformity and soundness in accounting principles would help assure it of its legitimate prerogatives in judging the facts, circumstances and risks, which in turn should dictate the method of application of accounting principles and practices.

Rule books eliminate professional judgment and independence

There are some who argue that elimination of undesirable alternative practices would result in a rule book that would eliminate the exercise of professional judgment.

The fact is that it takes very little professional judgment to evaluate accounting practices if all that is involved is to look around to see what methods are being followed by other companies and are considered to be acceptable as reflected in their published reports. No judgment is involved when the CPAs may accept any one of various alternative practices selected on the basis of what happens to be available.

On the other hand, considerable ability is required on the part of the profession to establish sound criteria in the form of uniform accounting principles. Professional judgment is required to apply those criteria properly in the wide variety of existing circumstances and conditions. With the elimination of alternatives, the accountant and management could concentrate their decision-making and judgment on appraising and assessing the facts.

Those who oppose comparability allege that its proponents want to apply uniform methods without regard to judgment or without recognition of the differences in facts in each case. This allegation is erroneous; the use of judgment and a proper interpretation of the facts is always necessary. This, however, does not lessen the need for uniform principles to serve as guidelines in the application of judgment.

Insofar as the independence of the CPA is concerned, far from detracting from his independence, uniformity in accounting standards, principles, and criteria would render him more independent. Under some existing conditions, a CPA may be powerless to exercise his independent opinion about what is sound because generally accepted accounting principles encompass a number of alternatives that the CPA is supposed to accept, whether he considers them sound or not.

Dictatorship by the large accounting firm

There are those who say that the adoption of more uniformity in accounting standards and the elimination of alternatives would be tantamount to a dictatorship of the large firms over the individual practitioners.

On the contrary, uniformity in standards would give the small firms and local practitioners far more authority and independence. Under present circumstances, the very large public accounting firms have a distinct advantage, with their continuous contacts with what is going on in accounting throughout the country. The large firms have more information concerning what all the alternative practices are, while the local accountant, who has an office, say, only in Chicago or in Moline, may not have this information. Far from being a disadvantage to the local or smaller accounting firms, uniform principles would be a distinct advantage to such firms insofar as they must compete in the professional world with the knowledge and resources of larger firms.

"CCD" doctrine

Then there are the advocates of "CCD"—conservatism, consistency, and disclosure. These accountants downgrade the need for more uniformity and consider financial reporting adequate if there is disclosure of the alternative practices selected and such practices are consistently followed, particularly if the practices are on the side of conservatism.

These arguments are fallacious. We do not correct reported earnings or their image in the public mind by disclosing that pension costs have not been fully provided for. Also, something that is wrong is wrong, even if it is consistently wrong, although the net effect on certain figures may be modified. As desirable as conservatism is under certain conditions, we should not tolerate an error merely because it is on the conservative side. Conservatism in today's balance sheet can mean a lack of conservatism in tomorrow's earnings statement and may represent a lack of courage to apply sound accounting. Like conscience, conservatism gets a lot of credit that belongs to cold feet.

If we aren't careful, you see, we can carry this reasoning to a ridiculous extreme — that it does not matter that something is wrong, as long as it is consistently wrong, as long as the error is disclosed, and particularly if it is wrong in a conservative way.

As accountants, whether working within industry or as its independent auditors, we cannot discharge our responsibility to the public we spoke of earlier by resorting to this type of unprofessional rationalization.

In summary

The achievement of comparability in financial statements involves the establishment of some uniform accounting standards and sound criteria that the accountant can use to apply accounting practices to particular situations as he performs the difficult task of judging and assessing facts. How much reserve is needed for doubtful accounts, what provisions should be made for possible loss from obsolesence and excess stocks of inventories, and a host of other questions involve room for a tremendous range in judgment — without adding a senseless range of accounting-principle alternatives to choose from, once the facts have been determined.

Would uniformity in accounting standards impose a strait jacket on the businessman or on the independent CPA? Far from it. Rather, such uniformity would release both management and the CPA from the prison of alternative practices that entrap businesses in a competition to use those practices that will make each look better in the market place than its competitors. Freed from this prison, the businessman could assess the facts the way he sees them, applying accounting principles that he knows are the same for him as for others.

The CPA could assert his independence. He would not be faced with competition from "accounting discount houses" who offer an ever-wider range of alternative accounting practices. The uniform standards would permit him to use independence of judgment and would permit him to make judgments of the facts without having his presentation destroyed by inferior but "acceptable" alternative practices.

Thus uniformity, rather than a strait jacket, means freedom for all of us, those of us who represent management and those of us who represent the public accounting profession.

Our free enterprise system with its rights and privileges has given us the freedom to report upon ourselves. In addition, the independent review of that reporting by public accountants is also performed basically within the framework of our free enterprise system, as opposed to government control. Naturally the public expects and assumes that it is being protected. If the public comes to the conclusion that it is being misled, it will demand and get more safeguards through additional government control, whether we like it or not. Arguments about "common practice" or "general acceptance" will not help us as a profession or as individuals. When the sports public was misled by the basketball betting scandals, its wrath was not satiated by the fact that several players and teams were involved; rather, its anger became greater and the players, as well as the teams, paid the price individually. Rudyard Kipling saw this general truth when he said, "The sins ye do two by two, ye pay for one by one."

A public relations booklet published by a leading securities firm tells the layman-investor that he need not worry when the financial statements are certified by independent accountants. The following statement from that booklet emphasized the responsibility which we all carry on behalf of the public:

> "A generation or more ago, before present accounting standards and improved accounting principles had gained wide acceptance, considerable imagination went into the preparation of balance sheets. This naturally made the public skeptical of financial reports. Today there is no substantial ground for skepticism. The certified public accountant, the listing requirements of the national stock exchanges, and the regulations of the Securities and Exchange Commission and other governmental regulatory bodies have, for all practical purposes, removed the grounds for doubting the good faith of financial reports."

Is it not urgent that we as accountants remove any deficiencies that we feel exist in today's financial reports, when the public is told that it can rely so extensively on these reports? Can we justify any lengthy transitional or evolutionary period in establishing sound accounting principles that report the facts clearly and consistently for all companies?

If we hide behind the collective cloak of industry practice or professional association, obviously nothing gets done. There is no conscience in a group; it exists and exerts a force only in the individual. If we are to make progress, each of us must seek out the right answers, rather than asking, "What are others getting away with?" or "What will the SEC allow?" As a profession, we will get nowhere if each individual seeks only to play it safe or to do as the woman driver who always drove with the emergency brake on so that when an emergency happened, she would be ready. We must have the courage to face criticism from those who like it the way it is.

At the risk of being labeled a preacher, let me say that what we are talking about is the broad, moral issue in business. Others in the world are challenging the American way of free enterprise and the profit motive. Is it the best way for us and for our children?

We can defend our position and will demonstrate that this is the best way if we remain efficient and imaginative and recognize and honor our obligations, morally and legally, to the public interest that now exists in business and in the financial information it provides.

It has been said that there are two ways to get to the top of an oak tree — you can sit on an acorn or you can climb a tree. I most definitely feel that we of the accounting profession have a responsibility to climb; and I also believe, based on efforts by our profession in recent years, that the thinking of a majority of our profession concurs.

Establishing accounting principles and the role of research

Before a Research Seminar of the Graduate School of Business, Washington University, St. Louis, Missouri, March 8, 1966—Olson

The research studies published since the creation of the Accounting Principles Board have, for the most part, represented satisfactory work, but they have not had much effect on the Opinions issued by the Board.

I WAS PLEASED to receive an invitation to attend this research seminar and to participate in your discussion of establishing accounting principles and the role of research. I believe that the concept of a seminar of this type is excellent and I congratulate those who are responsible for the idea.

The accounting profession is a young profession. In the last two and a half decades it has expanded tremendously in numbers and in the breadth of the services it performs.

The public accounting segment of the profession arose principally to serve the needs of the public interest in business. That public interest is now very broad. There are close to 20 million people in this country who are stockholders in American business; millions more are beneficiaries of various trusts and pension funds, which hold vast ownership interests in business. There are a great many creditors.

Those who constitute this ownership and those who provide the funds for business operations ultimately control the destiny of business by their decisions. To a very large degree these decisions represent evaluations of the performance of individual businesses based on their financial statements. The primary purpose of the public accountant's existence is to provide an independent view of management's financial representations. This requires that the public accountant be completely independent of management, even though management can often influence to a great degree his continued association with his client, thereby affecting his very livelihood.

The degree of independence that is essential to the public accountant is, I believe, unique, although independence of mind and viewpoint is essential to men of all professions in carrying out their responsibilities. This characteristic would certainly appear to be an essential quality of the good teacher, researcher, or student.

As practitioners, teachers and graduate students we should have much more in common than our need to maintain an independent and creative viewpoint. We should be struggling with the same theoretical and technical issues. To do this we must share our experiences. There may be a larger gap between the world of the practitioner and the world of the teacher in our profession than exists in some of the older professions such as law and medicine. This is one reason why I believe that seminars such as this one can be so important to our progress as a profession. The kind of dialogue that we can have today should help broaden the perspective of all of us.

I hope that each of us will forget any predispositions we may have toward the question of accounting principles, approach the matter dispassionately, and address ourselves, not to winning an argument, but to determining the correct answer. A big deterrent to the resolution of problems in accounting is that many of us become emotionally committed to a particular position, and end up being more concerned with who is going to win rather than with reaching the right answers.

The Problem

Generally accepted accounting principles

The standard used for the last thirty years in judging whether the financial statements of a company fairly present its financial position and the results of its operations has been "generally accepted accounting principles." The standard opinion of the independent public accountant reads as follows: "In our opinion, the accompanying financial statements present fairly the financial position of XYZ Company as of December 31, 1965, and the results of its operations for the year then ended in conformity with generally accepted accounting principles applied on a basis consistent with that of the preceding year."

However, the term "generally accepted accounting principles" does not appear to have been satisfactorily defined nor does it have any clear meaning, either to those who use it or to those who read it. In October, 1964, the Council of the American Institute of Certified Public Accountants adopted various recommendations relating to this term, which included the following:

1. Generally accepted accounting principles are those principles that have substantial authoritative support.
2. Opinions of the Accounting Principles Board constitute substantial authoritative support.
3. Substantial authoritative support can exist for accounting principles that differ from opinions of the Accounting Principles Board.

The AICPA has recently published a research study with which I believe many of you are familiar. This study concludes that there are a number of sources for determining whether an accounting practice has substantial authoritative support:

1. Practices commonly found in business.
2. The requirements and views of stock exchanges as leaders in the financial community; similarly, the views and opinions of commercial and investment bankers are entitled to weight.
3. The regulatory commissions' uniform systems of accounts and accounting rulings, which exercise a dominant influence on the accounting practices of the industries subject to their jurisdiction.
4. The regulations and accounting opinions of the Securities and Exchange Commission, which have

controlling authority over reports filed with the Commission.

5. The affirmative opinions of practicing and academic certified public accountants.
6. Published opinions by Committees of the American Accounting Association and of the American Institute of Certified Public Accountants (such as the Accounting Principles Board).

Support for a wide variety of accounting practices, many of them inconsistent, can be found in the sources listed above. Many alternative practices that are followed for similar transactions that took place under similar circumstances are all considered to be in accordance with generally accepted accounting principles. As a result, financial statements often are not prepared on a comparable basis between industries or even among companies in the same industry, and in many cases variations in the practices followed by two companies may have more effect on financial comparisons between them than result from differences in the facts and circumstances.

We do not need to get into those alternatives now; the fact is that they do exist and we can discuss them later if you wish. Their results may be devastating to investors who are making decisions on which stock to buy or sell, to creditors and lenders who are trying to appraise the relative credit capacity of businesses, and to business and the public in general. The financial soundness and earning power of business is a very important economic factor, affecting political decisions in the area of fiscal policy and touching the lives of everyone. It is important to all that the barometer that measures business profits and conditions be reliable.

Fragmentation of authority for accounting principles

The fact is that accounting principles have not been established on a truly authoritative basis by anyone. Industry and accounting associations and stock exchanges have evidenced varying degrees of interest in establishment of sound accounting principles. Unfortunately, however, the differing interests and points of view have created frequent and sometimes sharp controversy. This has been particularly true where important questions are at issue; the greater the need for improvement, the larger is the number of groups that are affected and the stronger the pressures become for doing nothing. The effect of these differences in viewpoint has been to discourage effective leadership and decision-making by nongovernmental organizations.

Various Federal regulatory agencies have considerable authority over the financial accounting and the reporting to the public of companies subject to their jurisdictions. These agencies ignore or support the viewpoints of various elements of the accounting profession as they see fit. In some areas they select from alternative practices and in other areas they accept all practices. They have both published and unpublished accounting policies and rules, with no effective means of appeal from their decisions in accounting matters. There is no overall harmonizing or coordinating authority insofar as accounting prescribed by these agencies for published financial statements is concerned.

Thus, both nongovernmental organizations and governmental agencies are involved in establishing accounting principles. However, with their confused mixture of responsibilities and authorities, and with the tendency of some of these organizations to avoid taking public positions in controversial areas, there is a serious question where the accounting profession can turn to accomplish the necessary results.

The Accounting Principles Board

Although there are many thoughtful accountants who feel there is no unusual urgency for improvement in accounting and for clarification of accounting principles, there is now a broad agreement in the profession that improvements are needed. It is also fairly clear from events in the past two or three years that there is a greater sense of urgency on the part of a large number of accountants and a feeling that very determined efforts will be required to correct the various weaknesses in accounting.

The first significant official recognition by the American Institute of Certified Public Accountants that more rapid improvement was necessary came in 1959 with the creation of the Accounting Principles Board. Most of you are probably generally familiar with this Board. It is the group created to issue official pronouncements on the part of the Institute on accounting matters. It superseded the former Institute Committee on Accounting Procedure, which had issued a series of fifty-one Accounting Research Bulletins. The Board consists of a group of 21 prominent people (gradually being reduced over the next several years to 18), including representatives from both large and small accounting firms, from universities and from industry.

The Board was created as a result of a report to the AICPA's governing body, the Council, by a Special Committee on Accounting Research. This Committee had been appointed subsequent to an address by Alvin Jennings, then president of the Institute, at the annual meeting of the Institute in 1957. There had been a growing awareness at that time of the need for a better means of developing authoritative statements on accounting principles for the guidance of industry and the accounting profession. Dissatisfaction with financial reporting was becoming increasingly evident and had been the subject of much discussion in business circles and in the financial press.

In recommending the establishment of an Accounting Principles Board, the Committee said there should be:

> ". . . continuing effort to determine appropriate practice and to narrow the areas of difference and inconsistency in practice. In accomplishing this, reliance should be placed on persuasion rather than on compulsion. The Institute, however, can and should take definite steps to lead the thinking on unsettled and controversial issues."

Coincidental with the organization of the APB was a reorganization of the accounting research activity of the AICPA. Accounting research studies were to be made on various subjects. The results of these studies were to be published and widely distributed as a prelude to change or modification in accounting practice and to the issuance of authoritative pronouncements or opinions by the Board.

Let us look briefly at what has been accomplished in the way of research and official accounting pronouncements since the Accounting Principles Board was created in 1959. The following research studies have been published:

No. 1—"The Basic Postulates of Accounting," by Maurice Moonitz (September 1961).

No. 2—"Cash Flow Analysis and the Funds Statement," by Perry Mason (November 1961).

No. 3—"A Tentative Set of Broad Accounting Principles for Business Enterprises," by Robert T. Sprouse and Maurice Moonitz (April 1962).

No. 4—"Reporting of Leases in Financial Statements," by John H. Myers (May 1962).

No. 5—"A Critical Study of Accounting for Business Combinations," by Arthur R. Wyatt (June 1963).

No. 6—"Reporting the Financial Effects of Price-Level Changes," by the Staff of the Accounting Research

Division of the AICPA (October 1963).

No. 7—"Inventory of Generally Accepted Accounting Principles for Business Enterprises," by Paul Grady (March 1965).

No. 8—"Accounting for the Cost of Pension Plans," by Ernest L. Hicks (May 1965).

The quality of these research studies, in general, has been good. They are comprehensive in nature and the facts and reasoning upon which most of the conclusions were reached are set forth.

Other research studies are in process and presumably will be completed over the next two or three years. These studies involve the accounting for income taxes, intercorporate investments, foreign operations, goodwill and business combinations, industrial product research and development, and operations peculiar to extractive industries. Research is also being done on the concept of materiality, income, and retained earnings, and the objectives of financial statements.

Six Opinions have been issued by the Accounting Principles Board in the six and a half years since its inception. These are as follows:

No. 1—"New Depreciation Guidelines and Rules" (November 1962) —There was no research study on this subject, and it involves a relatively minor accounting matter resulting from the issuance of new regulations by the Internal Revenue Service.

No. 2—"Accounting for the 'Investment Credit' " (December 1962)— There was no research study on this subject but it was discussed extensively by the members of the APB and was issued on a timely basis in an attempt to avoid alternative practices for a new item. (Subsequently amended, and largely nullified, by Opinion No. 4).

No. 3—"The Statement of Source and Application of Funds" (October 1963)—Research Study No. 2 was on this subject, and this Opinion, along with encouragement from the New York Stock Exchange, has resulted in such statements being included in many annual reports to stockholders.

No. 4—Amended No. 2 (March 1964)—Certain prominent AICPA members, along with the Securities and Exchange Commission, accepted an alternative practice specifically disapproved in Opinion No. 2. As a result, the APB issued Opinion No. 4, recognizing as acceptable two opposite practices.

No. 5—"Reporting of Leases in Financial Statements of Lessee" (September 1964)—Research Study No. 4 was on this subject, but the APB did not adopt the principal conclusions of the study. This Opinion evades the real issues involved and does not deal effectively with the problem.

No. 6—"Status of Accounting Research Bulletins" (October 1965)— This Opinion relates to the bulletins issued by the prior Committee on Accounting Procedure and gives formal recognition to some existing alternative practices and eliminates a few previous requirements (one of which had required disclosure of essential financial information, and its elimination represents a serious step backward).

Also, there is an exposure draft now out on Opinion No. 7, which deals with the accounting for leases in the financial statements of lessors.

After the cancellation of Opinion No. 2 on the investment credit by Opinion No. 4, it is fair to say that none of the Opinions issued by the APB so far has been effective in eliminating any significant alternatives among accounting practices. Thus it still remains to be seen whether the Accounting

Principles Board can accomplish its purpose in any important problem area.

The investment credit story

Crucial to the matter we are discussing today is the question of the status of the Board's Opinions. There is a very interesting story pertaining to this question.

It all started with the controversy over the accounting for the investment credit in 1962. You have heard a great deal about this and I won't go into the accounting arguments. Compared with some other accounting problems that exist, such as those involving business combinations and goodwill or pension plans or deferred taxes, the investment credit might not have been considered a major accounting issue. But the battle over the accounting for the investment credit served to reveal very clearly the divergence of views among accountants over the general meaning of the auditors' responsibilities, and particularly over the proper methods for establishing accounting principles and improving standards of reporting.

The accounting question involved was a relatively clear one. Congress had enacted a new law by which companies were allowed a credit against taxes otherwise payable, computed as a percentage (basically 7%) of investment in new plant and equipment. Some accountants felt that the credit should be treated as a reduction of the cost of the property; others felt that it represented a reduction of tax expense and should flow through to income immediately. The majority of the Accounting Principles Board believed that, based on the legislative record, the wording of the law, and the general substance of the item, the proper method was to treat the credit as a reduction, in effect, of the cost of the related property and to spread the benefits of the credit to income as a reduction of depreciation over the life of the property. After considerable controversy extending over several months and a great deal of public discussion, the Board, with the required majority of two thirds, issued its Opinion No. 2, which stated that the deferral method was the proper one.

The battle between those who favored the issuance of this Opinion and those who did not centered around the question of whether there should be more than one method. Those who opposed the Opinion said that the Board should permit both methods since thoughtful men disagreed on which was right.

It is very probable that if all the large accounting firms had chosen to follow the Opinion and had qualified their auditors' reports where clients failed to follow the practice advocated in the Board's Opinion, the issue would have been settled then and there.

However, several large firms whose representatives on the Board had voted against the Opinion chose not to enforce it, but rather considered the alternative practice of flow-through as also being a generally accepted accounting principle on the grounds that it had "authoritative support." At the same time, the Securities and Exchange Commission issued an Accounting Series Release stating that, in recognition of the substantial controversy over the accounting for the investment credit, it would accept either method of accounting in financial statements filed with it. Furthermore, the SEC said it would accept those statements even though some auditors might take exception in their report when companies followed a method not advocated in the Board's Opinion.

The result was a chaotic situation; those members who had chosen not to follow the Board's Opinion and the SEC had succeeded in establishing alternative accounting practices for a brand new accounting problem. In 1964, the Board finally decided to issue Opinion No. 4, which stated that while the majority of the Board still felt that deferral was the preferable method, in recognition of the fact that there was substantial authoritative support for the flow-through method, the Board would consider that both methods constituted generally accepted accounting principles.

The question of status of APB Opinions

As a result of this fight over the accounting for the investment credit, a debate arose in the profession over the authority which the Opinions of the Accounting Principles Board should have, and over the meaning of the term "generally accepted accounting principles." A proposal was submitted to a meeting of the Council (the governing body) of the AICPA in May 1964. The essence of this proposal was that, when a pronouncement of the Accounting Principles Board had become effective, the pronouncement should be considered as constituting the only generally accepted accounting principle in the subject area for purposes of expressing an Opinion on financial statements. The adoption of such a proposal would preclude the kind of action that had been taken by several firms in choosing to ignore the Board's Opinion on the investment credit on the ground that there was authoritative support for another method.

The introduction of this suggestion as a proposed resolution in the Council at its meeting in May of 1964 stirred perhaps the most extensive debate and discussion that body has ever held. A total of forty-one people spoke with respect to the resolution; some firms had as many as five or six persons speak.

Those who opposed the resolution seemed to base their opposition primarily on problems of implementing such a reporting requirement; they stressed the fact that the American Institute had no right to establish a definition of the term "generally accepted accounting principles" because this term is in the public domain and had meanings already established in contracts, indentures, and so on.

At the conclusion of the discussion, the resolution as originally drafted was discarded but a new one was introduced and passed by the Council, which read as follows:

> "Resolved that it is the sense of this Council that reports of members should disclose material departures from Opinions of the Accounting Principles Board and that the president is hereby authorized to appoint a special committee to recommend to Council appropriate methods of implementing the substance of this resolution."

This resolution simply required disclosure if an APB Opinion was not followed, and left the auditor free to give an unqualified opinion with respect to generally accepted accounting principles.

The Special Committee appointed to implement the resolution of Council worked hard during 1964 and came up with a recommendation to Council for handling disclosures of departures, which the Council unanimously adopted at its meeting in October 1964. The recommendation was that CPAs should see to it that departures from Opinions of the Accounting Principles Board (as well as departures from the Accounting Research Bulletins issued by the former Committee on Accounting Procedure) are disclosed either in footnotes to financial statements or in the audit reports of the CPA.

To most accountants, this action represented a substantial step forward; it gave the Opinions of the Accounting Principles Board considerably more status than other sources as authoritative support for accounting principles. For this action to be effective and meaningful, however, the Accounting Principles Board must now issue Opinions in controversial areas that will narrow existing differences in accounting.

The reports of the Special Committee created to implement the Council's resolution of May 1964 also made a number of other recommendations that the Institute has approved. Among other things, these reports urged that the Board promptly set forth its views with respect to the purposes and limitations of published financial statements and of the independent auditor's function, and that the Board move toward the reduction of alternative practices in accounting by adopting policies that would restrict alternatives and variations to those justified by differences in facts.

Deferred tax on installment sales

The Board did not deal effectively with the controversial issue of the investment credit, and a more recent event has underscored the difficulty of getting independent action from the Board on controversial issues. But this event and certain related happenings may have served to provide impetus for faster and more positive action by the profession in the future, as discussed in the paragraphs that follow.

Over the years divergent practices have developed and flourished in regard to the classification of deferred Federal income taxes relating to installment sales. For those of you who are unfamiliar with the technical accounting background, it can be briefly summarized as follows:

1. Many companies, primarily those in the retailing field but also to an increasing extent in the manufacturing industries, have installment receivables arising in the ordinary course of the business that are collectible over a period of more than one year.

2. Many of these companies reflect income from these installment sales in their financial statements in the period of sale, but defer the income taxes under the installment method and provide for the deferred income taxes in their financial statements.

3. The general practice is to include the receivables in current assets, even though they are not due for 2, 3, 4 or 5 years, since they are considered to be in the "operating cycle" as defined in Chapter 3A of Accounting Research Bulletin No. 43.

4. Some companies have classified the deferred taxes relating to the installment receivables as current liabilities since the related receivables are in current assets while others have classified similar deferred taxes as noncurrent liabilities.

The effect of this divergence in practice was assuming greatly increased significance by 1965, and it was likely to increase even further. With the expanded use of revolving credit plans and various other installment payment plans by merchandising companies and with the relatively recent regulations of the Internal Revenue Service permitting sales under revolving credit plans to be treated as installment sales for income tax purposes, many companies were accumulating an increasingly large amount of deferred income taxes on installment sales. For example, on January 31, 1965, Sears Roebuck had $454,000,000 of such deferred taxes.

Financial analysts and investment bankers have generally indicated that the classification of deferred taxes is important from both the investors' and creditors' point of view. The problem, therefore, is not theoretical. The classification of these taxes, where the amounts involved are material, has a significant effect on the determination of a company's working capital and the credit rating it receives.

As a result, last spring the Accounting Principles Board placed the subject on its agenda for consideration in connection with the issuance of its Opinion No. 6, "Status of Accounting Research Bulletins." In the exposure of Opinion No. 6, which was distributed widely in July 1965 for comment, the following paragraph was added to the Chapter of Accounting Research Bulletin No. 43 that deals with working capital:

> "Whenever it is appropriate to record deferred income taxes, such deferred taxes should be classified as a current liability to the extent that they are related to current assets which give rise to the tax deferment."

The APB received a number of comments from industry with respect to this paragraph, strongly objecting to it. Support for the proposed requirement, however, had come from Mr. Andrew Barr, Chief Accountant of the Securities and Exchange Commission.

Last October, when the Accounting Principles Board met again, the Board, in view of the comments it had received, decided to defer the question and directed that further study be undertaken. (The partner of our firm, George Catlett, who is a member of the Board, objected strenuously to deferring this question.) All that had happened in a period of three months was that a number of comments from industry had been received objecting to the proposed requirement. Substantially the entire Board, I understand, had initially felt that the current treatment of the deferred taxes relating to installment sales was obviously the only correct one when the related receivables were in current assets.

This incident certainly raised some serious questions concerning the ability of the Board to act effectively on accounting questions.

In two cases, therefore, in a little over two years the Accounting Principles Board had not demonstrated ability to deal independently with really controversial issues. It had reversed itself on the investment credit and allowed both methods, and had deferred action on the deferred tax issue.

The SEC Acts

Little action could now be expected from the Accounting Principles Board prior to the end of 1965 on the question of classification of deferred taxes relating to installment sales. So, either it was necessary for the Securities and Exchange Commission to act or nothing would be done. The problem in waiting was that Gresham's Law appeared to be taking hold; with increasing accumulations of these deferred taxes, more and more companies indicated that they would continue, or even change to, the long-term classification, leaving the receivable in current assets. Soon the practice would be almost universal.

But now the Securities and Exchange Commission acted. In response to a petition by our firm, in December 1965 it issued its Accounting Series Release No. 102 requiring consistent balance sheet classification of installment receivables and the related deferred taxes; either both were current or both were noncurrent. Furthermore, it said that this Release would be effective immediately with calendar years ending December 31, 1965. There was no exposure of this draft nor did the SEC give interested parties an opportunity for presenting their arguments pro and con.

This action by the SEC is significant. In addition, some of the actions that took place prior to the issuance of the SEC's Release are also of significance to us in considering the problem of what can or should be done in the area of sound accounting principles. In the course of its consideration of the petition, the Securities and Exchange Commission requested a meeting with representatives of the Accounting Principles Board. The meeting, held in late November, was attended by the full Commission as well as its Chief Accountant.

From the outset, the SEC made it abundantly clear to the Accounting Principles Board representatives that it planned to take quick and positive action with respect to deferred taxes and installment sales. It was obvious that the Securities and Exchange Commission had called the meeting not to ask the Accounting Principles Board's advice but rather to tell the Accounting

Principles Board its conclusions. Further, it would appear that the purpose of the meeting was designed with a longer range objective—to instill in the Accounting Principles Board a sense of urgency in its handling of problems under consideration.

It was brought out that the Chief Accountant of the Securities and Exchange Commission had asked the American Institute of Certified Public Accountants to consider and come up with an answer to this problem of deferred taxes on installment sales as long as fifteen years ago, in 1950. The SEC let it be known that it intends to see that such action is taken as is necessary to carry out its responsibilities under the laws which it administers. (Editor's note—The APB in Opinion No. 11 endorsed the view of our firm and the one endorsed by the SEC.)

Summary of the Situation

Here, then, is the situation as it appears today:

1. There are a number of very important alternatives in accounting practices, which are producing significant differences in financial reports among companies and which in turn, I believe, are reducing significantly the usefulness of financial statements.
2. At present, there is a considerable amount of criticism of financial statement practices by bankers, the financial press and others. This kind of criticism, if allowed to continue without action, can undermine the basic confidence of the public that the financial representations of American businesses have enjoyed. Our system of public ownership of business and of credit is built on the cornerstone of public confidence.
3. It is extremely difficult for twenty-one men from all parts of the country, such as those who serve on the Accounting Principles Board, with all types of interests and under extreme pressures, to act effectively on truly tough questions. They have faced two really controversial issues. They took action on one, the investment credit, but later had to back down. They failed to act on the other, the classification of deferred taxes relating to installment sales. In the latter case, their free choice of future action has, in effect, been denied them by the action of the SEC.
4. Lurking in the background is the vast (largely latent) Federal authority to control accounting. This authority is vested in the Securities and Exchange Commission under the securities laws, and also in other regulatory agencies, which have jurisdictions over particular industries and thus have various powers to control the accounting requirements of companies in their jurisdictions. These include agencies such as the Federal Power Commission, the Interstate Commerce Commission, the Civil Aeronautics Board, and the Federal Communications Commission.

In total, I think we would say that relatively little direct action has been taken by these agencies to control accounting, outside of prescribing certain uniform systems of accounts. The most significant, insofar as security holders are concerned, have been the actions of the SEC. However, the actions of the SEC have generally not been in the form of public announcements of the formal kind, such as that dealing with the deferred tax issue, but rather a behind-the-scenes approach. Decisions on individual accounting matters by the SEC in connection with registration statements, mergers, and so on, have become precedents that have been unknown to many until they filed statements with the SEC.

In the absence of strong and positive action by the Accounting Principles Board, however, the authority of these Federal regulatory agencies is indeed ominous.

5. The research studies that have been published since the creation of the Accounting Principles Board have, for the most part, represented good work, but their results so far have generally not found their way into concrete Opinions. There are some present indications, however, that the Accounting Principles Board is giving increasing attention to these research studies. The Board is now contemplating a pronouncement on accounting for the cost of pension plans and is making extensive use of the research study on this subject.

6. There are indications that the Board is taking the recent statements and action by the Securities and Exchange Commission to heart. It has increased its scheduled meeting dates for this year. It has reviewed its agenda and has accelerated target dates for the completion of certain important projects. It has generally evidenced an increasing sense of urgency in its activities. It may be unfortunate that it took six years and a "kick in the pants" from the SEC to accomplish this, but the important point is that we may now have greater hopes for progress. If the Accounting Principles Board measures up and performs as it can and should, the initiative in establishing accounting principles will remain with the profession. The next few years will probably provide the answer.

The Accounting Court

There is a possibility, therefore, that the Accounting Principles Board will improve its effectiveness in dealing with current problems on a timely basis and thereby carry out its responsibilities. If the accounting profession were to do a better job along these lines, the seriousness of the present problem would be minimized. It is undoubtedly true that in the long run the Federal regulatory agencies will give more weight to the views of the accounting profession if the profession does not procrastinate, and does not continue to allow a wide variety of practices to be available and acceptable.

There is, of course, no assurance that the regulatory agencies will follow Accounting Principles Board Opinions. It is also true that these agencies have been gradually assuming more authority over the accounting and reporting practices of a significant part of American business. There is now no effective and independent tribunal in the Federal government or any place else where the accounting profession, representatives of business, and other interested parties can have a public hearing and a formal record of the proceedings for the purpose of establishing appropriate and fair accounting principles and practices on a basis that is acceptable to the Federal agencies.

In the face of present Federal power, what possible courses of action exist for controlling and harmonizing such power in this area and assuring that everyone is given a fair hearing in the determination of accounting principles? In view of the present uncertainties, and while there is still time for deliberation and consideration, our firm has explored the possibility of a Court of Accounting Appeals, responsible to the public and operating in the executive branch of the Federal government. We are not now recommending such a Court, but are asking all those who are interested in improvement in the financial information supplied by business to consider all of the possible alternatives that exist, including this one. Let me just take a few minutes to outline how such a Court might operate, and then we can open the seminar to questions and discussion, not only of the question of the Court, but of any other problems and issues that I have discussed here by way of background.

Our firm has prepared a booklet that contains a draft of a possible bill that would create a United States Court of Accounting Appeals. This bill was prepared by legal counsel. The law firm that drafted the bill and another large law firm in New York have issued written opinions in which they have stated that if this bill were enacted into law by the Congress of the United States and signed by the President, it would be constitutional and valid and would provide an orderly method of accomplishing the objectives set forth in the bill. Neither firm, however, was asked to express, nor did express, an opinion as to the desirability of the bill.

The bill contemplates a tribunal, which would not be a part of the Federal judiciary system but would be an independent agency in the executive branch of the Federal government. It would be called a Court and its five members appointed by the President would serve for terms of ten years and would be designated as judges. There is precedent for this terminology. The United States Board of Tax Appeals is an independent agency in the executive branch of the United States Government, and its name has now been changed, as you know, to the Tax Court of the United States, and its members are designated as judges.

The Court would have both appellate and limited original jurisdiction with respect to the five Federal agencies I previously mentioned.

The draft of the bill would not grant to the Court any jurisdiction over accounting matters that the various Federal agencies do not already have. Its function would be:

1. To provide an effective means by which accounting rules prescribed by the various regulatory bodies such as the SEC could be reviewed on the record and affirmed, modified or reversed by a single tribunal, and
2. To permit such tribunal, in its discretion, to institute accounting rule making when an agency improperly refuses to do so. In this way, it would be possible to balance and harmonize the specific requirements of each agency within a unified, consistent pattern of accounting principles and practices. Federal regulatory agencies would thereby help to firm up accounting standards rather than contribute to their fragmentation and deterioration.

The Court would not eliminate the need for the Accounting Principles Board. Far from taking away from accountants any rights and responsibilities that they now have, the Court could give them additional stature. Where the agencies are now frequently able to establish accounting practices without a public hearing (such as Accounting Series Release No. 102 issued by the SEC on deferred taxes relating to installment sales), the Court would afford accountants a public forum in which to advance and support their professional reasoning. A strong, unified profession, speaking with a single voice with regard to accounting principles and clearly explaining its reasoning, would undoubtedly carry substantial weight with the Court.

Because of our form of government, under which certain powers are reserved to the states, the jurisdiction of the Court would be limited to other Federal agencies. It is likely, however, that the consistently well-reasoned views of such a Federally established Court, having jurisdiction over accounting in a large part of the nation's business, would receive careful consideration from state regulatory authorities and judicial courts.

The bill as drafted would include the following significant features with respect to accounting rule making:

1. At the agencies—

a. Decisions in rule-making procedures instituted by a Federal agency for the adoption, modification or appeal of accounting rules would be made by the agency on the record, after an opportunity for a hearing in conformity with the Administrative Procedure Act.

b. Any person subject to the jurisdiction of the agencies, any CPA or licensed public accountant who gives opinions upon the financial statements of any such person, or any association of such accountants could petition an agency to institute rule-making procedures, which would have to be instituted or the petition denied within 30 days.

c. Any such person could be a party to the rule-making proceedings.

2. At the Court—

a. Any person whose petition to an agency to institute rule making was denied could petition the Court to institute original rule making on the record, after opportunity for a hearing in conformity with the Administrative Procedure Act.

b. Upon timely petition by a party to the agency proceeding, the Court would review an accounting rule of the agency on the basis of the record and affirm, modify or reverse the rule or remand it to the agency for further proceeding.

c. In the case of a review of an agency decision, such agency and all parties to the agency proceeding would be parties to the review and would be entitled to file briefs and to be heard upon oral argument. Any other agency covered by the bill could file a brief as a friend of the Court and at the Court's discretion could be heard upon oral argument.

3. Judicial review of the Court decisions would be available in the same way as for an administrative agency.

One thing should be noted. The establishment of such a Court would *not* constitute an extension of governmental authority. Governmental authority over financial statements and accounting principles is already established under present laws. Rather, the establishment of such a Court would provide a degree of control over the agencies authorized to act in this area in such a way as to provide greater assurance of fairness and consistency in the application of authority that governmental organizations now possess.

Conclusion

CPAs cannot function effectively as independent examiners of financial statements unless they have sound standards to use as a basis for their opinions. It seems reasonable to assume that a solution to the problem will of necessity emerge, but the part to be played by the accounting profession, by the teaching profession or by the researchers has not yet been determined. In closing, the question is not what managements or accountants or commissioners would prefer in order to maintain their relative prerogatives as they exist. The question is what is best for the investors, the public and the other users of financial statements.

Achieving progress

Before the Berkeley Symposium on the Foundations of Financial Accounting, sponsored by the Schools of Business Administration, University of California, Berkeley, California, January 13, 1967—Catlett*

The accounting profession can overcome its "gaps" and achieve constructive progress.

WITH RESPECT TO the current criticism of, and dissatisfaction with, financial reporting, there undoubtedly is room for improvement. The situation in which we find ourselves today has, in my opinion, resulted from three principal causes. Some time ago, we heard a lot about the "missile gap," and more recently the "antimissile gap" has been mentioned in the press. In my view, the accounting profession has been the victim of three "gaps" of its own.

The first of these is the "time gap." Financial accounting and reporting to parties other than management have not kept pace with the needs of our society. If you carefully analyze the actual progress that was made during the period from 1940 to 1960, you will find that very little was accomplished during this war and postwar period. This is borne out to some extent by Carman Blough's historical analysis this morning. Not only were many of the old problems left unsolved, but new ones, such as those relating to leases, pensions, mergers and tax allocation, were also unsolved. Significant progress was made in the 1930's, and the same hopefully will be true of the 1960's, but the 20-year gap in between, when great social and economic changes occurred, put us so far behind that the attempt now to overcome the accumulated deficiencies is still in danger of being too little and too late, and the quality of the corrections may suffer from the time pressures involved in trying to catch up. Thus, we are suffering from a lack of timely progress in financial reporting to meet our changing environment.

Next, we have the "responsibility gap." The responsibilities of CPAs in giving opinions on financial statements, as compared to the responsibilities of managements and others, have really never been sufficiently well established and understood. This

* These remarks were made as a part of a discussion of a paper, "Conflicting Objectives and the Necessity of Tradeoff" by D. E. Browne, Group Vice President—Finance and Administration, Lockheed Aircraft Corporation.

fact underlies many of the differences of opinion with respect to the determination of accounting principles. This fact is reflected in legal actions which have been settled out of court and others that are now in court. Where are the responsibilities for principles and standards among the American Institute of Certified Public Accountants, the Securities and Exchange Commission, managements who issue financial statements, and CPAs who give opinions on such statements? Legal actions are generally taken against management and CPAs, and management may in some cases look to the CPAs for final responsibility. This lack of understanding of the relative responsibilities of various groups is a problem that is basic to many of the difficulties which the accounting profession now faces.

Finally, there is the "theory gap." I recognize the difficulty of establishing a complete and integrated accounting theory that would logically give good answers to all of the practical problems. It has often been said that what is good theory should be good practice and vice versa. However, there is a serious gap between what is considered to be sound theory and what is considered to be sound practice. We have never successfully built a bridge between the solutions to our everyday problems and the somewhat vague concepts on realization, matching costs and revenues, accrual accounting, and many other matters of theory. Until the gap between theory and practice is effectively closed, the solutions to our problems will tend to be arbitrary and disjointed rather than a part of an integrated plan.

Attracting talent

There is one point on which my view is completely the opposite of Mr. Browne's. He states that the desire for uniformity and standardization to achieve comparability is a serious deterrent to the profession in obtaining the proper type of manpower. My experience and observations have indicated that the best calibre of students will be attracted by the profession in future years *only* if the profession establishes and enforces sound and uniform standards. Without such standards there cannot be a true profession, and many students today are well aware of what is needed in the development of the type of profession with which they would like to be associated.

Management's position

I would not in any way minimize the responsibilities of management with respect to financial accounting and reporting. However, this responsibility includes the necessity of giving investors, creditors and others the best possible financial information upon which to base their decisions. Also, managements have every right to rely upon their CPAs to guide them in their actions and to defend them in litigation. The only defense in the long run is not custom, which has evolved in a haphazard manner, but uniform standards that can be demonstrated to be sound.

Achieving progress and accommodating change

There can be no disagreement by anyone with the statement: "Accounting, if it is to retain any semblance of utility, must be prepared to accommodate change." Mr. Browne then concludes that experimentation is necessary before less desirable alternative treatments can be eliminated and that, since the Accounting Principles Board is attempting to lock principles in concrete, it can never be a constructive force in the accommodation of change. We, of course, do not have time today to debate this point. However, in my opinion the Accounting Principles Board represents the only nongovernmental solution to our current problems in the area of accounting principles and in its absence the government is almost certain to take over the function. Part of the difficulties faced by the Board arise from the necessity of putting out fires while trying to build the firehouse. The Board has now started to work on basic concepts and principles and the successful completion of this project is essential to any long-range success of the Board's program.

There was plenty of experimentation in accounting for pension plans, and the Opinion of the Board on that subject was an attempt (even though unpopular with some people) to try to obtain a reasonable degree of order out of what could be characterized as accounting chaos. Whether the Board does properly accommodate change remains to be seen. There is no good reason that it could not do so.

Mr. Browne contends that we can move no faster than our environment will permit. I would merely add that we must also move as fast as our environment requires.

One of Mr. Browne's comments is so well expressed and is so much in agreement with my own views that I want to repeat in part what he said:

> "In directing progress in accounting, we must recognize that we live in a multivalued society. The goals of one group having legitimate interests in accounting are not those of other groups. Nor are these differences merely in order of priorities. Such differences in many cases disclose outright conflict. . . . We cannot progress unless we learn to compose these differences. And we must recognize that composing differences need not involve compromises. Attempts to satisfy all can only lead to such divergent routes that no progress can be made. We should note, too, that the goals of the various interested groups are in a constant state of change."

That viewpoint is another way of stating a very basic premise—we must establish what is the fairest presentation of the facts to all segments of society and effectively reflect this in financial accounting and reporting to the public.

Comparability

I know of nothing in accounting discussion today that is more maligned, misunderstood and misused than the term "comparability." Those who oppose this concept set up a straw man by asserting that comparability would be based on an arbitrary and unimaginative rule book prescribed by narrow perfectionists. The accounts and methods presumably would be more or less permanently frozen and would force a wide diversity of situations into a common mold. They then conclude, as Mr. Browne has, that obviously everyone would be misled. The fact is that those accountants who favor more comparability believe that uniform standards and principles, if properly established, (1) will produce sufficiently comparable results to be more useful; (2) will be structured so that they are sensitive to changed conditions; (3) will permit differing practices that best reflect various circumstances, but with adequate criteria for selection of the appropriate practice; (4) will furnish a sounder base for comparing the effectiveness of management; and (5) will develop confidence in the results on the part of the public.

Current values

The use of current values in accounting is something that is very logical in theory but very difficult to apply and control in practice. I have no doubt that the trend toward current value accounting, which already exists to some extent, will continue, because in principle there is much to be said for it. Success or failure will depend upon how well it is done and how well it is kept under control. Failure could bring on further governmental intervention. The accountants in this country have not quite recovered from the fiasco in this area in the 1920's.

This is a problem that cannot be settled by merely saying that the cost basis has been good enough and ought to be continued. However, for any progress in this area, ways and means must be found for gradually reflecting current values in accounting on an objective and sound basis. Thus, the implementation is critical.

* * *

As Mr. Browne indicates, management and the accounting profession have a common problem. They have brought many of their current difficulties upon themselves by lack of foresight and of a real desire to achieve the necessary improvements. Problems that needed solutions were permitted to slide along without being faced. The question is not who is subservient to whom, but rather whether the accounting profession with the assistance of management and other interested parties in our free enterprise system can settle their own problems satisfactorily on a positive and constructive basis.

Accounting for the cost of pension plans

Before the annual meeting of the Illinois Society of Certified Public Accountants, St. Louis, Missouri, June 23, 1967—Olson*

A discussion of the highlights of Accounting Principles Board Opinion No. 8 and its impact on accounting, auditing, and financial statements.

* George R. Catlett presided at this meeting as President of the Illinois Society of Certified Public Accountants.

ACCOUNTING Principles Board Opinion No. 8 on accounting for the cost of pension plans became effective for fiscal years starting in 1967, and for all CPAs who perform audits it should involve study and discussions with clients, and in some cases with their actuaries, so that the Opinion will be properly applied.

I want to make it clear that I am not an expert on pension plans or any of the complicated actuarial, tax and fiscal factors that are involved. My exposure to this new opinion has probably been very similar to what many of yours has been—dealing with a few sticky questions from clients or associates.

Many of these terms, such as "unit-credit method," "defined-benefit plan," "defined-contribution plan," "vested benefit," "deposit-administration contract," "pay-as-you-go," leave me feeling a little like the 15-year old girl who found herself at the perfume counter of a large department store one day. The clerk brought out something called "My Sin," then showed her a bottle labeled "Ecstacy" and another called "Night Passion." Finally, the young girl blushed and stammered, "Haven't you got anything for a beginner?"

Well, what I have to say on pensions is for us beginners, but I hope the discussion will be helpful.

Background of APB Opinion No. 8

Over the past twenty years there has been a very substantial growth in private pension plans in industry, growth both in terms of the numbers of people covered by the plans and in the benefits that they provide. Businesses and unions have both demonstrated a responsible concern for the well-being of retired persons. In the meantime, the costs of these plans have become significant considerations in the measurement of the financial position and earnings of companies, creating an ever greater need for sound methods of accounting for these costs.

Costs of many of the earlier plans had been simply accounted for on a pay-as-you-go basis. Over the years, the pressures to fund the plans on some responsible fiscal basis, together with the availability of valuable income tax deductions for amounts set aside in such funds, were important factors contributing to the recognition of the principle that the cost of pension plans should be charged against profits during the working lives of employees. But practices varied greatly and no clear-cut controlling accounting philosophy existed.

In 1956 the Committee on Accounting Procedure of the American Institute of Certified Public Accountants (AICPA), the predecessor of the Accounting Principles Board, took official cognizance of the fact that "variations in the provisions of pension plans in the United States, in their financial arrangements, and in the circumstances attendant upon their adoption, have resulted in substantial differences in accounting for pension costs." In its Accounting Research Bulletin (ARB) No. 47, the Committee expressed the view that "costs based on current and future services should be systematically accrued during the expected period of active service of the covered employees, generally upon the basis of actuarial computations." The Committee stated, however, that opinion on this issue had not yet crystallized and that "accordingly, for the present, the Committee believes that, as a minimum, the accounts and financial statements should reflect accruals which equal the present worth, actuarially calculated, of pension commitments to employees to the extent that pension rights have vested in the employees. . . ."

ARB No. 47 was implicitly a transitional pronouncement, pointing to the ultimate objective but allowing time and permitting latitude in arriving there. However, if anyone hoped that the transition period would be brief, their optimism was not justified. The old problems of extensive variations in accounting continued.

At one extreme were companies that adhered to the pay-as-you-go concept; in other words, the cash basis. This approach was based on the theory that plans could be terminated at the option of the employer and, therefore, that no liability accrues.

Most major companies did make provisions for pension costs that were adequate over a period of years to cover normal (or current-service) costs plus at least the interest on unfunded past-service costs. The problem was, however, that in many instances the provisions were not made according to any systematic pattern.

A particularly vexing problem for CPAs resulted from the treatment of actuarial gains, including unrealized appreciation of pension fund securities. Such gains would build up and some companies used them as a secret reserve to "cushion" costs, sometimes creating an illusion of constancy in earnings growth, a dangerous practice because of the premium that the market place attaches to stability in the growth of profits.

Because of the increasing importance of pension costs in the financial reports of business and the variations that existed in accounting for these costs, the AICPA concluded several years ago that something needed to be done to clarify and to narrow the accounting practices in this area. The culmination of the AICPA's efforts in this regard was the issuance in November 1966 of Accounting Principles Board Opinion No. 8, entitled "Accounting for the Cost of Pension Plans."

Opinion No. 8 followed the publication by the AICPA Director of Accounting Research in 1965 of an accounting research study entitled, "Accounting for the Costs of Pension Plans," by Ernest L. Hicks, CPA.

That research study was an excellent one and was very useful to the Accounting Principles Board in its deliberations preceding the issuance of the Opinion.

Significant Provisions of Opinion No. 8

Opinion No. 8 is a relatively lengthy and, at first reading, a rather complex Opinion, employing technical terminology with which many of us may not have been familiar. This was inevitable, since the Opinion deals with a matter that has significant accounting, actuarial, legal and financial ramifications. It will be my intent in the remainder of these remarks to cut through the technicalities and eliminate details, concentrating instead on the principal issues.

The objective of Opinion No. 8 is to provide a rational and systematic basis for recognizing pension costs on an accrual basis that results in consistent annual charges. The overall theme of the Opinion's accrual basis is that the cost of retirement benefits for employees under pension plans is a cost to be spread over the productive lives of the employees. The cost of retirement is thereby matched against the revenues that result from the goods and services produced by the employees.

The Opinion recognizes the broad concept of segregating the cost of pension plans between current (normal) service and past service—a concept that has been used by actuaries and accountants in their respective functions for a long time. As a result of the discussions and deliberations in issuing the Opinion and in applying its provisions to clients since issuance, accountants have learned that this distinction between current and past-service costs is a rather elusive one. The line may shift depending on different actuarial methods and considerations.

The Opinion uses both the terms "past" and "prior service" in distinguishing certain costs. For purposes of this discussion I will use only the term "past service" as encompassing all the costs assigned, under the actuarial cost method used, to the service of employees for periods prior to the initial adoption of a plan and for periods prior to a modification or an amendment of the plan.

Accounting for cost, minimum/maximum

The crucial paragraph for accountants is paragraph 17, which defines the recognition that should be given to the costs of pension plans in financial statements. The paragraph sets up a permissible range for the accrual of pension costs.

First, normal or current-service cost must be accrued systematically and consistently under any one of several acceptable actuarial cost methods, specifically excluding the terminal funding and pay-as-you-go methods. Normal cost is the cost related to the service of employees subsequent to the adoption or modification of the pension plan.

Second, past-service costs, which involve costs assigned to the service of employees for periods prior to the adoption or modification of the plan, are also to be accrued by current and future charges to income within the following range:

> The maximum provision may be based on a ten-year amortization from date of adoption, substantially as allowed by the Internal Revenue Service. It is safe to assume that this will not be a major battle line over pension costs.
>
> The minimum provision is to be the lesser of (a) interest on the unfunded past-service cost plus an additional amount, if necessary, so that the unfunded (or actually unaccrued) amount of the actuarial value of vested benefits will be 5% lower at the end of the year than at the beginning; or (b) amortization over a 40-year period from adoption of the plan.

Thus, if accrued pensions (which may or may not have been funded) exceed the present value of vested benefits, the effective aggregate minimum is simply current service plus interest on unfunded past service. However, pressures from many sources such as government and unions toward earlier and more significant vesting, may make the "interest-only" provision inapplicable in more and more cases, thereby effectively providing some amortization of past service by enforced recognition of vesting provisions.

If your client is dedicated to the minimum provision, I would recommend that you encourage the 40-year amortization of past-service minimum rather than the lower of 40 years or the interest-plus-an-amount-for-the-excess-of-vesting over funding minimum (hereinafter referred to as vesting excess). First of all, the 40-year minimum is a valid minimum in all cases and trying to pick the lower of the two each year, which is the absolute floor, could result in fluctuating costs. Second, it may save on the amount of annual actuarial determinations required, since the amount of vesting excess would then be no longer critical to accounting for pension costs. Third, figuring out how to compute the amount of the provision to be made under the vesting excess formula may be fairly complicated, and if interest plus 5% vesting excess amortization turns out to be more than a straight 40-year amortization of past service, it doesn't help anyway.

Actuarial cost methods

Several paragraphs of the Opinion and an Appendix deal with actuarial cost methods, which I will not discuss here. In summary, the Opinion recognizes that there are a number of actuarial methods that, although originally designed as techniques for funding, are also useful in determining pension cost for accounting purposes. Generally, the Opinion recognizes any of these methods as suitable bases upon which to make accounting computations for purposes of APB No. 8 (excluding terminal funding) if it is systematic, rational and consistently applied.

Excluding the premium methods, which are geared to insurance company funding, the two principal methods or actuarial philosophies most likely to be encountered are the unit-credit method, which simply recognizes as cost for a year the present value of the benefits resulting from that year's service (cost is a rising curve for each employee but aggregate cost rises only as average age rises) and the entry-age normal method, which introduces certain projections of employee composition, turnover, and salary increases, and thereby tends to be a leveler.

Amounts assigned to past service will differ, of course, depending on the method chosen. Other methods such as individual level premiums do not need to distinguish past and current service. The essential point here is consistency in method and in significant underlying actuarial assumptions used.

The Opinion provides that any difference between the pension cost accrued and the pension cost paid by a company should be reflected in the balance sheet as accrued or prepaid pension cost, with appropriate consideration being given to the allocation of income tax effects. Pension cost accrued for a year should be adjusted for interest on prior accrued or prepaid pension costs.

Actuarial gains and losses

We now come to a most significant provision of the Opinion. Actuarial gains and losses should be consistently recognized on a spreading, or averaging, basis. This is automatically accomplished under some actuarial cost methods. Otherwise, they should be taken care of through a separate adjustment and spread over a reasonably long period (10 to 20 years). An alternative approach that accomplishes the objective is to apply the gains or losses to any unfunded past-service cost.

Unrealized appreciation of fund assets should be recognized on a systematic basis that avoids any undue effect of short-term market fluctuations. The Opinion indicates that 75% of market may be used. Some companies may also use a five-year moving average. Still others may use an expected long-term growth rate, which would be adjusted as experience indicates.

As can be seen, the treatment to be accorded actuarial gains and losses and appreciation in fund assets results in a systematic and consistent charge to income and eliminates the opportunity to "manage" the pension provision by discretionary recognition of these factors when, as and if desired.

Disclosure

With respect to disclosure, the Opinion provides that the following information be shown in the financial statements or notes:

1. A statement that such plans exist, identifying or describing the employee groups covered.
2. A statement of the company's accounting and funding policies.
3. The provision for pension cost of the period.
4. The excess, if any, of the actuarially computed value of vested benefits over the total of the pension fund and any balance sheet pension accruals, less any pension prepayments or deferred charges.
5. The nature and effect of significant matters affecting comparability for all periods presented, such as changes in accounting methods (actuarial cost method, amortization of past and prior-service cost, treatment of actuarial gains and losses, etc.), changes in circumstances (actuarial assumptions, etc.), or the adoption or amendment of a plan.

You will note that the Opinion does not provide for disclosure of unfunded past-service costs, as is presently required by the SEC under Regulation S-X. The Board did not consider such disclosure necessary, and it might even be misleading. The amount can vary significantly depending on the actuarial cost method employed. It is a little like disclosing future payrolls. Further, it is not a significant factor as long as proper accruals are being made in accordance with the Opinion. At this date, however, the SEC has not amended its formal requirements, and we cannot be sure what position it will take.

A question arose when the Opinion was being drafted whether the amount of disclosure being required is really necessary or meaningful to most readers as long as proper provisions are being made. After all, such disclosure is not required with respect to other costs that frequently may be more material. Discussions with the SEC, however, indicated that it would insist on at least this much disclosure; and there was a desire to eliminate, or at least minimize, differences between reports to security holders and in the filings with the SEC.

Changes in methods

The Opinion recognized that properly disclosed changes may be made by companies in accounting for pension costs. These may result from changes in the actuarial cost method, the amortization of past-service costs, and the treatment of actuarial gains and losses, within the limits imposed by the Opinion. The effect of any changes, however, should be applied prospectively, not by prior-year charges or credits to retained earnings.

These same principles are established for transitions to comply with the Opinion. Whatever has been done in the past, any costs not yet recognized that would have been recognized had the principles set up in the Opinion been followed, now become past service, subject to recognition in the future within the maximum/minimum rules set up earlier. The minimum wages for your past pension cost sins, therefore, may be interest only, but forever.

Various other matters covered in the Opinion include employees to be included in cost calculations, plans covered (generally all plans that define retirement benefits), and the effects of funding.

Evaluation of the Opinion

This is one of the best and most effective Opinions that the Board has issued. It demonstrated that the Board could deal with an intensely complicated subject, and that compromise was possible without diluting too significantly the overall soundness of the provisions of the Opinion.

This Opinion should substantially reduce the area of differences among companies in accounting for pensions, and puts pension accounting on a reasonable accrual basis. It will largely remove the use of pension costs as profit levelers or profit growth assurers. The secret reserve is gone. There should be more system and consistency in pension costs.

Certain features of the Opinion may cause problems in the future but, on the whole, it appears that the Board has done a good job on a difficult and controversial subject.

Working papers

A discussion of Statement No. 39 of the Committee on Auditing Procedure of the American Institute of Certified Public Accountants, appearing in *The Journal of Accountancy*, March 1968—Olson

Working papers are an indispensable tool in our audits, but they do not constitute the objective of what we do as auditors.

THE OBJECTIVE of the CPA in his role as an auditor is to form and express an opinion on the financial statements or other financial information he has been engaged to examine. In the final analysis, that opinion really exists only in the auditor's mind. The substance and integrity of the opinion depend upon the auditor's professional competence and upon the knowledge he has gained of the facts underlying the financial information.

Thus the test of the soundness of an opinion runs to the question of whether the auditor is personally satisfied that the financial information upon which he is reporting meets the standards against which such information is being measured.

The auditor does not discharge his responsibility simply by preparing good working papers. However, working papers are important to the auditor in meeting that responsibility.

Importance of working papers

The preparation and review of working papers ordinarily account for a significant part of the time, cost, and effort of performing an audit. This function is also an integral part of the process by which we train our assistants and help them in their professional development.

The procedure by which the auditor arrives at a competent opinion involves the review of controls and systems, the testing of transactions to evaluate the effectiveness of those controls and systems, the gathering of facts, the resolution of exceptions, and the reasoning toward a conclusion. The fact of the matter is that this process would be difficult to accomplish unless the auditor employed pencil and paper and made some records in the course of his work.

Furthermore, certain procedures are commonly carried out by assistants for whose work the auditor is responsible. A record of this work is an important tool by which the auditor meets his responsibilities for supervision and review. Finally, working papers provide evidence that can assist the auditor in demonstrating that he had a valid and competent basis for the opinion he rendered, should he be called upon later to defend his opinion.

Background of Statement on Auditing Procedure No. 39

Earlier committees on auditing procedure of the American Institute of Certified Public Accountants have recognized the importance of good working papers in auditing. "Generally Accepted Auditing Standards—Their Significance and Scope," issued by the committee in 1954, devoted several paragraphs to the subject. Statement on Auditing Procedure No. 33, the committee's comprehensive consolidation in 1963 of its earlier pronouncements, also stressed the importance of maintaining adequate working papers.

The reference to working papers in SAP No. 33, however, was brief. The intent at the time was that a statement of broad standards relating to working papers would be issued at a later date for the guidance of the profession. This was the origin of Statement on Auditing Procedure No. 39, issued in October 1967 and approved unanimously by the 21 members of the Committee on Auditing Procedure.

The members of the Committee reached agreement on the principal conclusions and broad guidelines in SAP No. 39 fairly rapidly. However, the Committee found it difficult to phrase the statement in a manner that would clearly reflect the proper role of working papers. While working papers are an important and perhaps indispensable tool in our audits, they do not constitute objectives of what we do as auditors. The Committee gave extensive consideration to wording the statement so that it conveyed as clearly as possible the role and significance of working papers in an audit.

The Committee was also mindful of legal implications in the issuance of a statement on the subject of working papers, and accordingly consulted with the Institute legal counsel in the course of its deliberations. The Committee recognized that in carrying out its responsibility to assist the profession in improving its standards of service it must not create foolish or needless legal hazards that would help neither the profession nor the public which it serves.

General provisions

SAP No. 39 describes the two main functions of working papers as being to aid the auditor in the conduct of his work and to provide important support for the auditor's opinion, including his representation concerning compliance with auditing standards. The Statement acknowledges that the support for an auditor's opinion embraces an environment that extends beyond the working papers alone.

The Statement underscores the fact that the auditor is the owner of his working papers. This is supported by statutes in several states and by legal precedent in others. Further, the working papers should not be considered as a part of, or as a substitute for, the client's accounting records. The Statement reminds the auditor of his responsibility to provide safe custody of his papers for a period of time "sufficient to meet the needs of his practice and to satisfy any pertinent legal requirements of records retention."

Textbooks on auditing and the auditing manuals of CPA firms deal extensively with specific content, form, and organization of working papers. The Committee concluded that such matters of detail were outside the area of auditing standards, and therefore SAP No. 39 does not prescribe the detail content of working papers. Furthermore, the Statement emphasizes that working papers must suit the circumstances and needs of the auditor on individual engagements; hence their quantity, type and content may vary greatly from one engagement to the next.

Working paper guidelines

Of particular significance are the six guidelines set forth in paragraph 5 of the Statement, which describe in broad terms what working papers generally would include or show. Every CPA should consider these guidelines carefully in the conduct of all of his audit engagements. While somewhat general in nature, the guidelines are comprehensive and encompassing in their applicability.

Three of the six guidelines are responsive to the three standards of fieldwork comprehended by generally accepted auditing standards. These guidelines state that working papers would indicate observance by the auditor of the fieldwork standards by showing:

1. That the engagement had been planned and the work of assistants supervised and reviewed.
2. That the scope of the work had been considered in the light of a review of the effectiveness of the client's system of internal control.
3. The procedures followed and testing performed in obtaining evidential matter; this record may take any form so long as it permits reasonable identification of the work performed by the auditor.

Three additional guidelines state that working papers, as a general rule, would:

1. Contain data sufficient to show that the financial information being reported upon was in agreement with (or reconciled with) the client's records.
2. Show how exceptions and unusual matters disclosed by the auditor's procedures have been resolved.
3. Include appropriate commentaries indicating the auditor's conclusions concerning significant aspects of the engagement.

If thoughtfully considered by the CPA, these six broad guidelines for working papers should help him discharge his responsibilities as an auditor more effectively. At the same time, observation of these guidelines by the CPA will help him demonstrate the competence of his opinion, should he be called upon to defend it. The guidelines should provide assistance to the CPA in exercising his judgment without, at the same time, imposing on him any unnecessarily burdensome details.

The auditing standards of consistency and materiality

Before a conference on empirical research in accounting sponsored by the Institute of Professional Accounting, Graduate School of Business, University of Chicago, May 23, 1968—Olson

Perhaps businessmen and auditors are approaching their responsibilities in the area of financial reporting too much on the basis of minimum requirements.

THE PROBLEM of consistency should be viewed in its proper perspective. Consistency is a significant consideration in the preparation of financial statements because of the availability of alternative "acceptable" accounting practices, with very few criteria defining the applicability of the various practices to particular situations. The auditing standard that requires the independent auditor to report on consistency is the safety valve, the means for enforcing disclosure of changes that a company makes within the wide range of acceptable alternative accounting principles.

Thus, consistency is a secondary problem, and although it is an important one under today's conditions, we should not put consistency at the forefront of problems requiring solution in accounting. The principal problems are the absence of objective criteria to guide the accountant in the selection of a particular accounting practice in a given set of circumstances and the general availability of a variety of accounting approaches to identical situations. Hopefully, the matter of consistency will become less significant as the efforts of the Accounting Principles Board of the AICPA succeed in narrowing the range of alternative accounting practices.

Possible factors affecting disclosure

Decisions by the independent auditor concerning the propriety or adequacy of disclosure of changes in accounting principles may be affected by various factors, and professional judgment is required in assessing all of the factors in any given situation.

1. *Change from an undesirable to a preferable practice*—If there is a change from a practice that the auditor regards as undesirable, the auditor may judge materiality for purposes of disclosure somewhat

differently than in situations where no clear preference between methods exists. Where neither practice is clearly the preferred one, the disclosure will ordinarily be in terms of the effect of the change in relation to net income reported for the current year, and materiality may be judged primarily by reference to this relationship. However, where the change is from an undesirable to a preferred practice, the most significant and useful information for the reader would appear to be the effect that the new method would have had on the results reported for the previous year if it had been applied to the results for that year. Is not the reader of the financial statements entitled to the "best" figures for both years in making his decisions? In such situations, the effect of the change on the current year's net income is not a proper point of reference in making decisions relating either to materiality or disclosure.

2. *The importance of earnings trends*—A more vital concern than the pure relationship of the effect of a change on either the current or prior-period net income may be the effect of the change on the reported trend in earnings. The effect on net income of a particular change in accounting practice may be less, say, than 5%, but the effect of the change might be to report an increase in net income, whereas with no change in accounting practice a decrease in net income might have been reported. Since there appears to be broad agreement that investors assign considerable value to stability in earnings and in earnings growth, auditors should probably give more attention to the effects that changes in accounting principles may have on trends than to absolute relationships of effects of changes on net income in judging materiality for purposes of disclosure.

3. *Prospective effect of changes*—Changes in accounting principles sometimes have no significant effect on current financial statements but may have a significant potential effect on results to be reported in future years. For example, a change from the FIFO basis to the LIFO basis of valuing inventories would ordinarily have little effect on net income in the year of change unless there were very significant changes in price levels in that year.

Under present reporting standards, the independent auditor is not required to comment on changes of this kind in rendering his opinion on consistency. However, he is required to disclose the change in his report if it is not disclosed in a note to the financial statements. The requirement imposed on the auditor in this case is a questionable one and should be reconsidered. The auditor's function is to express an opinion on whether historical financial facts are fairly presented in conformity with generally accepted accounting principles applied consistently with the prior period. Auditors should not express opinions with respect to future events, nor do they have any professional competence to do so. There is no assurance that a new management might not change back to the FIFO method or that the change from FIFO to LIFO would ever have a material effect.

It would seem desirable to disclose changes in practice that could have significant future effects but have no material current effects. However, it is difficult to see how omission of such disclosure could be considered inadequate to an understanding of the financial statements currently being reported upon, thereby requiring comment by the auditor.

General disclosure of accounting practices

A possible method of achieving better disclosure of changes in accounting principles or practices might be to adopt a broader approach. So long as the undesirable conditions of alternative accounting practices exist, corporations might be requested to disclose the accounting principles and practices used in the preparation of their financial statements. A number of companies have adopted such a procedure. This approach would probably assure more adequate disclosure of changes in accounting principles when changes occur, although it would represent no cure for the central problem in financial reporting today, the flexibility that exists in the use of accounting principles.

Thoughts on materiality

The concept of materiality may have contributed to some undesirable conditions, since the application of the concept may not have been entirely consistent with its origins in accounting. Ideally, materiality should be a consideration only in achieving convenience and reasonable practicality in the issuance of financial statements. At some point decisions must be made to cut off the accounting process and to issue the financial statements, with the understanding that further revisions will be made only where the aggregate effect of subsequently disclosed adjustments is significant. This employment of the concept of materiality is a proper one.

However, where materiality becomes the focal point of controversy between the auditor and his client, the client pushing the auditor to the limits of materiality and the auditor deciding where he must "draw the line," the concept may lead to abuses.

If a company insists that a matter should be immaterial to the auditor, should it not then also be immaterial to the company? The company may be in the best position to judge the importance of a particular item and if it is truly immaterial, why does not the company (absent inconvenience) make the adjustment suggested by the auditor? The company's resistance may in some cases suggest evidence of its materiality.

The question of materiality brings a more fundamental issue into focus. Perhaps businessmen and auditors are approaching their respective responsibilities in the area of financial reporting too much on the basis of minimum requirements. Too often the questions are asked: "What does the Opinion of the Accounting Principles Board require? What does the Securities and Exchange Commission allow?" Only when we address ourselves, not to minimums, but to the highest standards of accounting will we solve the potential difficulties created by the concept of materiality. If financial statements are to improve and if our profession is to grow in quality, we must all consistently strive for our ideals. Materiality will then become a less significant issue.

Developing accounting principles — do we need a compass or a barometer?

Before the graduate study conference sponsored by the California CPA Foundation for Education and Research at Stanford University, August 11, 1968—Catlett

While a barometer may be helpful in measuring the pressures on all sides of controversial questions, a compass with a magnetic pole of soundly conceived objectives will lead us through the stormy seas to positions that can be successfully defended as being truly in the public interest.

I APPRECIATE having the opportunity to be here this evening to discuss with you the various problems we are facing today in trying to improve accounting principles. As indicated in the program for this meeting, the efforts of the accounting profession to establish sound principles have been marked with both milestones and tombstones. The epitaphs on the latter, if accurately written, would be quite revealing.

Evolution and progress

The development of accounting principles and practices as they exist in actual practice has been interesting to observe. I do not believe, given the present conditions in the United States, that adequate progress is going to be made as a result of some vague evolutionary process or of some type of a consensus approach. Anything less than strong leadership based on sound objectives is certain to fail.

The necessary leadership can come from the accounting profession, the business community or the government. The accounting profession now has its opportunity, but if it fails more governmental intervention would seem to be inevitable.

Accountants are becoming more involved in litigation of various types, some of which represents cases that are resulting in court decisions. This could be expected, as there are more audits, more exposure, and more responsibility being placed on CPAs. This is a painful process, particularly for the firms and individuals involved, but it is going to result in more clearly defined lines of responsibility for the profession than have previously existed. While it is difficult to determine how all of this is going to come out, the net effect may well be a strengthening of the profession and putting a greater premium on high standards. One fact is becoming evident; the courts are not necessarily going to accept the standards established by the profession as an adequate defense for a member of the profession unless the standards meet the tests of reasonableness and fairness and give the public what they have a right to expect from financial statements. A profession responsible to the public cannot limit its own responsibilities by unilateral action.

Work of the APB

When the Accounting Principles Board was established in 1959, the general plan was for it to first consider and determine the basic concepts and principles, and then settle the problems in the light of the framework that had been established. The Board now has a subcommittee that, with the assistance of the Institute's research staff, has prepared a draft of a document on the basic concepts and principles of accounting. There is some evidence that this venture will not be any more successful than previous attempts, because it is likely to end up trying to support and rationalize what is now occurring rather than establishing what is needed.

The Board, in the meantime, has been forced to take up pressing current problems and solve them on a somewhat disjointed basis in the same manner as the former Committee on Accounting Procedure. The premises and concepts of the author of each research study and of each member of the Board are still those that he has developed himself; thus each person involved is starting his reasoning and logic from a different point. Some of the problems would be difficult to solve satisfactorily even if the Board had reached agreement on the premises from which it starts; but when there is no agreement on premises, the problem solving gets all tangled up with the different concepts of each of the individuals involved.

For various reasons, some good and some not, the Board in the first few years of its existence did not accomplish very much. There was some delay while waiting for the completion of research studies. The investment credit fiasco was unfortunate. Some of the earlier Opinions were not ones to give distinction to the work of the Board.

In the last three years, however, the Board has done a much better job in its work. Its management and organization are greatly improved. There are more than 20 working subcommittees. Every Board member is on about four or five subcommittees. Instead of the full Board meeting four times a year for two days each, as it once did, it is now meeting about seven or eight times a year for three days each. The subcommittees also meet frequently. The Institute's research staff is improving its effectiveness. The attitude of the Board today is that it has an important job to do and it wants to move ahead to achieve concrete accomplishments.

Three of the recent Opinions published, on pension plans, the income statement and income taxes, represent major achievements and a great deal of hard work. The Board faced some difficult problems and dealt with them squarely.

The Board occasionally gets away from some of the practical everyday problems and looks to the long range. One of these is the reflection of the effect of price-level changes in financial statements. The Board has done considerable work in this regard and expects to issue a pronouncement on this subject next year.

Reaching solutions

In approaching our problems today, there is much evidence to indicate that solutions do not come from the natural emergence of the most logical and sound practices.

The whole concept of "general acceptance" as the basic standard for accounting principles is subjected to a multitude of pressures—pressures for more profits or less profits, pressures by groups and agencies of all types, competitive pressures, political pressures, pressures for the status quo—and many more could be listed. The tendency for deterioration to the lowest common denominator is a result of pressures. To try to achieve progress under these conditions requires a barometer, because these pressures are the ones that greatly influence "general acceptance" and "substantial support," and what constitutes a "consensus," as well as what actions various groups and agencies are willing to take. The retention of this concept would ultimately lead us down the road to failure, and as the ship sinks everyone could sing "Everybody's doing it."

I do not abhor the idea that pressures do play a part in our democratic processes. People and organizations with different points of view and various interests do have a right to express what they think should be done. Organizations establishing accounting principles should be certain that all points of view, with the underlying reasoning, are received and given proper consideration. However, the decisions should be based on sound premises and conclusions and not merely on what powerful pressure groups may prefer for their own purposes.

I have for some time been advocating, without any success, that the APB should hold public hearings for all major subjects on its agenda. The APB has operated in too much secrecy, and many people in the business community have been critical of the APB because of its inaccessibility. Public hearings would give all interested parties an opportunity to present their views, and this procedure would represent an excellent safety valve that might prevent an explosion resulting from too much pressure building up. (Editor's note—The first public hearing was held by the APB on May 25 and 26, 1971, and George R. Catlett presided at that hearing.)

Efforts of APB need direction

The accounting profession in general and the APB in particular need a compass to give direction to their efforts to improve financial accounting and reporting. The need is so obvious to me, but the lack of interest on the part of so many other people must indicate either that I am completely off base in my thinking or that I have no ability to convey my views to others.

An understandable and meaningful description of the objectives of corporate financial statements, beyond mere generalizations, can be written. These objectives must be thought out and recorded in such a manner that they can be an effective guide to the development of sound accounting principles and practices. No committee of the American Institute has ever done this. The Accounting Principles Board, after almost nine years of existence, finally has a draft of a document that purports to be on this subject, and this draft does not serve this purpose either. There have never been authoritative decisions regarding what the true objectives are. These decisions should be made by a recognized and qualified professional body, such as the Accounting Principles Board, and a comprehensive description of these objectives should be used as a magnetic pole to which all accounting principles and practices can be directed and oriented. Each step of the way should be charted and tested to be certain that the compass is always pointing in the right direction.

This approach will permit piecemeal improvement and will, at the same time, maintain a consistent course of action. One of the frustrating aspects of trying to achieve progress now is the argument that it is not logical to make one change without also making many other related changes; but it is not practicable to make many changes at once.

If we really have a compass, the job then is to determine what concepts, principles, guidelines, criteria, etc. will produce answers that best serve the objectives. The professional ship must sail through rough seas on a true course if the results to be achieved are to withstand the tests of time and usage. Soundness must prevail over custom. All interested parties, such as corporate managements, governmental agencies and creditors, can present their views and participate in the discussions. In the end, however, some authoritative body must lay down the basic ground rules by which the game is to be played. There should be plenty of room for professional judgment in applying the guidelines.

And we should not use disclosure in voluminous fine print as a crutch for, or an excuse against, proper accounting. Sound concepts and principles which will produce the most useful, reliable and comparable financial statements are needed. If this can be achieved, we will not need so many footnotes.

A medical authority said recently that when the eyes are closed, the hearing becomes more acute. We had better open our eyes and figure out where we are going rather than closing our eyes and listening to all of the reasons about why changes are so difficult to make.

What needs to be done?

We should ask ourselves how the accounting profession can assure success in doing what needs to be done on a timely basis. Here are a few conclusions that I have reached:

1. The American Institute and the Accounting Principles Board must assume even more aggressive leadership in improving accounting principles and financial reporting if the likelihood of governmental agencies gradually taking over this function is to be avoided. Governmental agencies probably would not do as well as the Board could do, and we would end up with a mass of rules and regulations.
2. The Board has gradually been establishing better liaison with some industrial and other groups and with certain governmental agencies. This should be continued and improved.
3. The activities and pronouncements of the Board should be given full support by Institute members, and it is likely that support would then be received from industry, governmental agencies and other interested parties.
4. Integrated accounting concepts and theories should be established and the accounting principles and practices must be fitted into that framework in a logical manner. The starting point for this effort must be a clear and comprehensive description of the purposes and objectives of corporate financial statements. Goals must be established. Some people consider that it may be necessary to solve the problems first and then construct the underlying theories to support them, but I do not agree with that viewpoint. It would be better if we first decide what we are trying to do before we decide how to do it.
5. The quality of our research must be improved. Too often we fail to recognize that fact-finding is not a substitute for thought. Also, research is usually directed to the past (with the influence of inhibitions and customs that caused the problems in the first place) rather than to what the users of financial statements really need in the future.
6. The accounting profession must not fall into the trap of prescribing detailed procedures. Professional judgment must always be used if we are to make our maximum contribution to society. Thus we need uniform principles and guidelines but not rigid rules.
7. Tradition and precedent have their place, but they can also represent

stagnation. They are not a substitute for constructive analysis, creative thought, and effective progress.

8. "Harmonious evolution" sounds attractive, but it is quicksand, which leads to failure in trying to achieve a consensus. Let's use a compass pointing toward our goals and not a barometer reflecting the pressures.

George Bernard Shaw once said: "The reasonable man adapts himself to the world; the unreasonable man persists in trying to adapt the world to himself. Therefore, progress depends on the unreasonable man." The accounting profession today needs leadership more than at any time in the past, and this must include some unreasonable people who are not satisfied with the present situation.

While a barometer may be helpful in measuring the pressures on all sides of controversial questions, a compass with a magnetic pole of soundly conceived objectives will lead us through the stormy seas to positions that can be successfully defended as being truly in the public interest.

The committee on auditing procedure—past, present, and future

Before the 19th Annual Kentucky Institute on Accounting, University of Kentucky, Lexington, October 26, 1968—Olson

The profession should pay more attention to auditing matters and give them the kind of attention that has been given to accounting principles during recent years.

I WOULD LIKE TO discuss with you the activities of the AICPA's Committee on Auditing Procedure—what it has done in the past, what is now being done, and what may be in store for that Committee in the future. This is the Institute's senior technical Committee with authority to issue statements on auditing procedure on behalf of the profession. I have been a member of that Committee for more than three years. It has been a most rewarding experience for me personally, and I believe that over the years this has been one of the most productive groups of those within the accounting profession.

The Past

Membership and organization

The Committee on Auditing Procedure has been composed of 21 members from both large and small firms and from universities. The membership has recently been increased to 24.

The Committee meets for three days each quarter, but numerous subcommittee meetings are held between the regular meetings of the full Committee. However, there is some question whether this schedule of meeting dates is truly adequate for the needs of the present.

The first 37 Statements on Auditing Procedure

The first Statement issued by the Committee on Auditing Procedure dealt with the so-called "extensions" of auditing procedure. The Statement resulted from one of the first major adverse proceedings against a public accounting firm in this country, the McKesson & Robbins case. The Statement elevated to the level of generally accepted auditing procedures two important procedures, confirmation of receivables and observation of inventories.

Over the first 35 years of its existence the Committee issued a total of 37 statements, or an average of about one statement each year.

Perhaps the most significant accomplishment during this period was the issuance in 1963 of Statement on Auditing Procedure No. 33. This Statement codified the previous statements of the Committee. SAP 33 may be the most useful single, comprehensive, authoritative document ever issued by any committee or board of the AICPA. It is an invaluable guide to generally accepted auditing standards and particularly to all aspects of audit reporting standards.

The Present

During the year ended October 1967, the Committee concentrated on completing two statements that had been in process for some time, namely SAP 38, which dealt with the CPA's association with unaudited financial statements, and SAP 39, which laid down some broad guidelines for working papers. Both Statements were issued late in 1967.

Unaudited financial statements (SAP 38)

SAP 38, on the subject of the auditor's association with unaudited statements, was exposed to the AICPA membership on a wide basis in draft form in the latter part of 1967, and this exposure resulted in extensive comments leading to a number of revisions before it was issued in final form.

SAP 38 dealt with one of the most controversial subjects that the Committee had tackled. The Committee worked on it for three or four years, through various subcommittees and subcommittee chairmen. More than a dozen drafts were circulated to the full Committee, each leading to extensive discussion. It is one of the few Statements on Auditing Procedure to which dissents have been recorded. One member qualified his assent and one member dissented directly.

Few statements issued by the Committee have affected such a broad portion of the practice of the general membership of the AICPA. Since its issuance, the AICPA has received hundreds of letters and one state society threatened to bring action on the floor of the Council meeting to have the statement rescinded, all of which was to be expected.

The Committee has come in for some ridicule, most of it good natured, as a result of SAP 38. It is being referred to as the "Unaudited Procedure Committee." We are being asked how much "unauditing" do we have to do in order to call the statements "unaudited." One member of the Committee who disagreed with the disclaimer requirement told me that, if I put a disclaimer on a set of statements saying that I had not audited those statements, he wanted to attach a disclaimer saying that he hadn't audited them either.

The basic problem to be dealt with is this. When the CPA is associated with any set of financial statements, the user immediately associates verification or audit credibility with those statements. Yet there is a broad and useful practice by CPAs, particularly for smaller businesses, which consists of assisting business with the preparation of financial statements without audit. Many of these businesses do not have the competence and the know-how in areas such as generally accepted accounting principles and the disclosures required for a fair and useful presentation.

Thus, the objective of the Committee on Auditing Procedure was to delineate carefully the service of preparing or assisting in the preparation of financial statements as a special accounting service rendered by the CPA and to differentiate it from that of auditing. What is the best way to do this so that the users of financial statements will not be misled regarding the nature of the service? The answer is not a clear-cut one and judgment is involved. Whenever judgment comes into play on an important issue affecting a big practice, controversy is bound to arise.

The basic provisions of SAP 38 are as follows:

1. A signed disclaimer of opinion by the CPA should accompany all unaudited financial statements (each marked "unaudited") where the auditor has participated in their preparation, and has delivered them to the client. The only "plain paper" statements now permitted are those where the CPA has merely accommodated his client by typing them.
2. The listing in the disclaimer of limited procedures performed in connection with the preparation of unaudited statements is prohibited except in certain restricted situations, such as in negative assurance letters for underwriters and in similar situations. Wherever such procedures are listed, the use of the report must be expressly restricted to the parties specified in the disclaimer. The purpose of this requirement is to attempt to eliminate the so-called "second-class" audits that bankers and others often could not understand, lengthy recitals of procedures and reports that look like audit reports but are not audit reports at all.
3. The auditor is not required to carry out any auditing procedures in connection with unaudited financial statements. This does not mean that individual CPAs cannot take such precautionary procedures as they wish in order to minimize the risk of association with misleading statements. However, the Committee believed that it would be contrary to the purpose of the Statement to suggest that certain auditing procedures were required, because this would, in fact, create the second-class audit that the Committee was setting out to eliminate.
4. The Statement requires that, if the CPA has received information that indicates to him the financial statements are not fairly presented in conformity with generally accepted accounting principles, he should ask the client to make an appropriate revision or state his reservations in his disclaimer.
5. The Statement says that all the disclosures necessary for a fair presentation should be set forth in unaudited statements. There is one exception to this in the Statement: where statements are prepared solely for internal use, such as monthly statements prepared for a client, such disclosures may be omitted if the CPA states in his disclaimer that the statements are to be restricted to internal use by management.

There are other provisions in SAP 38, but these are the principal ones. While SAP 38 may need modification after a few years of application in practice, I believe it will be found sound and useful in distinguishing the service of preparing unaudited financial statements from that of auditing, and in eliminating confusing "second-class" audits.

We can't expect users of financial statements to understand something halfway between an audit and an "unaudit." When a doctor gives you a physical examination, you trust the doctor to give you the tests that he considers are needed. You can't expect the user of financial statements to understand how one set of financial statements is half-safe or one-quarter safe. Either it is audited or it is not. In any event, that is the philosophy that prevailed in the Committee, but there undoubtedly are some who disagree with the Committee's judgment.

Working papers (SAP 39)

The other Statement that the Committee issued last year may actually be more important to us in the long run, particularly in our capacity as independent auditors. This was SAP 39, which laid down some guidelines on working papers. This Statement has caused no particular controversy. While the guidelines for working papers in SAP 39 may sound like an endorsement of motherhood, nowhere had these standards been set down before.

The process by which we arrive at a competent professional opinion in auditing involves the review of controls and systems, the testing of transactions to evaluate the effectiveness of those controls and systems, the gathering of facts, the disposition of exceptions, and the reasoning toward a conclusion. This procedure would be very difficult to carry out unless we employed pencil and paper and made some record in the course of our work. Furthermore, if procedures are carried out for us by assistants for whose work we are responsible, the record becomes an important tool by which we carry out our responsibilities for supervision and review; one of the generally accepted auditing standards.

Of particular significance are the six guidelines set forth in paragraph 5 of SAP 39, which describe in broad terms what working papers generally would include or show. These guidelines appear simple and somewhat general in nature, but they are actually fairly encompassing.

Three of the six guidelines are responsive to the three standards of fieldwork comprehended by the term "generally accepted auditing standards." In other words, working papers would generally indicate observance of these standards by showing:

1. That the engagement had been planned and the work of assistants supervised and reviewed;
2. That the scope of the work had been considered in the light of a review of the effectiveness of the client's system of internal control; and
3. The procedures followed and testing performed in obtaining evidential matter. This record may take any form so long as it permits reasonable identification of the work performed by the auditor.

In addition to these guidelines relating to the auditor's observance of the three generally accepted standards of fieldwork, three other guidelines state that working papers generally would:

1. Contain data sufficient to show that the financial information being reported upon was in agreement (or reconciled) with the client's records;
2. Show how exceptions and unusual matters disclosed by the auditor's procedures were resolved; and
3. Include appropriate commentaries indicating the auditor's conclusions concerning significant aspects of the engagement.

These are the six guidelines that the Committee concluded would help the CPA discharge his responsibilities as an auditor and that, if observed, would help the CPA demonstrate the validity of his opinion, should he be called upon to defend it. The guidelines in no manner restrict the CPA in exercising his judgment, nor do they impose any unnecessarily burdensome detail. In fact, the Committee was careful not to get into details, and the Statement emphasizes that there is no intent to prescribe such detail, pointing out that working papers must suit the circumstances and needs of the individual audit engagement.

Reports following a pooling of interests (SAP 40)

The Committee has recently completed and the Institute is now distributing SAP 40, entitled "Reports Following a Pooling of

Interests." This is a relatively noncontroversial Statement and merely updates the auditing literature to conform with present accounting requirements.

You will recall that as a result of APB Opinion No. 10, restatements of prior-year financial statements presented for comparative purposes subsequent to a pooling of interests is mandatory; the alternative method of presenting the separate financial statements of the constituents to a pooling was eliminated. Portions of SAP 33 needed to be revised to reflect this change, and this is the subject matter of SAP 40. The Statement points out that, where restatement has not been made, there is an inconsistency.

A footnote to SAP 40 states that the Accounting Principles Board is reconsidering the entire subject of accounting for business combinations, including the concept of pooling of interests, and that it is contemplated that an APB Opinion will be issued on this subject.

Subsequent discovery of facts

One of the most difficult subjects under consideration by the Committee on Auditing Procedure at the present time is a proposed statement on the question of correcting financial statements and revising the auditor's opinion when, subsequent to the issuance of a report, facts are discovered that existed at the time the report was issued and that, if known to the auditor, would have caused him to have issued a different report on the financial statements. Someone has proposed the title of "Egad" for this Statement.

This project originated as a result of a legal action against auditors in which the plaintiff has alleged that the auditors failed to take action to prevent readers from continuing to rely on an auditor's report that, the plaintiffs charged, the auditors had learned was in error. Since that time, another case has been developing that may raise a similar charge.

There has been general agreement among Committee members from the beginning of this project that, if an auditor receives knowledge that financial statements upon which he has reported were materially in error and those statements continue to be relied upon, then the auditor has a responsibility to take some kind of action in the direction of preventing continued reliance on those statements.

However, it has been extremely difficult to write a Statement that provides useful guidelines, and at the same time doesn't create unnecessary or impossible hazards for the auditors. For example, the wording must distinguish clearly between "facts existing at the time of issuance of a report" and "subsequent developments." In addition, the Statement should not apply to subsequent resolution of contingencies or similar problems that had been disclosed in a qualified auditor's report or footnotes. Such developments might call for amended financial statement disclosures in some cases, but they are not the kind of matters to which the proposed Statement should apply.

One of the dangers against which the Committee has tried to guard is any implication that the Statement would impose a general surveillance responsibility upon the auditor after he issues his report. Such a responsibility would be impractical and impossible to discharge on any broad basis, and is one that users of auditors' reports should not expect.

There are a variety of circumstances under which an auditor might have to act. There may be cases where the client cooperates fully, the client cooperates in the investigation of "subsequent information" but not in making disclosures, or the auditor may receive no cooperation whatsoever, even in making his investigation. The Statement needs to consider all three situations.

In addition, there are questions in defining materiality for taking action. For example, materiality probably should be assessed not only in terms of amounts but in terms of the time elapsed since the issuance of the financial statements, since the time factor affects the likelihood of continued reliance on the statements.

After extensive discussion and numerous drafts, the Committee now has a draft that probably will be exposed to various AICPA members and groups for comment. I hope that Kentucky CPAs who receive copies of the exposure draft will study it carefully and send us their comments. It will be an important document, which can affect all of us.

Negative assurance

Another Committee project that should be of considerable current interest is one on the subject of negative assurance letters, letters saying that based on limited procedures nothing has come to the auditor's attention that led him to believe that the statements were not presented in conformity with generally accepted accounting principles.

SAP 33 states that the issuance of negative assurance-type letters on unaudited financial statements is inappropriate except to ". . . security underwriters in which the independent auditor reports on limited procedures followed with respect to unaudited financial statements . . . pertinent to a registration statement filed with the Securities and Exchange Commission."

The members of the Committee agree that it may be undesirable to base a reporting standard on who gets the report, rather than on objective criteria. But it has been difficult to decide on the best course of action. Two options would appear to be available to the Committee:

1. Eliminate negative assurances altogether in connection with unaudited financial statements, whether for underwriters or others. If this were done, some other type of letter might be substituted that would state positively what was done and what the findings were, but which would not include a sweeping "negative assurance" regarding the unaudited financial statements as a whole.
2. Issue a statement superseding the present provisions in SAP 33 which would set up tighter restrictions on the issuance of negative assurance letters on unaudited financial statements, but which would not single out one group as recipients. It would be broader in the sense that more parties could get negative assurance letters, but it would be more restrictive regarding the conditions under which they could be issued.

This project has been given top priority because of increasing requests from underwriters for negative assurance as a result of the now famous BarChris decision.

The negative assurance letter has unprofessional overtones, since it provides one with the ability to give a kind of opinion even if he does no work at all. In fact, the less work you do, the more negative assurance you can give. Even if one isn't an accountant, he could say that he didn't find anything wrong with the financial statements; or he could do so just by dropping in and saying "Hello" to the receptionist. It is, therefore, very vulnerable to abuse and, of course, more importantly, it is vulnerable to misinterpretation by users.

For this reason my view is that we should seriously consider the first alternative mentioned, that of doing away with the sweeping negative assurance-type of letter and substituting something more professional and positive. In retrospect, it was probably a mistake for the accounting profession to get involved in giving negative assurances to underwriters in the first place. It may be questioned whether the underwriter, if he feels that audit assurances on financial statements are necessary, is really fulfilling his responsibilities completely, since he is getting a letter that disclaims an opinion on the financial statements taken as a whole. If the accounting profession had insisted initially that auditors have only one quality of assurance to give, and that is based on an audit, and that we have no half-audits that an outsider could really understand anyway, the system would probably have accommodated audits of stub periods. Arguments about time requirements in connection with registrations should not have been persuasive.

There is a danger that the whole system of negative assurance letters may appear to an outsider as a self-serving one. The negative assurance, as compared to an audit, reduces the cost to the client of registering securities. The underwriter thinks he is being protected and diligent, and the auditor thinks he is protected because he disclaims responsibility for the statements taken as a whole. Is the public that is buying the securities being looked after by such a circular approach?

It seems to me that there are some specific things the auditor could be asked to do on short stub periods. For example, he might be asked to look into the condition of receivables or the inventory and make inquiries and audit tests as directed, set these matters out in a letter, and report positively what he found without any sweeping negative assurance on the statements as a whole. Longer stub periods such as nine-month periods probably should be audited in most situations.

This is likely to become a very hot and controversial issue before it is concluded. It is hoped that a useful statement will be issued that will help upgrade the standards of service of our profession, particularly in connection with registration statements.

Revision of short-form report

A project has been in process for some time to revise the standard short-form auditors' report. The purpose of the project is to clarify the wording of the report so that it means to the reader what the auditor intends it to say. A couple of drafts have been circulated, but the reactions of the Committee have not been very favorable.

One of the difficulties in trying to clarify the wording of the short-form report is that we auditors may not really know what we are saying. This is so because the profession lacks clear definitions of the auditors' responsibilities and of the objectives of financial statements. It is very difficult to make our report clear or to communicate clearly if we don't know for sure what we are trying to say.

It may be that we should first give more attention to defining financial statement objectives and the auditors' responsibilities and, having done so, we could address ourselves more effectively to the wording of the short-form report. In any event, I believe it may take some time before agreement is reached to change significantly the words in the standard form of the auditors' report.

Other projects

There are a number of other projects that the Committee is working on. Let me list them and describe them very briefly:

1. *Internal Control*—A subcommittee is working on the entire area of internal control, its relationship to audit scope, and reports on controls.

   Auditors' opinions on internal control have been appearing in published annual reports of companies in a few cases, particularly banks. However, there is no clear definition of the standards against which the adequacy of internal control is to be measured. Such reports also may have undesirable implications of providing assurance on unaudited financial statements that may not be warranted. In addition, the adequacy of internal control may depend on the qualifications of particular people as much as on the design of the control system itself. In any event, the issuance of these opinions in published reports is a mistake, I believe, until we get some better definitions of standards and have made a better determination of the words that should be used in such opinions.

2. *Reports based in part on other auditors' reports*—Another project has been established to review the matter of the top auditor of a consolidated company basing his report in part on the reports of other auditors who have examined the statements of segments of the total enterprise. What, specifically, are the responsibilities being assumed by the top auditor when he bases his report in part on work of other auditors? Should the names of the other auditors be specified in the auditor's report? What disclosure should be made of the proportions audited by each firm? To what extent is it acceptable for the auditors of the consolidated statements to base their reports on those of other auditors? Can it be done if 75% of the assets have been examined by other auditors? These are the kinds of questions being considered. This subject is also under consideration by the professional society in Canada.

3. *Independence*—In another project the Committee is considering the wording that should be used where the auditor lacks independence. AICPA Ethics Opinion No. 15 was issued several years ago when the new independence rule was adopted by the profession, and that Opinion contains an example of a report that an auditor might render in instances where he was not independent. Subsequent to the issuance of SAP 38 on unaudited statements, the Ethics Committee instituted a reconsideration of this Opinion, and asked the Auditing Procedure Committee to consider the matter. I believe most members of the Committee feel that the loss of independence is so fundamental that it pervades all of the auditing standards and everything the auditor does, that the financial statements concerned belong in the same broad category as unaudited statements, and that certainly the philosophy, if not the words, of SAP 38 should apply.

   Wording in an auditor's report suggesting that he has made an examination in accordance with generally accepted auditing standards except that he is not independent is not appropriate. This is like saying that I made an audit, but I am a carpenter and therefore not a competent auditor.

4. *Confirmation of receivables and observation of inventories*—Confirmation of receivables and observation of inventories are being reexamined by a subcommittee. As you know, if an auditor has not confirmed receivables or observed inventories but has completely satisfied himself by other means, he is now required to explain in his report that he did not perform these steps and then say that he is satisfied himself by other means. This was put into the rules to put a special burden on the auditor who chose to follow other auditing procedures. However, these procedures are now well established and it is difficult to see how the reader is supposed to interpret such a disclosure. There is a danger that the

reader, and even some auditors, will think of this disclosure as a qualification, when in fact it is not. More important, there are many other well-established auditing procedures, such as confirmation of accounts payable, inspection of securities, reconciliation of bank accounts, "vouching" additions to property, and checking depreciation provisions, that may be just as critical in an audit as those relating to receivables and inventories. There is no requirement that in these areas the use of procedures other than the most conventional ones needs to be disclosed.

5. *Other matters*—The Committee is working on a number of other matters, some of which have resulted from current legal cases affecting auditors. For example, a new subcommittee has been organized to examine the types of request for "comfort" that are being received from underwriters as a result of the BarChris decision. Another subcommittee has been organized to reexamine Chapter 11 of SAP 33 on subsequent review; this project also arose out of the BarChris case. There are a dozen or more audit guides in process, dealing with such matters as finance companies, hospitals, stockbrokers and colleges and universities. A subcommittee of the Committee on Auditing Procedure examines these guides before they are published to make certain they do not conflict with existing auditing standards or contravene something that is in an advanced stage of development within the Committee.

The Future

Many major legal actions have been taken against auditors recently, and there have also been a number of legal or regulatory actions taken against other members of the investment community. All of these cases generally involve the broad question of the fair dissemination of corporate information.

There is a real question whether we, as a profession, fully understand the seriousness of these developments. The Committee on Auditing Procedure has done a good job, but more needs to be done, since CPAs need much more guidance in auditing than they have received. Most of the actions against auditors have involved the quality of their auditing procedures or their reports. It is time that the profession paid more attention to auditing matters and gave them the kind of attention that has been given to accounting principles in the last several years.

I do think there is an interplay here, however. The looseness in generally accepted accounting principles has undoubtedly eroded the attitudes toward accountability on the part of management and auditors, and hence may have created some laxness in auditing. What difference does it make if a particular write-off is made when a change in accounting principles could achieve the desired result anyway. Thus, solutions in the area of accounting principles may also be important to the strengthening of auditing standards.

Nevertheless, there should be much more research on the part of the Institute in the area of auditing. There may be some question whether we even have all the right subjects on the agenda. There is no auditing research activity within the profession that comes close to the research activity being conducted under the auspices of the Accounting Principles Board and the Accounting Research Division of the Institute. It is difficult to see how the profession can continue to justify such disproportionate attention to these two areas.

There are problems, for example, in achieving more reliability in quarterly reports of public companies, on the basis of which many important investment decisions are made. Should there be regular interim audits or should our procedures be adapted so that we can give some more continuous type of assurances? Perhaps we should be studying the question of continuous auditing.

As a basis for improving our auditing performance, we need to develop a statement setting forth the objectives of auditing and the philosophy of auditing responsibilities.

Thank you for giving me this opportunity to discuss with you the activities of the Committee on Auditing Procedure.

Better objectives needed to improve accounting principles

Adapted from an article in *The Journal of Accountancy*, October 1969—Catlett

Significant progress in financial reporting can be accomplished if the accounting profession has sufficient determination, independence and vision to establish the necessary goals and work toward them in an effective manner. Accounting principles should not be determined by compromise and negotiation and established by unsupported edict.

THE ACCOUNTING PROFESSION in recent years has made a valiant effort to improve the accounting principles that underlie the financial reporting of business enterprises. The program of the Accounting Principles Board is unprecedented in its scope and in the resources dedicated to it. The members of the APB are devoting a tremendous amount of time to this program. Nevertheless, the achievements to date leave a worrisome question concerning whether there has been sufficient progress in terms of present-day requirements and whether the APB is accomplishing what needs to be done.

What is the goal?

The APB has been giving particular attention to the elimination of alternative practices and to the narrowing of differences in financial reporting. However, the mere reduction of alternative practices should not be the primary goal, since the elimination of practices does not necessarily result in the best ones surviving. In some areas, a minority practice may be preferable, but it also may be the simplest to abolish. It is just as easy to be uniformly wrong as it is to be uniformly right, and sometimes easier, particularly when attempts are made to achieve a "consensus" on what is preferable and to use "general acceptance" as the guiding light.

Generalizations, such as the much quoted desire of "making like things look alike, and unlike things look different," also becloud the issue with respect to comparability of financial statements. Looking alike does not always represent a proper reflection of the facts in either of two cases; also, looking different does not give any assurance that the differences between two cases are fairly presented.

The goal of the APB should be the establishment of uniform accounting principles on a sound and authoritative basis in order to have a fair presentation of the financial facts. This goal can be attained only if there is a clear and concise statement of the objectives and concepts that should be used as the foundation upon which to build a solid set of principles. These base points could then be followed in solving accounting problems in a consistent and coordinated manner.

The APB, as well as its predecessor committee on accounting procedure, has been so busy "putting out fires" and dealing with a large and ever-increasing backlog of current problems that it has never established an adequate basis upon which to build. This deficiency results not only in the waste of a great deal of time in debating each subject on a more or less isolated basis, but also in makeshift conclusions that could in the end defeat the entire effort to improve accounting principles. The accounting profession has tended to fall into the trap of working furiously on how to do something before establishing what it is trying to do. This approach can be compared to building a room for a house without having either a foundation or plans for the house.

The APB should be dedicated to the identification and establishment of principles to meet present needs rather than to the refinement and extension of what presently exists. Reiteration of what exists, with patches applied to cover up the holes, serves only to magnify the many inconsistencies and outmoded customs that have accumulated over the years. The rationalizations, which are fabricated under the guise of accounting theory to support some of the existing practices, are subject to serious question.

The view is occasionally expressed that the basic objectives and concepts which would be the framework for a set of sound principles cannot be established on an overall basis, but that each problem (such as leases, pension plans, tax allocation, intercorporate investments, and business combinations) must be solved separately and then the concepts and principles will evolve. This reverse procedure has been followed by the APB and its predecessor committee, and the ultimate futility of this approach is evident from the continuing frustration and controversy which result from unsupported conclusions. The accounting profession should awaken to the urgent need for clear-cut objectives, which have not yet been identified and defined.

Another view is that progress can be made only by evolution of practices through usage and acceptance, and that improvements will emerge by the irresistible force of their desirability. Neither history nor human nature supports this line of reasoning. In fact, evolution does not produce such a result, and this is one of the reasons that so much government regulation exists today. When a laissez-faire approach to accounting is combined with the present-day pressures for growth, performance, and earnings, deterioration in the principles followed is much more likely to occur than improvement. The only way progress can be made is to carefully and clearly establish the most desirable goal and then work diligently to get there, step by step, on an authoritative, coordinated, and professional basis.

Purposes and objectives of financial statements

Proper solutions for our current problems that will stand up for any reasonable period of time cannot be determined unless there is a foundation upon which to build. Such a foundation must include a comprehensive statement of the purposes and objectives of financial statements. Many questions need to be answered. What is the general objective of financial statements and what characteristics would make them most useful and result in the fairest presentation of the facts? What is the purpose of a balance sheet? What kinds of assets should be recognized and, in general, how should they be valued? What types of liabilities should be shown? What is the purpose of the income statement? What represents income realization? When do costs become expenses to be charged off?

Whether goodwill is an asset for accounting purposes depends upon what kinds of assets are to be recognized. Whether marketable securities or long-term intercorporate investments should be carried at cost, at fair value, or on the equity basis depends on the general concepts for asset valuation. Whether financing leases are liabilities to the lessee depends upon what is the most meaningful basis of determining obligations.

The APB and the entire accounting profession are rapidly heading into a period when the objectives must be established and the pieces put together on a rational and consistent basis. Investors and other users of financial statements will not continue to accept the pronouncements of a profession that has not developed sensible and understandable objectives in the light of the current needs of those who use financial statements.

Ten research studies have been published by the AICPA Director of Accounting Research on a wide variety of accounting problems, and several more are in process. With no agreement on the objectives and basic concepts, and with none having been established by the APB, the authors have found it necessary to assume or establish their own before proceeding to recommended solutions for particular problems. The effectiveness of the research has been considerably impaired because of this lack of a common set of base points. Thus, the research has flown off in all directions. And as a result, the studies have generally been criticized as representing personal viewpoints and either being too far ahead of what is presently acceptable or merely supporting what is already occurring.

Assets as an illustration

The accounting for assets can be used as an illustration of the kinds of questions that need to be considered in establishing overall objectives before trying to solve individual problems.

What kinds of assets should be recognized for accounting purposes? Many items of economic value are generally not shown as assets. This is evident when a company's common stock is selling for substantially more than the recorded stockholders' equity. This difference may result from carrying certain assets below their current fair value, but more frequently the difference is represented by the many intangible values that are not accounted for in terms of assets and stockholders' equity.

When should assets be recorded in relation to the legal, economic, and business aspects of transactions? What factors should be considered?

At what amount should assets be recorded? There is a general presumption in present accounting that assets are to be carried at cost. Consistent with the heavy reliance now placed on transactions with independent parties for the recognition of assets, valuation has generally been based on exchange prices generated in these transactions. But should the so-called cost basis of accounting become an insurmountable hurdle to progress? As a matter of fact, there are several departures from the cost basis in practice now. The term "asset" when used in relation to "financial position" has a connotation of value that cannot be ignored.

The past reliance on cost for the initial valuation of assets has rested on two grounds: (1) experience indicates cost is generally reflective of value at the transaction date, and (2) cost is objectively determined and subject to verification. However, as the time interval increases between the initial transaction that brings the asset under the control of the business and the subsequent financial reporting dates, cost may lose its close relationship to value. Thus, cost may become less significant. There are a whole series of propositions that should be considered; for example, the closer the valuation of assets is to current values and to current costs determined in a reliable manner, the more useful and significant is the information presented.

"Realization" as a test of the carrying value of an asset may be as much of a problem when an asset is carried at cost as when it is carried on another basis, above or below cost. While cost is an objective test of value at the date of acquisition, that basis does not have any particular relevance to realization when viewed at a later date. Many of the ancient rules relating to realization are under pressure of change, but an overall plan based on sound concepts is needed for improvement to be achieved on a lasting basis.

Valuation of assets is related in some respects to the recognition of income; and while these two problems have certain aspects which should be considered separately, they both should be related to one overall objective.

Locked in by outmoded conventions

The difficulties involved in trying to overcome some of the practices presently in existence seem to be almost endless. Excuses of all kinds exist for not making significant changes. The reasons that are put forward for maintaining the status quo are baffling.

Most of the so-called fundamental concepts and principles that presumably support the existing conventions and practices are a hodgepodge of theories. Some of these theories are the ones that have created and perpetuated many difficult problems, and such theories are hardly the ones to follow in solving those same problems.

Financial statements are used for different purposes and in different ways by a great many more people than was the case thirty years ago. Stewardship accounting is less significant, and the presentation of accounting data for making decisions regarding the future is more important. Vestiges of "venture" accounting still are with us, even though investors today are far more interested in current values and the earning power of a business enterprise. Yet, we seem to be locked in by many conventions (some of which are nothing but old bookkeeping rules) regarding the cost basis, realization concepts, liability determinations, and many other customs, which may have once served a useful purpose but are now out-of-date.

The argument is frequently advanced that a change cannot be made in one area, because the new approach would then be inconsistent with the current practices in other areas. Yet it is obvious that new approaches cannot be made in all areas at once. Thus, this all-or-nothing attitude is really a perpetual roadblock to significant progress. If overall objectives and concepts were clearly established, as discusssed above, then each step could be fitted into a master plan, and progress would be made on an organized and consistent basis that could be understood and explained.

One of the dilemmas facing the APB or any other organization that tries to develop improved accounting principles is the problem of usefulness vs. verifiability. Since the AICPA committees, governmental agencies, and stock exchanges have generally been influenced by enforcement problems and the possible danger of "abuses," verifiability has tended to win out over usefulness. Perhaps auditors have been more concerned with auditing problems than with accounting principles. For example, continued adherence to the cost basis and many of the realization rules may be more influenced by verifiability than by usefulness in meeting today's needs. While verifiability and conservatism have had considerable effect on many of our conventions, and they cannot be ignored now, the time is long overdue to take a fresh look at the obvious need for a modern and reasonable basis for present-day financial statements.

Professional judgment

What part does professional judgment play in the determination and application of accounting principles? The answer to this question always seems to be a subject of fruitless debate, with the advocates for each of the various approaches to accounting principles claiming that they favor the maximum use of professional judgment.

The best abilities and competence available, both within and outside the profession, should be focused to contribute in the most constructive manner in establishing uniform principles. The biases and preconceived conclusions of individuals must somehow be minimized, without at the same time having the compromises of group action so dilute the effort that the results are ineffective.

If an adequate set of uniform accounting principles could be established, much more professional judgment would be required to apply them than is the case at the present time. Many of the present accounting practices are based upon what is customary, and little judgment is required merely to follow what other companies are doing and what other CPAs are accepting.

Implementation criteria would be needed for applying the set of principles in order to have reasonable application to the wide variety of circumstances which exist. However, these guidelines should be consistent and in harmony with the principles, and such guidelines should not represent unsupported and capricious dogma. A proper balance is needed between the determination of sound principles and the exercise of professional judgment in applying such principles.

Avoidance of arbitrary rules

The accounting profession at the present time is in great danger of ending up with an odd assortment of arbitrary rules. Some of the leaders of the profession seem to be more interested in adopting a regulatory and police-type attitude to "plug holes" and to inhibit so-called "corner cutting" and "abuses" than in establishing proper principles. There is a tendency to overreact because of the unusual cases and to establish oppressive rules for everyone. A uniform set of principles of the right type would do more in the long run to avoid "abuses" than could be accomplished by a shelf full of rule books.

The APB has dealt in a substantive way with three major subjects that have significantly involved accounting principles. These subjects are accounting for leases—Opinions No. 5 and No. 7; accounting for the cost of pension plans—Opinion No. 8; and accounting for income taxes—Opinion No. 11. None of those Opinions is related to any basic objectives or overall concepts previously adopted by the APB or to any very convincing demonstration of why the conclusions reached produce the most useful results for investors and other users of financial statements. Those Opinions left open some serious questions, and they all will require reconsideration by the APB.

Opinion No. 9 on reporting the results of operations has little to do with accounting principles, since it relates primarily to the form of the income statement and the classification of the items therein, rather than to the underlying accounting. This subject, including the problem of prior-period adjustments, should be related to the overall purposes of financial statements, but such purposes have not yet been established.

Opinion No. 15 on earnings per share contains many arbitrary rules. That Opinion does not deal with accounting principles and sets forth only detailed guidelines for the computation of statistics (even though they are important ones) in a manner that the APB considered to be the most meaningful to the readers of financial statements. However, the conclusions are not related to previously established base points of any kind.

In fact, the APB's conclusion that the philosophy of that Opinion should be limited to computations of earnings per share and not reflected in the accounting and the financial statement presentation has the dubious effect of isolating such computations from accounting principles.

The Opinions of the APB should be based primarily on principles supported by properly determined objectives and concepts. The applicable principles should be set out clearly and separately in each Opinion. The Opinions need to include some guidelines and criteria for implementation purposes, so that there is a reasonably uniform approach in actual application. But the implementation rules should not be mixed up with the principles and should not overshadow the principles. As an example, neither an accounting principle nor its effective application should be based on a percentage, because principles cannot possibly be determined in that manner. The nature of a transaction, and not its size (assuming the amounts involved are material), should determine the principles to be followed in accounting for it.

For example, one of the problems presently facing the accounting profession is whether pooling-of-interests accounting should be continued and limited to combinations of companies of prescribed relative sizes, determined by specific percentages. Another question is whether the appropriateness of equity accounting for intercorporate investments should be affected by percentages of ownership of the outstanding equity securities of the other company. The accounting profession can never sustain, as a principle, that a transaction at a 20 percent level should be accounted for in one manner and at a 19 percent level in another manner, with vastly different effects on financial position and results of operations.

New alternatives sometimes required

The desire to eliminate alternative practices for the same types of transactions and the need to establish more uniform principles may cause us to forget that progress sometimes requires the creation of new alternatives. If alternative practices already exist, it may be possible to eliminate one or more of them. However, when progress requires a new alternative that has had little acceptance in practice, and particularly if the new alternative represents a major change, the new and old alternatives may need to coexist for some period of time.

Thus, the primary objective of the APB is not necessarily to reduce alternatives but to eliminate undesirable alternatives and to seek improvements, which may sometimes require new approaches. If new alternatives are not permitted, and if it is not recognized that new approaches cannot immediately replace previous practices, progress will cease to occur in many areas of accounting.

Examples of areas where experimentation and new alternatives may be needed are: discovery-value accounting for certain natural resource industries; fair-value accounting; price-level accounting; full-cost accounting in the extractive industries; equity accounting for intercorporate investments; accounting for intangible assets; the determination of certain types of obligations; and revenue recognition.

Effect of compromise

In any group of accountants, such as the members of the APB, honest and sincere differences of views exist regarding the best solution for the problems under discussion. A democratic approach to achieving progress requires compromise; and, we would hope the progress is in the right direction. However, compromises necessary to achieve sufficient agreement (two-thirds of the members in the case of APB Opinions) can be fatal if the effect is to dissect the principles in a "tug-of-war." Principles can be identified and selected. They should not be compromised; they cannot be negotiated; and they will not survive if established only by unsupported edict.

While accounting principles are not scientific truths that are discovered by research, such principles do need to be related to carefully determined objectives and concepts. Two principles might each be supported by logic and reason, depending upon the objectives sought, but a position part way in between would not be a principle at all. The partial-purchase, partial-pooling accounting for a business combination is a current example of an attempt to rationalize an in-between answer, and the result is an aberration that defies any reasonable explanation.

Arbitrary percentages and prescribed periods of time used in the determination or application of accounting principles are usually the result of a compromise that is not based on any principle. Pooling-of-interests accounting, as an example, has not been supported by a logical concept, and the results have been a chaotic condition which has been severely criticized in the public press and which has cast a cloud over the reliability of corporate reporting.

Leadership in the accounting profession, as in other phases of human endeavor, is the result of the efforts of individuals. Collective action, which is necessary in the case of a group such as the APB, must necessarily result in compromise, but the wrong type of compromise can seriously impair the objectives being sought. As is well-known, the larger the group, the greater the need to compromise, particularly when a two-thirds vote is required for positive action. The profession will suffer if the effectiveness of its leadership and the results of its attempts to develop sound accounting principles are stifled by compromise.

Conclusion

The most productive approach that the APB could take on behalf of the accounting profession would be, first, to clearly and concisely set forth on an authoritative basis the objectives upon which to build a foundation, including the purposes of financial statements today—not at some indefinite time in the future. This program should be accomplished with the full cooperation and assistance of all interested organizations and agencies in the business and financial community, academic institutions and government. Then the basic concepts and principles necessary to carry out these objectives and purposes would be established. After that, the appropriate practices and methods would be determined on the basis of the principles involved in each of the problem areas. The arbitrary criteria and rules, to the extent necessary for a reasonably uniform application and implementation, would be indicated, but these would be kept to a minimum and identified separately from the principles.

To those accountants who take the position that the approach I have discussed is not practicable and cannot be carried out, my answer is—an admission of such inability represents an abdication of the responsibilities of CPAs in reporting on financial statements, a breakdown in the leadership role that the accounting profession has assumed, and an undesirable reflection upon the financial reporting of all business enterprises, which depend so heavily upon public acceptance of the reliability of their reports.

Significant progress can be accomplished on a lasting basis if there is sufficient determination, independence, and vision to establish the necessary goals and work toward them in an effective manner. If this program is carried out on a hit-or-miss piecemeal basis that does not hang together as a part of a framework based on well-conceived goals, the outcome is certain to be not only off the target but also too little and too late. The accounting profession has a tremendous opportunity to be of constructive service to our society for a long time to come, but this cannot be accomplished without better objectives.

Accounting for business combinations and goodwill

Three articles printed in *The Review of Securities Regulation* in 1969 and 1970, during and after consideration of this subject by the Accounting Principles Board—Olson

These articles are of significance because they reflect important background information and viewpoints at that time.

Part I (October 21, 1969)

THE SIGNIFICANCE OF business combinations—by acquisition, merger, or consolidation—is too apparent to require comment. Equally apparent should be the need for consistent accounting procedures that will permit intelligent evaluation of proposed and completed combinations. Existing procedures do not fulfill these requirements, a failure that has been noted by both members and staff of the SEC. The burden rests on the accounting profession to come forward with proposals for reform.

"Purchase accounting" and "pooling accounting," two radically different concepts of accounting for business combinations effected through exchanges of stock, are considered acceptable by the accounting profession today. What is more, variations are permitted in the application of the basic concepts, producing additional ambiguities in accounting results.

A variety of motives produces business combinations, among them the desire for growth, diversification or the solution of income or estate tax problems. A central objective in all combinations, however, is an improvement in business performance resulting in increased earnings to reward investors who put their capital at risk. Under existing accounting procedures, the earnings and financial position reported by an enterprise resulting from a business combination may reflect not only operating performance but also the method of accounting adopted in the particular case.

Inadequate accounting for business combinations may make sound proposals appear economically undesirable and obscure the defects of others. The existence of accounting options precludes meaningful comparison of alternative investments and significantly impairs the usefulness of financial statements.

Purchase accounting

Under purchase accounting, a business combination is viewed as a purchase, a transaction in which one business buys another. Under this approach, the fair value of the consideration exchanged is measured and accounted for in the statements of the continuing or resulting enterprise. The separable resources and property rights of the acquired or absorbed company are recorded at their fair values at the time of the transaction, as determined from details of the transaction or from appraisals. The difference between the total value of the consideration given, which is the value assigned to the acquired enterprise, and the value of its separable resources and property rights (less liabilities) is generally referred to as goodwill. Goodwill is recorded as an asset on the balance sheet of the continuing enterprise, and herein lies a principal difficulty with purchase accounting.

No one questions the existence or value of goodwill, but accounting for goodwill has baffled accountants for generations. It has an elusive quality that defies meaningful traditional accounting measurement. Goodwill embraces those intangibles that affect a company's earning power, such as management, technical know-how, brand names, marketing organizations, and labor relations. These values are inseparable from a business and are most concretely evidenced by the market price of a company's stock.

Goodwill values generally are not recorded in financial statements except when goodwill is acquired in a business combination accounted for as a purchase. Under current accounting rules, goodwill recorded as an asset on the balance sheet of the continuing enterprise and determined to have an unlimited life may be carried as an asset indefinitely or be amortized by charges against earnings over an arbitrary number of years. Amortization or write-down of goodwill is required only if a limited life or loss of value is foreseen.

Realistically, purchased goodwill merges with the goodwill of the continuing company, and determination of the life or continuing value of the purchased goodwill becomes artificial and meaningless. How can the expected life of goodwill be measured? Who can determine whether purchased goodwill has lost or is losing its value after it has merged with the total goodwill of the combined enterprise? The existing rules do not reflect the nature of goodwill and the accounting that results is predictably uninformative.

Under the purchase accounting approach, earnings of the acquired or absorbed enterprise appear in the accounts of the continuing enterprise only from the date of the combination. By the same token, the retained earnings of the continuing company reflect the earnings of the acquired company only from that date. However, in proxy statements involving acquisitions, the SEC generally requires presentation of statements of income combined on a pro forma basis, in addition to the regular financial statements.

Pooling-of-interests accounting

Pooling-of-interests accounting views a business combination not as a purchase of one company by another but as a "marriage" of the constituents to the transaction. No new basis of accountability is established. The amounts at which assets and liabilities are recorded in the accounts of both or all predecessor companies simply are carried forward to the accounts of the continuing or resulting enterprise. There is no accounting in the financial statements of the continuing enterprise for the fair value (at the time of the transaction) of the separable resources and property rights of the absorbed business. There is no accounting for goodwill, and a multitude of problems is thereby circumvented by the continuing enterprise.

From the time of combination, the constituents to a pooling are viewed as though they had always been together. In financial statements issued by the continuing enterprise, earnings of all constituent companies for the entire current year and for all previous years are combined. Statements of financial position are combined, and retained earnings reflect the aggregate balances of the retained earnings of all the predecessor companies. A company can combine with another company on a pooling basis late in the year (or even early in the subsequent year but before financial statements are issued) and include in its earnings the income of the acquired or absorbed company for the complete year as well as for preceding years.

Popularity of pooling

As initially conceived, pooling-of-interests accounting had rather limited application. It was to be applied only to combinations of two businesses of roughly equal size that retained both the management and ownership interests of both constituent enterprises. However, the criteria restricting its use proved ineffective, and pooling-of-interests accounting became increasingly popular. It is now considered an acceptable alternative to purchase accounting for almost all combinations effected by issuing voting stock. These alternatives, together with the options relating to amortization of goodwill, have served to confuse accounting for business combinations.

The popularity of pooling-of-interests accounting is easily explained. It eliminates the difficulties of accounting for goodwill, as well as the embarrassment of dealing with goodwill on the books of the continuing enterprise. Goodwill that is amortized creates an additional charge against earnings; if not amortized, it remains as a dubious asset on the balance sheet and is of little significance in evaluating a company's financial position. In addition to bypassing the difficulties of accounting for goodwill, pooling of interests avoids current valuation of tangible assets and the generally higher depreciation charges resulting from the write-up to current values. The product is a brighter earnings picture for the combined entity.

Comparison of methods

The choice of method can produce wide divergences in the financial position, earnings, and growth trends presented in the financial statements of the continuing enterprise. The differences are best demonstrated by a simple illustration.

Assume that ABC Company acquires XYZ Company on December 31, 1969, in a share-for-share exchange of common stock. Assume further the following facts:

	ABC Company	XYZ Company
Book value of tangible assets	$5,000,000	$1,000,000
Liabilities	1,000,000	0
Stockholders' equity	4,000,000	1,000,000
Retained earnings	2,000,000	500,000
Earnings for the year ended December 31, 1969	$ 500,000	$ 250,000

Valuations made at the time of combination	
Fair value of tangible assets	$2,000,000
Goodwill	1,000,000
Total consideration given by ABC	$3,000,000

Under purchase accounting, the current fair value of the tangible assets of XYZ Company ($2 million) and the amount of its goodwill ($1 million) would be added to the book value of the assets of ABC Company for a total book value (including goodwill) of $8 million. Under pooling-of-interests accounting, the predecessor book values would simply be combined for a total of $6 million.

Stockholders' equity under purchase accounting would be $7 million, combining the equity accounts of the predecessor companies and adding the $1 million goodwill and the $1 million excess of fair value over book value of the tangible assets of XYZ Company. Under pooling-of-interests accounting, stockholders' equity would be a combination of existing amounts, or $5 million. Under purchase accounting, retained earnings of the continuing ABC Company would be $2 million, while under pooling-of-interests accounting retained earnings of the constituents would be combined for a total of $2.5 million.

Earnings for the year 1969 for the continuing ABC Company under purchase accounting would be $500,000, since earnings of the absorbed XYZ Company would be reflected only after the date of the transaction. Pooling-of-interests accounting would combine the earnings of both entities for the year for a total of $750,000.

The two methods of accounting can result in completely different statements of prospective earnings. The nonrecognition of goodwill under pooling-of-interests accounting relieves prospective earnings from a charge for its amortization if, indeed, an election is made to amortize goodwill. Nonrecognition of the difference between the fair value and the book value of tangible assets means that prospective earnings will not be charged with depreciation or other absorption of this difference. In the absence of any changes in post-combination operating results, reported earnings will simply be the aggregate of ABC and XYZ earnings. Under purchase accounting, current valuation of assets and recognition of goodwill produce depreciation charges (and may produce amortization charges) that will adversely affect future statements of earnings.

Assume in the previous illustration that under purchase accounting (a) the goodwill is to be amortized over 20 years; (b) the excess of fair value over book value of the tangible assets is applicable to equipment having a depreciable life of ten years; and (c) the net earnings of the two companies continue at the same level as for 1969. The table below shows the difference in the earnings for 1970, the year following the combination, as they would be reported under the two accounting methods.

	Purchase Acounting	Pooling-of-Interests Accounting
Annual earnings before adjustments resulting from business combination—		
ABC Company	$500,000	$500,000
XYZ Company	250,000	250,000
	$750,000	$750,000
Adjustments resulting from business combination—		
Amortization of $1,000,000 of goodwill over 20 years	—50,000	0
Depreciation of $1,000,000 excess of fair value over book value of tangible assets over 10 years	–100,000	0
Annual earnings as reported after business combination	$600,000	$750,000

The two accounting methods may show completely different earnings trends. Under purchase accounting, the income statements would reflect the earnings of XYZ Company only from the date of the business combination, December 31, 1969. Under pooling of interests, income statements presented for all prior periods would include the earnings of both ABC and XYZ.

Assume that the earnings of the companies are as follows for the four-year period ending December 31, 1970:

	ABC Company	XYZ Company
1967	$300,000	$250,000
1968	400,000	250,000
1969	500,000	250,000
1970	750,000	

The difference in earnings trend reported for these years by the continuing company under the two methods of accounting are illustrated below:

	Purchase Accounting	Pooling-of-Interests Accounting
1967	$300,000	$550,000
1968	400,000	650,000
1969	500,000	750,000
1970	600,000	750,000

The earnings trend pictured under purchase accounting is the more optimistic, although the statement of earnings for 1970 is brighter under pooling of interests.

Chaos

The present situation can only be described as chaotic. Either purchase or pooling accounting is available for almost all business combinations effected by voting stock. What is more, combinations that in substance are cash transactions can be made to appear as stock transactions and accounted for as pooling of interests; one method is to use treasury stock acquired for cash.

Financial presentations of earnings of a continuing company become especially confusing when some acquisitions are accounted for as purchases, with earnings included only from date of acquisition, and other acquisitions are treated as poolings, with earnings included for all periods presented. A similar hodgepodge is created in the company's balance sheet in such cases.

When the consideration consists of both cash and voting stock, combinations sometimes are accounted for as part pooling and part purchase. The assets of the acquired company are partially revalued and a portion of its goodwill is recognized. A portion of the results of operations and earnings of the acquired company are included for all prior periods in the report of the continuing company, while the remaining earnings are recognized only from the date of the transaction. The accounting profession cannot expect users of financial statements to make intelligent decisions from such data.

Pooling-of-interests accounting lends itself to a number of questionable uses. Where there is a large difference between the book value of tangible assets and their fair value, a substantial but spurious profit can be reported. For example, the book value of land held by a real estate development company may be a small fraction of its real value. If the acquisition of such a company is accounted for as a pooling of interests, the land can be carried over at its book value, immediately sold by the continuing company, and the profit credited to earnings. The substance of such a transaction is to issue capital stock and credit the proceeds of the issue to earnings.

In another questionable use, a company unable to achieve an earnings goal can delay issuance of financial statements and acquire another company under a pooling of interests. The profits of the acquired company for the entire year may then be included in reported earnings.

But the susceptibility of pooling accounting to manipulation and the limitations of historical cost figures are overshadowed in importance by the confusion inherent in the existence of alternative accounting procedures. The accountant's role is not to encourage or discourage individual combinations or the merger movement generally. He should provide the financial information on which decisions can be made. It is basic that an investor's appraisal of a combination or of the surviving company should not be influenced by the choice of accounting method.

Research Studies

The American Institute of Certified Public Accountants (AICPA) has published two Research Studies on the problem of accounting for business combinations and goodwill. The first, "A Critical Study of Accounting for Business Combinations,"[1] was published in 1963. The second, "Accounting for Goodwill,"[2] appeared in 1968.

The 1963 Study dealt primarily with the question of whether both the pooling of interests and purchase methods of accounting were appropriate to the reporting of business combinations. The Study concluded that business combinations are essentially exchange transactions whether the consideration is in cash or securities, and that pooling of interests is not an informative or appropriate method of recording this exchange. It recommended that purchase accounting be used for all business combinations involving independent entities, except in those rare

1. Arthur R. Wyatt, Accounting Research Study No. 5.
2. George R. Catlett and Norman O. Olson, Accounting Research Study No. 10.

instances when no constituent to the merger appeared to be the dominant surviving company. In such situations, the Study proposed that the resulting enterprise be accounted for as a new entity, assigning fair values as of the date of the transaction to the assets of both or all of the constituent companies. Consideration of these recommendations was delayed pending a study of the problem of accounting for goodwill, a problem that would become much more acute if pooling-of-interests accounting were eliminated.

The 1968 Study also concluded that pooling of interests was not an appropriate method of accounting, that purchase accounting should be used for all transactions involving independent entities, and that a "fresh start" or new entity approach should be taken where none of the constituents to a combination emerged as the clearly continuing entity. This Study gave extensive consideration to the nature and characteristics of goodwill. It concluded that the proper method of accounting for goodwill, after current valuation of all acquired separable resources and property rights, is to deduct goodwill from stockholders' equity, either by a charge to capital surplus or retained earnings or by showing a deduction for goodwill on the face of the balance sheet.

In our hypothetical acquisition of XYZ Company by ABC Company, the balance sheet of ABC Company immediately after the acquisition would be as follows if the acquisition was accounted for by purchase accounting and goodwill deducted from stockholders' equity:

Book value of tangible assets of ABC Company		$5,000,000
Fair value of tangible assets of XYZ Company		2,000,000
Total assets		$7,000,000
Liabilities of ABC Company		$1,000,000
Stockholders' equity		
ABC Company	$4,000,000	
Fair value of XYZ Company	3,000,000	
	$7,000,000	
Less—purchased goodwill	1,000,000	6,000,000
Liabilities and stockholders' equity		$7,000,000

Under this approach, the purchased goodwill does not appear as an asset in the balance sheet, and there would be no charge for amortization of goodwill against earnings. However, there would be charges against earnings of the combined enterprise for the depreciation of the ordinarily higher values assigned to the separable resources and property rights of the acquired company through the use of current as opposed to book values.

Those who oppose the study's conclusions regarding the proper accounting for goodwill argue that goodwill is an asset that should be capitalized on the balance sheet and amortized by charges to income, just like any other asset. The Study argues that purchased goodwill is not utilized or consumed in the production of earnings and that the cost of purchased goodwill has no continuing and reliable relationship to its value. Therefore, goodwill is not the type of asset that belongs on the balance sheet, nor can it be amortized by charges to income except over a purely arbitrary number of years.

The pooling-of-interests procedure of retroactively combining the basic financial statements of the constituents to a combination would be eliminated. Earnings and retained earnings of the absorbed enterprise would be reflected in the basic financial statements of the continuing company only from the date of the combination. The Study further noted that companies should be encouraged to present, *as supplementary financial information,* combined pro forma statements of the constituent companies for periods preceding the combination. Such supplementary presentations would present earnings trends with greater clarity without undermining the integrity of the basic accounting procedures.

Prospects for improvement

A widespread controversy exists within the accounting profession and the business community concerning the acceptability of pooling-of-interests accounting and the proper method of accounting for goodwill. The divergences are illustrated by the comments of the advisory committee that assisted in the preparation of the 1968 Study on accounting for goodwill. These comments, which were printed with the Study, reflect a wide range of views and, in most cases, disagreement with one or more aspects of the Study.

The AICPA's Accounting Principles Board is officially charged with responsibility for formal pronouncements on accounting principles for the independent accounting profession. It is presently engaged in drafting an opinion on accounting for business combinations in the course of which it will consider, though not necessarily adopt, the complementary recommendations of the two Studies. The Board presently leans toward the complete elimination of pooling of interests, the use of purchase accounting for all business combinations, and the capitalization of purchased goodwill with amortization over a period not to exceed forty years. However, these are tentative conclusions and it is too early to judge what the final outcome of the Board's deliberations will be.

Accounting for business combinations has an impact on the interests of millions of stockholders and creditors. The extensive activity in acquisitions, mergers, and consolidations makes it urgent that a sound solution be found to the problem of accounting for business combinations and goodwill.

Part II (April 3, 1970)

The Accounting Principles Board of the AICPA has issued its long-awaited exposure draft on accounting for business combinations. The need for revision of existing accounting practices has been apparent for some time; the true road to reform has been in hot dispute. The exposure draft, which appears to be an effort to accommodate widely divergent approaches, has served to raise the temperature of an already heated debate. If adopted, the proposals would substantially alter existing practices and could drastically affect the course of business growth in the United States.

The APB's proposals, as set out in the exposure draft, have been mailed to thousands of accountants, businessmen, and government officials for comment by May 15.[1] If, in the light of these comments, the APB adopts the proposed changes, the new procedures would apply to the financial statements of all business combinations occurring after June 30, 1970.

The exposure draft proposes the retention of both purchase and pooling accounting, but not as alternatives in any given business combination. Detailed criteria are established to determine the appropriate method. Pooling criteria have been greatly tightened, but a combination that meets all the prescribed conditions for pooling must be accounted for in this way. All other combinations must be accounted for as purchases. A management with a preference for purchase accounting (in some instances the earnings trend may look better presented in this way) would have no difficulty in failing to meet one of the pooling criteria.

Pooling accounting

The conditions that must be met to qualify a combination for pooling treatment are summarized below, although their application to a particular transaction would involve a host of complex determinations.

1. The smallest company entering a business combination must be at least one third the size of the largest participant, as measured by relative voting common stock interests in the resulting company. The acquisition of a relatively small company by a

1. Copies of the exposure draft, "Business Combinations and Intangible Assets," can be obtained by writing to the American Institute of Certified Public Accountants, 666 Fifth Avenue, New York, New York 10019.

large firm, the dominant pattern in recent years, could no longer be accounted for as a pooling of interests.

2. The combination must be effected by the issuance of voting common stock for at least 90% of the voting common stock or all of the net assets of the acquired company. The use of other forms of securities would preclude pooling accounting, even if the security is a voting convertible preferred stock, which the APB classifies as a "common stock equivalent" and which must be considered as common stock in computing earnings per share.

3. Each of the constituents to a merger must have been an active, independent company for at least two years before the plan of combination is initiated. (A plan is initiated where it is announced or the shareholders are notified; an alteration of the plan constitutes a new initiation.) Acquisitions of subsidiaries or divisions of a group could not be treated as poolings.

4. Unless delayed by litigation or by regulatory authorities, the plan for the combination must be consummated within one year after it is initiated.

5. The relative interests of individual common stockholders in each of the constituents to the combination must not be realigned by the exchange of securities effecting the combination.

6. The stockholders in the continuing enterprise must neither be deprived of nor restricted in exercising their voting rights for any period.

7. A combining company other than the corporation issuing stock to effect the combination may pay only normal dividends and reacquire only a normal number of shares of treasury stock after the combination is initiated. Thus, there can be no "bail outs" of any common stock ownership interests before the transaction is consummated.

8. There must be no agreement directly or indirectly to retire or reacquire all or part of the common stock issued to effect the combination, or to enter into other financial arrangements negating "the exchange of equity securities." Thus, there can be no prearranged "bail outs" of ownership interests to be made after the combination is effected.

9. The merger must not provide for any future issue of additional shares or payment of other consideration on the basis of some contingency. Earn-out provisions, under which the terms of combination are subject to successful earnings performance for a given number of years after the transaction, would disqualify a transaction as a pooling.

10. The surviving company must not intend or plan to dispose of a significant part of the assets of the combining companies within two years after the combination, except to sell (a) duplicate facilities, (b) excess capacity, and (c) assets that would have been disposed of in the ordinary course of business of the separate company. This provision is meant to eliminate the generation of "instant earnings" from the sale of valuable assets at substantial amounts in excess of their book values immediately after a pooling takes place.

The draft describes in detail the procedures to be followed in pooling accounting. With some exceptions, they are substantially the same as those in current use. There is a specific prohibition against the existing practice of retroactively combining the financial statements of companies pooled after the end of the fiscal year but before the financial statements are issued.

Purchase accounting

Under the proposed purchase accounting procedures, the tangible assets and identifiable intangible assets are to be recorded on the books of the acquiring company at their fair values at the date of the combination. The excess of the consideration given above these fair values is to be considered goodwill. The goodwill must be capitalized as an asset on the books of the combined entity and amortized by charges against earnings over a period not to exceed forty years. In connection with valuing the total consideration, the draft warns against blind acceptance of stock market prices as indicators of the fair values of securities issued. It notes that market prices may be unreliable, as for example, where the market for the securities is thin.

While earnings of the acquired company would be reported only from the date of the acquisition in the basic financial statements of the combined company, the draft would require the presentation of supplemental pro forma information as to combined earnings for the year in which the merger occurs, and for the immediately preceding year where comparative statements are presented.

The draft also requires extensive disclosure, in footnotes to the financial statements, of financial effects and other data related to a business combination. These requirements apply to both methods of accounting.

Diverse viewpoints

The exposure draft departs from the conclusions of two extensive Research Studies published by the AICPA.[2] These Studies concluded that pooling of interests was not a valid concept of accounting and that all mergers should be accounted for under the purchase method. At the same time, the second Study, which concentrated on the problem of goodwill, concluded that it was improper to carry goodwill as an asset and amortize it by charges against earnings. Rather, the Study recommended that goodwill be deducted from stockholders' equity at the date of the combination. This treatment accounts for goodwill as an acquisition cost, but removes the distortion of future earnings that would result from its amortization. The cost of purchased goodwill bears no relationship to its continuing value. After combination, it merges with the ongoing company's goodwill, which does not appear on the balance sheet. It can neither be realistically accounted for as a separate asset nor amortized by charges to income on any but a purely arbitrary basis.

The APB's draft is difficult to read and the reasoning behind its conclusions is often obscure. It contains detailed instructions for the application of explicit criteria, but the overall impression is of arbitrary guidelines without cohesive underlying accounting principles. The composition and draftsmanship of the proposed APB Opinion probably reflect compromises of diametrically opposing views held by Board members.

The prospects

Under the proposed conditions, very few of the business combinations of the last several years would have qualified as poolings. An overwhelming majority would have failed on the size test alone. Most combinations would have had to be accounted for as purchases and, under the proposed rules, would have placed enormous amounts of goodwill on the balance sheets of business enterprises. Even under an amortization program of forty years, write-offs of goodwill would have resulted in very substantial reductions of earnings following mergers, and might well have had a chilling effect on the merger proposals.

The question before the APB is not whether mergers should take place, but how best to reflect what is occurring. The APB has been moved by the need for accounting reform and not by a desire to discourage mergers in general. However, if the draft becomes effective, its approach to goodwill could result in a sharp drop in the number of mergers.

The draft is likely to produce an unprecedented confrontation between the accounting profession and the business community.

2. See Olson, "Accounting for Combinations," *The Review,* Vol. 2, No. 18, Oct. 21, 1969; "Accounting Research Study No. 5" by Arthur R. Wyatt, and "Accounting Research Study No. 10" by George R. Catlett and Norman O. Olson.

The controversy is focusing on the combination of a stringent-size criterion for pooling and the mandatory amortization of goodwill when pooling is not available. It is too early to predict the results of the battle but its outcome is certain to affect not only the role of the Accounting Principles Board, in its efforts to carry out its responsibility for improving financial accounting and reporting, but also the future of business mergers.

Part III (September 21, 1970)

The Accounting Principles Board (APB) of the AICPA, its members deeply divided in their views, has finally issued its new rules for accounting for business combinations and goodwill. Spelled out in APB Opinions No. 16, "Business Combinations" and No. 17, "Intangible Assets," the rules establish multiple criteria designed to restrict the availability of pooling-of-interests accounting. In addition, Opinion No. 17 mandates that when mergers are accounted for as purchases, goodwill must be amortized by charges to earnings. The new rules, which are not retroactive, will apply to business combinations initiated after October 31, 1970.

Controversy and compromise

The proper accounting for business combinations and goodwill has been debated in the accounting profession for generations.[1] The arguments reached a crescendo in the months following the distribution, earlier this year, of the APB's exposure draft. As predicted,[2] the exposure draft produced an unprecedented confrontation between the accounting profession and the business community. The controversy centered around a restrictive size test (a requirement that the parties to a merger be of some reasonably comparable size if pooling accounting is to be used) and the mandatory amortization of goodwill when pooling is not available.

1. See Olson, "Accounting for Combinations," *The Review,* Vol. 2, No. 18, Oct. 21, 1969.
2. See Olson, "Pooling Exposure Draft," *The Review,* Vol. 3, No. 7, April 3, 1970.

When the APB met in June to consider the flood of comments received as a result of the exposure process, the initial 3-to-1 relative size test was relaxed to 9 to 1. When the Board met again in late July to consider the final wording of the Opinion, the size test was abandoned completely. The requirement for capitalization and amortization of goodwill under purchase accounting survived.

The new rules provide for the retention of both purchase and pooling-of-interests accounting, but not as alternatives in any given business combination. Detailed criteria must now be met if pooling of interests is to be used. All other business combinations must be accounted for as purchases.

The new rules are diametrically opposed to the conclusions of two extensive research studies published by the AICPA before the Board commenced its deliberations.[3] Those studies had concluded that pooling of interests was not a valid concept of accounting and that business combinations should be accounted for as the purchase of one business by another. The second study, which concentrated on the problem of goodwill, concluded that it was improper to include so ephemeral a value as goodwill as an asset in the determination of financial position or to amortize it by charges against earnings. The study recommended that goodwill be written off against stockholders' equity at the date of the combination. This treatment of goodwill would have reduced the pressure to continue pooling accounting (which avoids the goodwill problem) and could have led to adoption of purchase accounting for all business combinations. The determination of many APB members to tie purchase accounting to capitalization and amortization of goodwill was at the heart of the demand that developed late in the Board's deliberations for the preservation of pooling accounting to the greatest extent possible.

3. Wyatt, Accounting Research Study No. 5; Catlett and Olson, Accounting Research Study No. 10.

The intensity of the disagreement on the Board's final compromise is vividly demonstrated by the members' dissents. The two-thirds vote required for approval was eked out only through the device of two separate Opinions, one covering pooling of interests and the other the question of goodwill.

The product is a set of highly complex requirements that probably satisfy very few and are vigorously opposed by others. Some see the new rules as a step forward in providing reliable accounting information; others as a step sideways. Some accountants (a group that includes the author) view the action as a long step backward. There is little discernable enthusiasm from any quarter. Whether controversial rules affecting such an important aspect of financial reporting can survive without genuine underlying support from those charged with their implementation is a matter of conjecture. The application of the rules to business mergers in the months ahead should provide a clue.

Pooling criteria

Pooling-of-interests accounting views certain business combinations not as purchases of one company by another but as transactions occurring outside the corporate entity being accounted for—a mere pooling or sharing of risks among shareholders.[4] Opinion No. 16 limits pooling-of-interests accounting to those combinations effected by issuance of voting common stock. In addition, it lays down an intricate set of rules aimed at prohibiting gimmicks or merger terms that would tend to negate the fragile, "sharing-of-risks" concept upon which pooling accounting is based.

Use of 90% voting common stock. To qualify for pooling accounting a business combination must be effected by the issuance of voting common stock in exchange for at least 90% of the voting common stock interests of another company or for all of its net assets. Having acquired 90% of the voting common stock, the entire transaction would be treated as a pooling. The remaining 10% may continue outstanding as a minority interest or be acquired for cash or other consideration. No pro rata distribution of cash or other consideration to the holders of the 90% may be made.

Curiously, the issuance of a voting convertible preferred stock, rather than common stock, would disqualify the combination for pooling, even though the APB treats many such securities as the equivalent of common stock in computing earnings per share. This limitation is significantly extended by the requirement that the rights of the voting common stock issued by the acquiring corporation in the combination must be identical to those of the majority of the acquiring corporation's outstanding voting stock. The historical dividend patterns of combining companies often differ. The former pooling rules permitted the use of voting convertible preferred stock or a special form of common stock in a pooling and made it possible, for example, to continue a relatively higher dividend rate for the shareholders of the absorbed company. The effect of the new rules is that if a merger is to be accounted for as a pooling, disparate dividend rates cannot be continued for the shareholders of combining companies.

A number of specific criteria attempt to ensure the essential stock-for-stock nature of the transaction. They are as follows:

1. The combining companies may not change the equity interests of the voting common stock (by distributions to stockholders, exchanges or retirements) in contemplation of a combination within the two years preceding initiation of the plan of combination, or after initiation of the plan.
2. Each combining company may acquire its own voting common stock only for purposes other than business combinations. No more than the normal number of shares

4. See Olson, *supra,* note 1 at 834.

may be acquired after the date the plan of combination is initiated.

3. The relative interests of individual common stockholders in each of the constituents to the combination must not be realigned by the exchange of securities effecting the combination.
4. The stockholders in the continuing enterprise must not be deprived of, nor restricted in exercising, their voting rights for any period. The voting rights to which common stock ownership interests in the combined corporation are entitled must be exercisable only by the stockholders. Thus, common stock received in a pooling may not be transferred to a voting trust.
5. The combined corporation must not agree, directly or indirectly, to retire or reacquire all or a part of the common stock issued to effect the merger. The merger plan cannot contain any financial arrangements for the benefit of former stockholders of a combining company—such as guaranteeing of loans secured by the stock issued.

Qualifying transactions—To qualify for pooling, each of the combining companies must be autonomous, and must not have been a subsidiary or division of any other corporation within two years before the plan of combination is initiated.[5] A wholly owned subsidiary that effects a combination by issuance of its parent company's shares may use pooling accounting provided the other criteria are met.

The combination must be effected in a single transaction or be completed according to a specific plan within one year, unless delayed by the proceedings of a governmental authority or by litigation. This condition, together with the requirement that the combining companies must be independent of each other, will make it difficult to obtain the advantages of poolings in business combinations resulting from take-overs. "Independent" for this purpose means that, at the outset, a combining company must not hold an investment of more than 10% of the outstanding voting common stock of another combining company. An unsuccessful take-over where a company winds up holding 11% of another company's stock would appear to preclude subsequent pooling of those companies unless an additional 79% of stock could later be acquired on the same terms as part of the same plan within the year.[6]

Prohibition of contingent payments—The merger plan may not provide for any future issue of additional shares or payment of other consideration on the basis of some contingency. The popular "earn-out" provisions, under which the terms of the combination are tied to earnings performance for a given number of years, would disqualify a transaction as a pooling. By the same token, selling stockholders cannot be given protection by provisions for the issuance of additional shares in the event of a subsequent decline in the market price of the issuing company's stock.

The no-contingency criteria may prove to be a substantial obstacle to pooling accounting. Contingency provisions in merger plans help eliminate some of the immediate risks of combination to both buyers and sellers. In the case of acquisitions of small stockholder-managed companies, "earn-out" provisions have provided an effective means of assuring the continuation of competent management in the selling company. Presumably, the theory of the no-contingency criteria is that the "sharing-of-risks" would be negated during the period of contingency. But it borders on the absurd to permit contingency arrangements to decide the whole basis for

5. The two-year rule does not apply to a company created to comply with a governmental or judicial divestiture order.

6. Preexisting intercorporate investments of less than 10% may also create complex obstacles of pooling of interests, see Opinion No. 16.

the valuation of assets and the determination of earnings in a business combination.

Disposition of assets—If pooling accounting is to apply, there must be no intent or plan for the surviving company to dispose of a significant part of the assets of the combining companies within two years after the combination, except to sell (a) duplicate facilities, (b) excess capacity, and (c) assets that would have been disposed of in the ordinary course of business of the separate company. Further, where any such disposition takes place, the gain must be clearly segregated and labeled in the income statement as an extraordinary item. These provisions are meant to minimize the impact of "instant earnings" from the sale of valuable assets at substantial amounts in excess of their book values immediately after a pooling takes place.

The effectiveness of these provisions is questionable. The disposition of assets acquired is solely within the power of the surviving corporation once a combination has occurred, and no previous intent or plan to dispose of them is necessary. What is more, substantial gains on the disposition of assets out of the ordinary course of business, must be treated as extraordinary items under previous APB pronouncements in Opinion No. 9. The disclosure of profits on sale accomplishes little that is new.

Pooling accounting

If a combination meets the new qualifying conditions for pooling-of-interests accounting, the procedures to be followed, with a few exceptions, are substantially those which have existed for some time.

While a company can combine with another company on a pooling basis late in the year and include in its earnings the income of the absorbed company for the complete year, Opinion No. 16 prohibits the practice of padding earnings by retroactively combining the financial statements of companies pooled after the end of a fiscal year but before financial statements are issued. Whether this prohibition will eliminate an abuse or create more confusion is debatable. The effect on financial statements of post year-end poolings must be disclosed and the statements of such pooled companies must be restated and combined in all subsequent interim and annual reports issued by the combined company.

Opinion No. 16 clarifies the accounting for the costs of a merger accounted for as a pooling. Finders' fees, costs of preparing and publishing proxy statements, registration, legal and accounting fees and other merger expenses must be charged to earnings of the combined company in the year that the merger takes place and can neither be capitalized as an asset nor charged to a stockholders' equity account.

Purchase accounting

Business combinations that do not meet the new pooling criteria must be accounted for as purchases. Under the purchase accounting procedures, the tangible assets, identifiable intangible assets, and liabilities of the acquired company are to be recorded on the books of the acquiring company at their fair values at the date of the combination. The excess of the consideration given above the net amount of these fair values is considered goodwill and must be amortized against net earnings over a period not to exceed forty years.[7] While the quoted market price of an equity security issued to effect a business combination may usually be used to approximate the fair value of the consideration given, Opinion No. 16 warns against blind acceptance of a market price where there is a thin market or prices are extremely volatile.

Earnings of the acquired company are to be reported only from the date of acquisition in the financial statements of the combined

7. Since amortization of goodwill is not deductible for income tax purposes, the net effect on earnings of a 40-year amortization is comparable to a 20-year depreciation for plant and equipment.

company. However, the Opinion requires the presentation of supplemental pro forma information concerning the combined earnings of the companies for the year in which the merger occurs and for the immediately preceding year, where comparative statements are presented.

These rules are largely consistent with previously existing concepts for purchase accounting (with the notable exception of the new requirement for amortization of goodwill and presentation of pro forma combined earnings). However, in the past, actual accounting procedures, particularly in the allocation of the purchase price, have been somewhat fluid. The specificity of the procedures in Opinion No. 16 is likely to result in more careful allocation of amounts to individual assets and liabilities. Assessment of the fairness of the allocations will be a demanding task for the accountant. The task will be complicated by the fact that the new restrictions on pooling may require more frequent writing up of assets for financial statement purposes when their tax base remains unchanged by the merger.

Although valuation of the debt of the acquired company assumed by the combined company is an appropriate function under accounting, it is likely to present practical difficulties. The rules require that the debt be calculated at "present values of amounts to be paid determined at appropriate current interest rates." Due to rising interest rates and declining stock market prices, large amounts of debt securities, particularly convertibles, are now selling at amounts substantially less than their face values. Accordingly, the requirement is likely to produce large amounts of "debt discount" on balance sheets following mergers. While the recording of such discounts reduces by a corresponding amount the cost assigned to goodwill, the allocation to debt discount generally will have an adverse effect on reported earnings in the initial years after the combination. Debt discount will be amortized by charges to earnings over the term of the related debt, normally shorter than the 40-year amortization period required for goodwill.

Other troublesome effects may show up as the purchase accounting procedures are enforced. Many financial institutions hold relatively low-interest bearing mortgages and bonds with market values substantially below book values. When such an institution is acquired by another, the rules require the write-down of such investments to fair value at the date of combination. The result—an increase in the goodwill carried forward, with unpredictable effects on the timing of earnings of the combined company.

In contrast to the procedures under pooling of interests, direct costs of acquisition in a merger accounted for as a purchase are considered part of the cost of acquisition. The direct cost of registering securities issued is accounted for as a reduction of the fair value of those securities. Indirect and general expenses associated with business acquisitions are not considered part of the cost of acquisition and are to be charged to income at the time they are incurred.

Goodwill and intangibles

The general requirement for amortization of *all* intangibles in purchase accounting will reduce future reported earnings. The cost of acquiring "unlimited-life" rights such as sport franchises, broadcasting licenses, and highway-trucking routes must be amortized against the earnings they produce, even when the values of these properties may be rising.

But goodwill remains the most difficult problem in business combinations. Where purchase accounting is required by the new rules, the difference between the fair values assigned to the net separable resources and identifiable intangibles and the consideration given (merely a stock market speculative value) must be recorded as an asset and amortized by charges to earnings over a period not to exceed forty years. The new rules are likely to produce strenuous efforts to structure merger plans to meet the pooling criteria and to devise ingenious schemes to avoid the rigid and arguably improper requirements for accounting for goodwill. That disputes over goodwill are likely to continue unabated is evidenced by the dissents to Opinion No. 17.

In addition, difficult encounters are foreseeable between the accounting profession and certain regulatory agencies, notably those with jurisdiction over financial reporting by banks, whose regulations prohibit the recording of goodwill in the balance sheet.

Effective date and transition

The provisions of the new Opinions are effective for combinations initiated after October 31, 1970. The date of initiation is defined as the earlier of (a) the date the major terms of a plan, including the ratio of exchange of stock, are announced publicly or otherwise formally made known to the stockholders of a combining company, or (b) the date that stockholders of a combining company are notified in writing of an exchange offer. The new rules will not apply to any plan of combination initiated before but consummated after November 1, 1970, nor to mergers consummated before that date.

A "grandfather" clause provides that a company holding a minority interest in another company on October 31, 1970, may thereafter initiate a plan of combination and account for the plan as a pooling provided the combination is completed by October 31, 1975, and the other pooling criteria are met. In these circumstances, the 90% rule applies to the common stock outstanding on October 31, 1970, less that held by the combining company at that date. The former minority interest, if more than 10%, will be accounted for as a purchase and the remaining interest on a pooling basis, thereby continuing partial-purchase, partial-pooling accounting in these cases. For obscure reasons, such partial poolings will not be permitted for a company that acquires the remainder of an interest in a company in which it held a 51% or greater interest at October 31, 1970.

Disclosure

The opinions require extensive disclosure of financial effects and other data related to business combinations. The nature of the rules, together with the mixture of old and new procedures, including the special rules applicable to the five-year transitional period, will render such disclosures very difficult for even the most sophisticated investor to interpret. The desirability of a fair presentation of financial position and earnings without the need to resort to complex footnotes cannot be overemphasized. Complex footnote disclosures may only magnify the "information gap" between the sophisticated and the unsophisticated reader, and reinforce the disadvantage of those investors most in need of protection.

The profession at the crossroads

The new Opinions are the culmination of almost a decade of work by the accounting profession. The detailed rules finally issued by the APB represent a compromise of sincere but widely differing views with scant demonstration of how they may be expected to serve the needs of the investor. There appears to be little real conviction in the profession that the new Opinions represent a correct approach. Without the energies that flow from conviction, application of the new rules is likely to be problem-ridden and result in new crises and controversies.

The accounting profession's performance with respect to business combinations and goodwill raises a real question as to whether it is properly organized to establish adequate accounting standards. Its procedures must be reappraised in search of more objective bases for the determination of accounting principles than the ad hoc accommodation of conflicting views. One of the first steps must be that of defining the function of financial statements, so that the solution to individual accounting problems can be achieved in the framework of an overall plan.

Author's Note: The new APB Opinions are lengthy and complex. Detailed study of the actual text is essential for those preparing matters of record.

Accounting for business combinations

Before the Financial Executives Institute, Rochester, New York, February 25, 1970 —Olson*

Accounting should not be designed to prevent or enhance conglomerate growth. The purpose of accounting is to achieve fairness in financial reporting to all users of financial statements.

A BUSINESS phenomenon of the late 1950's was the emergence and growth of the so-called "conglomerate" companies. They attracted much attention and their securities were very popular in the marketplace.

During the last few years, however, substantial criticism has been leveled at the conglomerate companies. Agencies of the Federal government have been particularly critical, Congress has conducted investigations, and even the general business and financial press have been critical of the conglomerates. It is difficult to assess the effects of this criticism, but undoubtedly the deterioration of stock market prices of conglomerate companies reflects at least in part its cumulative impact.

Although the term, conglomerate, lacks precise definition, it might be described as a multimarket company that operates through many individual entities. If this is a fair definition, nearly two thirds of the 500 largest manufacturing companies listed by *Fortune* would be classed as conglomerates. Actually, almost every one of today's corporate giants is the product of one or more mergers. Without these mergers our nation's capacity to produce goods and services would very likely be only a fraction of what it is today.

It is not for us as accountants to judge the pros and cons of the merger movement or the advantages and disadvantages of conglomeration in business. Nevertheless it is my view that much of the criticism of conglomerate companies has either been unfair or represents criticism of all businesses, not just those that have grown through acquisition and diversification in recent years.

Accounting principles under attack

Like the conglomerates, the accounting

* This address was given prior to the publication of APB Opinion No. 16, "Business Combinations," and APB Opinion No. 17, "Intangible Assets," in August 1970.

profession has also been criticized, but this criticism has extended over a longer period of time. The accounting profession has been staggered in recent years by a rash of lawsuits involving charges of negligence, gross negligence, fraud, and even conspiracy to defraud. These suits involve the accounting profession's function as independent auditors, examining and expressing opinions on the financial statements of businesses.

The news reports of various unexpected financial disasters over the past year or two and of companies, managements and auditors being sued over their financial and audit reports have shocked the investment community and the public in general. "Shouldn't there have been more forewarning in the financial statements of impending disaster?" some ask. Understandably, these events have raised questions about the adequacy of financial reporting by business.

As you know, in almost every standard auditor's report published in the United States, the auditor expresses his opinion about the fairness of the financial statements in accordance with "generally accepted accounting principles." The term, generally accepted accounting principles, embraces alternative practices equally acceptable in many areas, even though application of the alternatives leads to a lack of real comparability in the reports on earnings and financial position of various companies.

The term, generally accepted accounting principles, has been in use for almost forty years, but there is no adequate statement of such principles available. It is the absence of such a statement and the existence of alternatives in many areas that have been the principal causes of criticism of accounting principles over the past ten to fifteen years.

The criticisms and pressures for reform have led the Accounting Principles Board to accelerate its activities in the last few years. The Board has worked extremely hard and has issued Opinions on several troublesome matters that have had significant effects on financial reporting, such as income tax allocation, reporting results of operations, and determining earnings per share. These Opinions have focused increased attention on the APB and on the accounting profession in general. Thus, there has been an increased general awareness of accounting principles which, in turn, has led to an increase in the level of criticism concerning such principles, in spite of the progress which has been made.

Convergence of criticism

The criticism of conglomerates by the press and of the accounting profession by the business community have converged within the last year or two. The intersection of these separate lines of criticism occurred primarily on account of the practices being followed in accounting for business combinations. These practices are available to and are used by all companies who enter into business acquisition transactions, but the problem of accounting for business combinations is of greater magnitude for conglomerates because of their size and the large number of their acquisitions.

Importance of accounting properly for business combinations

Proper accounting for proposed business combinations is important, even before the transactions are consummated, so that the individuals whose ownership interests are involved may have proper financial information upon which to decide whether to approve or oppose a particular transaction. In addition, those who would become stockholders in the continuing enterprise should have proper information upon which to decide whether to sell or retain their investments. Inadequate accounting for business combinations may give stockholders an erroneous impression concerning the basis of trading their interests, and thus may make sound proposals appear economically undesirable, while obscuring the defects of others.

Of equal importance is the effect that the accounting practices for a business combination may have on the financial position and earnings to be reported in subsequent years, and on the comparability of data among business enterprises. These practices bear directly on the amount of net income reported by the resultant enterprise and on its financial position, including the amount of stockholders' investment shown in the financial statements of the continuing entity.

Criticism of conglomerates for their selection of particular procedures for accounting for business combinations is really unfair, since these same accounting principles are available to, and are used by, companies not designated as conglomerates. The criticism should rather focus on the unsolved accounting problems.

The role of the accounting profession

As members of the accounting profession we should not be, and are not, motivated either to prevent or enhance conglomerate growth. Accounting is not designed to prevent anything. Its overriding central purpose is to achieve fairness in financial reporting. Any efforts by us as accountants to improve existing accounting rules must be motivated solely by a desire to achieve improvement in financial statements. If accounting principles are properly established, they should not interfere with the natural and normal growth of any company.

Accounting principles must have only one objective and that is to communicate to the reader of the financial report the economic facts surrounding the transactions. That objective should not include passing judgment on whether a transaction, such as a merger, should have occurred.

Difficulty of accounting for business combinations

Accounting for business combinations has become perhaps the single most troublesome accounting problem that exists today. There are several reasons for the difficult nature of the problem.

No other accounting problem so vividly demonstrates the need for a clear statement of the objectives of financial statements. As soon as we start discussing or arguing the pros and cons of various accounting alternatives in this area, we come to the realization that we don't agree on the objectives of financial statements. What is the balance sheet supposed to show—asset values in relation to liabilities? If so, what assets? What is the statement of earnings supposed to show? How is this statement used? There is surprisingly little agreement on the answers to these questions. Little wonder, then, that there is a lack of agreement on solutions to difficult accounting problems, such as the accounting for business combinations and goodwill.

Only when a business combination occurs, and one business enterprise acquires another, does accounting have to deal with the total value of an enterprise as it is determined in the marketplace. The glaring deficiency in accounting for economic values of separable resources and property rights becomes obvious in a business combination, since the owners of the acquired company will insist on being compensated for the full value of their assets, whether or not these values are fairly reflected in the balance sheet.

There are two principal reasons for the deficiency in accounting for asset values today, both of which come front and center in a business combination.

Effects of inflation—The accounting profession in the United States has generally ignored the effects of inflation. General price indexes have about doubled. Some of the construction indexes have gone up almost four times.

These changes in price levels mean that the carrying amounts for many assets in financial statements are understated and are far removed from current realities and present-day values. While this is a condition that exists for all corporations in varying degrees, the cumulative effect of the failure to recognize inflation is dramatized when a business combination occurs.

Inadequate cost accounting—In addition to the failure to recognize inflation effects, understatement of assets has resulted from inadequate accounting for costs in the acquisition and development of assets. If all of these costs were capitalized on a reasonably accurate basis, balance sheets would contain amounts for assets much closer to the value of the assets. In many cases these amounts, when adjusted for inflation effects, would be the best evidence of value that could be established.

The industries most affected by inadequate cost accounting practices are principally involved in natural resource development, although nearly all companies are affected to some extent. The principal sources of asset understatement due to inadequate cost accounting practices are: cost of discovery, development, and growth in natural resources industries; several costs of an indirect nature relating to plant construction; costs of product development in research activities; and the LIFO method of inventory accounting.

These deficiencies (which generally reflect the current deductibility of certain costs for income tax purposes), become most obvious when a business combination occurs. Significant adjustments must be made at the time of a business combination if the acquiring company is to record properly the cost of the assets acquired.

Goodwill

In addition to a lack of definition of financial statement objectives and the deficiencies in accounting for asset values, there is one other aspect to business combinations that makes accounting for it difficult. Only when a business combination occurs and one business enterprise acquires or gains control over another does accounting have to deal with the total value of an enterprise as it is determined in the marketplace. There are values attached to a business over and above values that can be assigned to the assets ordinarily measured in a balance sheet, that is, its separable resources and property rights. Such intangibles have generally come to be known as goodwill. This is perhaps the principal problem in accounting for business combinations, as we shall see later.

Purchase accounting

Originally, most business acquisitions were viewed as the purchase of one company by another. Under this approach the separable resources and property rights and liabilities of the acquired company are recorded as assets and liabilities of the acquiring or continuing company at their fair value at the date of the acquisition. The difference between the total value of the consideration given, whether in cash or stock, and the fair value of the acquired company's separable resources and property rights (less liabilities) is generally designated as purchased goodwill. Under purchase accounting, goodwill is set up as an asset. If that goodwill is deemed to have unlimited life it is sometimes carried without amortization, or it may be amortized to income over an arbitrary number of years. Goodwill that is recognized to have limited life is amortized to income over this life, or it may be written off or written down as an extraordinary item if subsequent unusual events indicate a loss of value.

This problem of accounting for goodwill in purchase accounting has baffled accountants for generations. It is questionable whether goodwill can be identified as having either a measurable limited life or an unlimited life. Realistically, making any estimate of the life of goodwill is impossible. Goodwill defies traditional accounting measurements and, therefore, present rules have produced a mishmash of results in accounting for goodwill.

Under purchase accounting, earnings of the acquired or absorbed enterprise appear in the accounts of the continuing company only from the date of the business combination.

Pooling-of-interests accounting

The confrontations with understated asset values, and the inadequacies in accounting for goodwill that developed at the time of business combinations, became progressively more difficult in a period of rising prices and stock market values. This led to the popularization in the 1950's of an accounting concept known as pooling of interests. This concept, in effect, circumvented the problems of accounting for fair values and goodwill.

As initially conceived, pooling-of-interests accounting was to have rather limited application. It was to be applied only to combinations of two businesses of roughly equal size that retained the management and ownership interests of both enterprises.

However, the criteria restricting the use of pooling proved ineffective and pooling-of-interests accounting became increasingly popular. It is now considered an acceptable alternative to purchase accounting for almost all combinations effected by issuing voting stock. These alternatives, together with the options available in accounting for goodwill under purchase accounting, have served to confuse thoroughly the accounting for business combinations.

Under pooling-of-interests accounting a business combination is viewed not as a purchase of one company by another but as a "marriage" of the parties to the transaction. Under this approach no new basis of accountability is established. The amounts at which assets and liabilities are recorded in the accounts of both or all predecessor companies are simply carried forward to the accounts of the continuing or resultant enterprise. There is no accounting in the financial statements of the continuing enterprise for the fair values of the separable resources and property rights of the absorbed business. Similarly, there is no accounting for goodwill.

Hence, pooling of interests circumvented a multitude of accounting problems which are confronted under purchase accounting. The difficulties of accounting for goodwill and for the increased value of separable resources and property rights under purchase accounting in an era of general inflation and rising stock market prices made pooling of interests increasingly popular. Goodwill that is amortized creates an additional charge against earnings. This was avoided. If unamortized, goodwill remains as a dubious asset on the balance sheet, of little significance in evaluating a company's financial position. This problem was avoided. Pooling of interests also avoided current valuation of tangible assets and the generally higher depreciation charges that result from the write-up of assets to current values. The result under pooling as contrasted with purchase accounting is a brighter earnings picture for the combined entity, particularly under the general conditions of inflation existing during the last 25 years.

Under pooling of interests, a combination where the constituents are viewed as though they had always been together, earnings of all constituent companies for the entire current year and for all previous years presented are combined. Also, retained earnings reflect the aggregate balance of the retained earnings of all the predecessor companies. A company combining with another company late in the year on a pooling basis (or even early in the subsequent year but before financial statements are issued) can include in its earnings the income of the absorbed company for the complete year.

Deficiencies and abuses in pooling

Pooling-of-interests accounting has fallen into disrepute. It has received a great deal of bad publicity and it may be that the pooling-of-interests method of accounting is beyond redemption. What are the deficiencies and accounting abuses in pooling?

Most important, pooling fails to account for the values exchanged. Companies may acquire businesses whose book values are low in relation to the fair value of the assets. For example, a company may pool a land investment company whose real estate holdings are carried on the books at $1,000,000 but whose true value is $10,000,000. Immediately after the pooling, the real estate is sold for $10,000,000 and a profit of $9,000,000 is recorded by the continuing company. It would appear that the substance of such accounting is to credit the proceeds of a capital stock issue to earnings rather than to capital.

There are other methods of obtaining instant earnings under pooling of interests. When a particular earnings goal has not been achieved, a company may combine near the end of the year with another under the pooling-of-interests method of accounting and include in the earnings for the year all of the earnings of the absorbed company.

Business combinations may also be accounted for as partial poolings and partial purchases when the consideration consists of both cash and stock. Under such part-pooling, part-purchase accounting, only a partial revaluation of property is made and only a portion of goodwill is recognized. Similarly, only a portion of the results of operations of the absorbed company is included in the statements of the resultant enterprise. It is difficult to see how the reader of financial statements can understand ridiculous hybrid financial reports prepared on the basis of this kind of accounting.

Cash deals can be made to look like stock deals. For example, a company may acquire its own stock for cash, use the treasury stock in a business combination and treat the combination as a pooling, even though the transaction was in substance effected by the use of cash. Similarly, a cash deal may be made to look like a stock deal by the downstream merger technique, whereby the acquiring company, in effect, is merged into the acquired company.

Nature of business combinations

Most of us will agree, I believe, that the alternatives that now exist between pooling-of-interests accounting and purchase accounting, together with the alternatives for accounting for goodwill under the purchase-accounting method, detract from the usefulness and the reliability of financial statements of companies that have grown by way of business acquisitions and mergers. These deficiencies need to be corrected if public confidence is to be restored in the financial statements of companies that grow by business combination.

What is the answer to our dilemma? To provide the answer we must examine two factors, the nature of business combinations, and the nature of goodwill.

Let us first examine the nature of a business combination. What really happens?

There is little dispute that when a business combination is effected by cash or debt, a purchase transaction has occurred, one company having purchased the assets and business of the other. There is no unanimity of view, however, about what happens when a business combination is effected by common stock.

Those who argue that there is a difference between a cash and a stock transaction contend that pooling-of-interests accounting is appropriate for business combinations effected by stock. They contend that there has been no acquisition of one company by another company, but that the exchange of stock is a transaction occurring outside of the business entities being accounted for. The transaction is merely an exchange of ownership interests. They state that nothing of substance has occurred requiring a new basis of accountability, and that there has been no exchange transaction in the usual sense. The business combination is simply a uniting of two or more businesses formerly conducted separately. Therefore, the assets and liabilities should be added together and all financial statements for current and prior periods should be combined. There has been no purchase, they contend, of one company by another such as happens when cash or debt is used.

Those who argue that there is no difference between a business combination effected by stock and one effected by cash contend that there is only a difference in the form of consideration used and that all are purchases. Most business combinations, they argue, involve a constituent that is clearly the continuing entity, and that the substance of the transaction, whether by stock or cash, is that one company takes over the business and assets of the other. Business combinations, they state, are the means by which the continuing company expands and grows. It follows that the principles of accounting for expansion and growth by business combination should be the same as those for expansion and growth from within.

I believe that the weight of the arguments support the theory that business combinations are purchases. One party to the transaction is ordinarily the dominant continuing one and can be clearly identified. I can find no difference in substance between those business combinations effected by stock and those effected by cash. Without a substantive difference in the nature of the transaction, I do not find any reason for basic differences in the accounting for business combinations simply because the form of consideration differs. Therefore, the proper accounting for business combinations is to be found in the general concepts underlying purchase accounting, rather than in those underlying pooling-of-interests accounting.

In rare cases there will be business combinations in which no party to the transaction can be identified as the continuing entity. The size of the constituents is similar and the managements of both are completely integrated at a high level. In these instances, rather than a purchase transaction having taken place (or a pooling transaction as some have contended), the transaction has actually resulted in the creation of a brand-new company. Thus, the appropriate accounting for these combinations is to be found in the principles of accounting for a new entity. How do we account for a new business? Generally, the assets are accounted for at their fair values excluding goodwill. Therefore, the assets of both companies would be revalued.

All business combinations, other than those rare exceptions to be accounted for as new entities, should be accounted for as purchases. This requires evaluation of the assets of the acquired company to determine their fair values, and such fair values should be recorded on the books of the acquiring company. Earnings of the acquired company should be included in the accounts of the acquiring company only from the date of acquisition, and, similarly, retained earnings of the acquired company should not be carried forward. It is recommended, however, that pro forma statements of combined income for the constituent companies, appropriately adjusted for new depreciation and interest charges resulting from the combination, be presented as information supplementing the basic historical financial statements.

Nature of goodwill

Elimination of poolings and the treatment of all business combinations as purchases would create astronomical amounts of goodwill on the balance sheets of U. S. businesses under present accounting rules. Should goodwill be accounted for simply as another asset—capitalized and amortized over some arbitrary period? This would appear to be an impossibility and, as I shall attempt to show, would be theoretically improper as well. What then should be done about goodwill?

No one questions the existence or value of goodwill, but accounting for it has been difficult. It has an elusive quality that defies meaningful traditional accounting measurement. Goodwill embraces all those intangibles that affect a company's earning power, such as management, technical know-how, market penetration, brand names, labor relations, etc. These values are inseparably tied to a business and are most clearly indicated by the market price of a company's stock. Therefore, goodwill values are subject to all the varied factors, rational and irrational, that influence stock market values.

We have defined goodwill as being the difference between the total value of a company (based generally on the market price of its equity securities) and the aggregate value of its separable resources and property rights. Goodwill may be more valuable than all other assets combined; in fact, in the case of many U. S. corporations the goodwill values are several times as large as the values of the various tangible and identifiable intangible assets.

What then is the problem? The fact of the matter is that goodwill is not "just the same as any other asset." And for this reason, an accounting treatment that differs from that accorded other assets may be warranted. Goodwill is an amount established by the marketplace in evaluating a present going business and the future prospects of that business. Its value is subject to all of the varied factors from peace to war that affect the stock market.

The following specific characteristics of goodwill are pertinent to the accounting therefor:

1. The value of goodwill has no reliable or predictable relationship to costs that may have been incurred in its creation. This generally is not true of other assets, except for certain intangibles such as patents. Some goodwill values may be created by expenditures which the company absorbs, but many favorable conditions and goodwill factors occur with no expenditures at all. Goodwill can grow instantly or cease to exist instantly, sometimes in the opposite direction to the trend in profits. Thus, its value is not ordinarily a reflection of costs incurred.
2. Individual intangible factors that may contribute to goodwill cannot be separately valued.
3. Goodwill attaches only to the business as a whole. It does not exist as a value apart from other assets. It is inseparable from the business.
4. The value of goodwill may and does fluctuate suddenly and widely because of the innumerable factors that influence that value. Goodwill does not have the stability of value possessed by most resources and property rights that makes cost accounting for such resources and property rights appropriate and useful.
5. Goodwill is not a value consumed in the production of earnings; it doesn't wear out. Rather, goodwill is a result of earnings or of the expectation of them, and its value is a measure of those expectations. Earnings are produced through the consumption or use of the company's individual resources and property rights, that is, those elements of value which usually appear in a company's balance sheet.
6. Only investors or owners establish the value of a business taken as a whole, and goodwill appears to be an element of value that runs to the investor or owner rather than to the business enterprise itself.

Proper accounting for goodwill

With these characteristics in mind, is it appropriate to account for goodwill values in the same general manner as we account for other assets—that is, by capitalization in the balance sheet and amortization by charges to earnings?

The concepts of goodwill that appear to underly the current practice of accounting for purchased goodwill are that goodwill is an asset whose value is susceptible to separate measurement after its purchase, and that the period of existence of purchased goodwill can be estimated and goodwill may be determined to have an unlimited or an estimated limited life. These concepts are incompatible with the characteristics of goodwill which were noted above.

Realistically, purchased goodwill merges with the goodwill of the continuing company, and determination of the life or continuing value of the purchased goodwill is artificial and meaningless. How can the expected life of goodwill be measured? Who can determine whether purchased goodwill has lost or is losing its value after it is merged with the total goodwill of the combined enterprise? Purchased goodwill is not susceptible to traditional accounting measurement.

We have two basic financial statements: the balance sheet, whose purpose or objective it seems to me is to convey some information concerning the value of the assets of a business in relation to its liabilities, so that its financial position can be adjudged (and we convey such information by the use of cost information rather than by continual revaluation); and the statement of income, whose function it is to show something about the earning power of a company.

Historically, except for the purchased goodwill in business combinations, only the separable resources and property rights have been reflected on the balance sheet. They provide the existing security for debts and the support for the equity. Concerning all the other valuable assets of a business, from good management to good labor relations, it is not an accounting function to measure them in the balance sheet. Rather it is the investor's responsibility to measure those values based, in part at least, on his evaluation of the financial information he receives, particularly the information about earnings.

To record purchased goodwill as an asset, representing perhaps only a part of the goodwill of the continuing enterprise, obscures financial position; amortization of goodwill to earnings obscures true earning power.

The proper accounting for purchased goodwill is to write it off at the date of the transaction either by a charge to surplus or by showing it as a deduction from stockholders' equity. Such accounting conveys the proper message, namely that this amount represents the amount of existing resources expended for the possibility of realizing future earnings. The goodwill will go back on the balance sheet when it comes back in the form of specific resources as a result of earnings from operations.

In summary, it is my recommendation that pooling-of-interests accounting be eliminated and that the concepts underlying purchase accounting be established as the only proper ones for business combinations, excluding those rare instances when a new entity is formed. Along with the elimination of pooling-of-interests accounting, however, must come a different treatment of goodwill. In my view, the proper treatment is to deduct goodwill from stockholders' equity at the date of the transaction.

What is being done?

Over the course of the last seven years the American Institute of Certified Public Accountants has published two Research Studies relating to this problem. The first, "A Critical Study of Accounting for Business Combinations," was published as Accounting Research Study No. 5 in 1963. The second, "Accounting for Goodwill," was published as Accounting Research Study No. 10 in 1968. Both of these studies concluded that business combinations are essentially purchase transactions, whether the consideration involved is cash or stock, and that pooling of interests is neither sound in concept nor an informative or appropriate method of recording the purchase.

The second study was made by George R. Catlett and myself. It dealt extensively with the question of goodwill and came to the conclusion, which I have cited before, that goodwill should be recorded as a charge to capital surplus or retained earnings, or be shown as a deduction from stockholders' equity on the face of the balance sheet.

The Accounting Principles Board has devoted a major share of its time for the last year and one-half to developing an Opinion on accounting for business combinations and goodwill. The Board has come up with numerous drafts and, in the course of this period, has adopted several different positions.

It is obvious that there is a considerable difference of view among Board members about the solution. This difference of view is reflected throughout the accounting profession and is highlighted in the comments of the advisory committee to the research study on "Accounting for Goodwill." The result of these divergent views and the pressure to get a solution, pressure from the SEC, as well as that generated by public criticism, have led to attempts to compromise the differing views.

The Board has reached a tentative position and this position is to be set forth in a draft that will be exposed widely in the very near future. Undoubtedly, the Financial Executives Institute will receive copies of the exposure draft for comment. The following conclusions are included in the position now being taken by the Board.

1. Criteria are set up whereby business combinations will be accounted for either by the purchase or pooling-of-interests method but not as alternatives. Under the proposed solution most combinations would be treated as purchases.
2. Poolings would be permissible where common stock is used but would be severely limited, the principal limitation being a size test.
3. There are various other conditions, such as that the plan is to be carried out within one year and that the combination agreement must not provide for any future issuance of additional shares or payment of other consideration on the basis of some contingency. In an effort to forestall instant earnings from undervalued assets, the Opinion would provide that the surviving combined corporation must not dispose of a substantial part of the assets of the formerly separate companies within two years.

Thus, pooling of interests would be substantially eliminated; perhaps less than 5 or 10% of business combinations would qualify for pooling-of-interests accounting. In addition, the draft Opinion would require the capitalization of goodwill wherever purchase accounting is followed, and such goodwill would be amortized over a period not to exceed forty years.

Conclusion

The position proposed by the Board appears to me to be an impossible one. Enormous amounts of goodwill will be created on balance sheets, and the amortization of such goodwill, in my view, may render some income statements useless. The size criterion for pooling is meaningless. Why should the acquisition of a large company call for a completely different concept of accounting from that used in connection with the acquisition of a small company?

There is probably little question that an

Opinion of the Board will be forthcoming. Necessarily, that Opinion will reflect some compromise of views. Unfortunately, the Board has now arrived at about the worst of all possible compromises, one which, in my view, makes no sense whatsoever. I believe it is impossible to get a practical, workable solution if capitalization and amortization of goodwill is going to be required and pooling of interests is to be virtually eliminated.

I hope that each of you will study carefully the exposure draft when it is distributed, and that you will write the Accounting Principles Board giving your views. Accounting for business combinations has an impact on the interests of millions of stockholders and creditors. The extensive activity in acquisitions, mergers, and consolidations makes it urgent that a sound solution be found to the problem of accounting for business combinations and goodwill.

The auditor in legal difficulty—what's the answer?

Adapted from an article in *The Journal of Accountancy,* April 1970—Olson

The long-run impact of the recent cases may be beneficial if the profession responds constructively and meets the public's need for more reliable financial information.

THE LARGE NUMBER of legal actions taken against auditing firms in recent years raises questions concerning how the auditor can avoid such difficulties. There are no easy answers, but answers must be found, and on a professional basis. Characteristic of professional responsibility is the critical element of judgment; professional issues are seldom black or white. The challenges to the profession and the opportunities open to it are enormous if it will but take a constructive approach to the difficulties that confront it.

The purpose of this article is to discuss this issue, principally along three lines: avoiding trouble; what to do when you find yourself in trouble; and, some thoughts at large for the accounting profession.

The author wishes to emphasize that the viewpoints expressed herein are the author's views and not those of the AICPA; they have reference to professional standards and not to legal obligations; and they are suggestions as to how the author believes things should be and not descriptions of conditions as they now exist.

Doing a first-rate job on every engagement

One basic proposition, on which we all must agree, is that there is no substitute for doing a topnotch job on every audit engagement. In our discussions of techniques for minimizing our legal liabilities, we sometimes give too little emphasis to this fundamental proposition. It deserves more emphasis by all of us.

A characteristic of our profession, as of other professions, is that significant specialized knowledge and a high degree of expertise are involved. The professional man who possesses this knowledge and skill is licensed by the public to serve the public.

Since the public is not expert, the public is largely at the mercy of the professional man. It would seem, therefore, to be in the public interest for the courts to take a serious view of the professional man's responsibilities, particularly as to his qualities of independence, objectivity, and integrity.

There is the hazard that the CPA may give a disproportionate amount of his attention to larger clients. He may feel that he could get into the most trouble with these clients. Such a policy is dangerous and can prove to be a big mistake. Some of the most publicized cases involving responsibilities to third parties by auditing firms have related to clients that have not been among the more prominent clients of those particular firms. CPAs can become involved in serious difficulties on relatively small engagements.

It is indefensible for a professional man to take the commercial view that he must serve best the client who is the biggest and most important and is most likely to enhance his reputation and fees. This is inconsistent with our professional responsibilities and may reflect on our posture of independence.

The fact of the matter is that in the smaller companies internal controls are sometimes weaker, management organizations sometimes not as competent and deep, and the competitive position often less well established. All of these conditions suggest the need for at least as much care, competence, and supervision on smaller engagements as on the larger ones.

Limits to professional work load

All of us in the profession are interested in growth, not only for the present benefits growth may bring, but in order to build for the future of younger men and women. Also, we are all interested in serving an ever-growing list of clients.

This desire for growth also poses danger. We must realistically appraise our situations to make certain that we can deliver the services to which we are committing ourselves in a manner that measures up to the standards established by our profession. We must resist the temptation to take on more than we can handle effectively.

Supervision and participation of experienced personnel

Closely related to the question of not taking on more than we can handle is the matter of supervision. Our profession has sometimes tended to turn too much work over to the less experienced personnel. Supervisors, managers, principals, or partners may sit back and not participate directly until an audit or other engagement is nearing completion.

There may be too much of a tendency to think of ourselves as business executives—that partners and supervisors should conduct themselves as chief executives or vice presidents. However, we are first and foremost professional men. Our first job, regardless of our level of experience and responsibility, is to give first-rate professional service to clients; and to do so we must supervise and counsel the younger staff continuously.

Our profession's tendency to keep experienced people in the office may reflect a bygone era when a tremendous amount of detail work was done by clerical-level personnel, before the current emphasis on analyses, tests, and controls. The opportunities for making auditing more dynamic and professional in character are enormous. Every client is different and businesses have all the capacity for diversity that individual human beings have. We shouldn't standardize every procedure and turn all the work over to inexperienced personnel. The judgment of the mature and experienced person is crucial to every audit.

Let's put ourselves in the place of the investor or creditor. What if it were our money? Shouldn't we give audits the same kind of attention that we would if we were looking after our own property?

Working paper evidence

The process by which the CPA arrives at a competent professional Opinion involves a review of controls and systems, the testing of transactions to evaluate the effectiveness of those controls and systems, the gathering of facts, the disposition of exceptions, and the reasoning toward a conclusion. This process would be very difficult to conduct unless the auditor employed pencil and paper and made some record in the course of his work. Furthermore, if procedures are carried out for him by assistants for whose work he is responsible, the record becomes an important tool by which he carries out his responsibilities for supervision and review—one of the generally accepted auditing standards that he represents in his report that he has followed. Also, working papers provide evidence which can be of assistance in demonstrating that the CPA had a valid and competent basis for his Opinion if he is called upon to defend it.

The Committee on Auditing Procedure of the AICPA issued its Statement on Auditing Procedure No. 39 (SAP No. 39), entitled "Working Papers," in October 1967. This Statement very appropriately does not attempt to spell out details. It points out that working papers must suit the circumstances and needs of the individual engagement and that the quantity, type, and content of working papers may vary greatly from one engagement to the next.

Nevertheless, the Statement identifies six guidelines that describe in broad terms what working papers should include or show. While the guidelines appear simple and somewhat general in nature, they are actually fairly encompassing.

Three of the six guidelines are responsive to the three standards of fieldwork comprehended by the term "generally accepted auditing standards." In other words, working papers would generally indicate observance of these standards by showing:

1. That the engagement had been planned and the work of assistants supervised and reviewed.
2. That the scope of the work had been considered in the light of a review of the effectiveness of the client's system of internal control.
3. The procedures followed and the testing performed in obtaining evidential matter. This record, the Statement says, may take any form so long as it permits reasonable identification of the work performed.

In addition to the three guidelines that relate to the three standards of fieldwork, three other guidelines state that the working papers generally would:

1. Contain data sufficient to show that the financial information being reported upon was in agreement with (or reconciled with) the client's records.
2. Show how exceptions and unusual matters disclosed by the auditor's procedures were resolved.
3. Include appropriate commentaries indicating the auditor's conclusions concerning significant aspects of the engagement.

These are the six broad guidelines that the Committee concluded, if thoughtfully considered, would help every CPA discharge his responsibilities and that, if observed, would help him to demonstrate the validity of his Opinion, should he be called upon to defend it. The guidelines in no manner restrict the auditor in exercising his judgment, nor do they impose any unnecessary burdensome detail.

SAP No. 39 acknowledges that an auditor may have support for his Opinion which encompasses an environment and facts beyond the working papers themselves. However, it is much easier for a CPA to sustain the position that he had a valid basis for his conclusion and that he had made an examination in accordance with professional standards, if the working paper evidence supports that contention. Some doubt, at least, is raised when the auditor states that he performed an audit step, but there is no record of it in his working papers.

Audit programs

Each audit engagement should be guided by a carefully considered program or plan, and the working papers should indicate in some manner that the steps outlined in the program have, in fact, been carried out. In addition, where there have been deviations from a program because of changes in conditions or for other reasons, the working papers or the program should indicate clearly that those changes had been made intentionally. For, as useful as a program can be in the conduct of an examination, the record of a program not executed can be disastrous.

Consider, for example, a situation where an audit program calls for a particular scope of audit testing in an area, but the scope is not carried out, and the working papers contain no explanation why the tests were not made. Assume further that the CPA finds himself in court over an issue and that the tests omitted might have disclosed a material misstatement that was not otherwise discovered during the audit. The auditor would appear to be in an untenable position. The program, in effect, says that in his own evaluation of the client's internal control the auditor considered a particular procedure to be necessary. How can he now defend not having performed the procedure? He would be in a better position to have had no program at all than to have had one, failed to carry it out, and failed to indicate that he had changed the program.

Disposing of exceptions

Closely related to the matter of executing the steps in an audit program is that of disposing of exceptions or unusual items disclosed by audit tests.

The general approach in auditing is to examine transactions on a sample-test basis. Where exceptions are disclosed by such testing, it is vital that the exceptions be disposed of satisfactorily and that the working papers indicate the disposition.

Let us assume that a CPA examines a series of 100 disbursements as a test of vouchers payable, cash disbursements, receiving and purchasing procedures. In the group of 100, he finds three exceptions where there were no receiving reports. This is duly noted in the working papers by the assistant who did the work and the CPA calls it to the attention of the chief accountant. Nothing further is done.

As it turns out, the company's chief accountant is engaged in a large fraud, diverting receipts of materials to a private warehouse and sending the company the invoices. In a situation such as this, the CPA is in a very vulnerable position, probably a weaker position than if his tests had failed to uncover the irregularity.

The auditor in this case should have pursued the exceptions and resolved them to his complete satisfaction; failing that, he should have reported them as unsupported disbursements in a letter to the top management or, depending upon the circumstances, to the directors.

Maintaining independence

We are all aware of our need to maintain independence, not only from a financial standpoint but in all aspects of our relations with clients.

Some aspects of independence may not have been given enough attention. For example, to the extent possible, provision should be made in each firm for some rotation of personnel on jobs. There is a danger that when one is assigned to an engagement too long he may lose some of his objectivity.

The client as well as the auditing firm can often benefit from the fresh approach of new personnel.

In addition, CPAs can enhance their independence by maintaining regular direct contacts with the boards of directors of their clients. This is particularly important for clients whose securities are publicly held. Directors should understand the general scope and purpose of the auditor's work, and the arrangements should be in writing. The directors should be made aware of any areas of controversy between auditors and management, such as those that might arise over accounting principles.

Probably the best way to establish and maintain regular contacts with directors is through an audit committee of directors whose specific responsibility is to meet and discuss matters with the auditors. Clients should be encouraged to establish such committees.

Know the rules but ask—does it make sense?

All CPAs should be thoroughly familiar with the accounting principles and auditing standards which the profession has established. However, the CPA's professional responsibility is not necessarily met simply because he has "touched base" with the technicalities of generally accepted accounting principles or generally accepted auditing standards. Statements might be misleading and the audit work inadequate even though no specific written rule has been broken.

Auditors run the risk of too narrow and blind adherence to rules and not stepping back to judge whether the results from an overall standpoint make sense. Perhaps the rules have been applied in such a manner that they do not add up to a reasonable result at all.

As professional persons, auditors should not operate on a philosophy that they have discharged their responsibilities when they have followed all the rules. Each of us should come to honest conclusions based on adequate knowledge in every situation and not dismiss matters by simply saying, "Well, I don't like it but I have done everything that the books call for." We should ask ourselves the question, "Are the results likely to be misleading to an uninformed but reasonable man?" He is the person who has been called the lowest common denominator of the judicial system, but his understanding of our responsibilities may be more decisive in court than the definitions we write for ourselves as a profession.

This is a difficult and intangible matter, but every CPA must be mindful of it. Perhaps it is more a matter of a frame of mind involving personal characteristics, courage, independence, and integrity. We need a personal philosophy that states that we won't go along with things just because another auditor did. This runs to the essence of professionalism.

Then there is the question of quality control in a practice. What can be done in this area will vary, depending on the size and nature of our individual practices, but all CPAs can do something.

For example, individual firms should arrange for some regular "audit" of the quality of their work. An interoffice or intraoffice working paper review program, wherein supervisors or principals are assigned to review engagements with which they have not been associated, can be very beneficial in identifying weaknesses in a practice and taking corrective action.

Most decisions in our profession involve judgment. Doctors when faced with a particularly difficult and serious case will try to obtain the independent views of other doctors. Each firm should encourage a spirit of openness about problems and create an atmosphere which encourages everyone to discuss problems with others in the firm. This is essential to maintaining quality control. These matters are too serious for an individual to let pride stand in the way of checking with others.

The client in precarious financial position

No discussion of this subject would be complete without mentioning the special care that may be needed when a client is in an obviously precarious financial position. It appears that in most cases affecting auditors that have been publicized in recent years, the client went bankrupt or investors or creditors otherwise lost large sums of money.

Undoubtedly, a great many mistakes have been made by CPAs over the years, but relatively few have led to serious problems. Often these mistakes are like trash in the hold of a ship; they come to the surface when the ship goes down.

One hesitates to recommend that the auditor take extra care in the apparently precarious situation, because this may suggest a presumptive attitude toward our work running contrary to our need for objectivity. Nevertheless, where a client's financial position is obviously weak, the auditor should take some extra precautions—not merely to protect his own interests but more importantly to minimize the effects of any impending financial disaster on those who have made investments.

Related to this problem is the problem of the ethically marginal client—the client whose officers are in trouble with the law for one reason or another—or the client who obviously "cuts corners" in his business dealings. As auditors we are qualified to examine financial facts objectively and to express opinions on them but we are not professionally qualified judges of human character. I would be opposed to including in our auditing standards any statement that the auditor should review a potential client's reputation. On the other hand, the auditor should use some judgment and take some reasonable and practical steps when he knows he has a client whose standards are such that he may not be able to deal with him in the good faith that characterizes most business and professional associations.

Realistic assessment of position

Even with the best of planning and performance, a CPA may find himself in trouble, and a few comments and observations are appropriate on what the auditor should do then.

When adversity strikes and our performance is challenged, what do we do, beyond notifying our insurance companies?

First of all, auditors must recognize that not all challenges to the quality of one's performance have substance. We must not act from fear and thereby allow ourselves to be blackmailed by a challenge to our reputations. Auditors are not guarantors of profits to the equity holder, and losses to investors are not necessarily in any way the responsibility of the auditor.

On the other hand, auditors must be careful not to be emotional or to get too defensive. The most important advice one can give is that the auditor should first make an independent, objective and completely realistic assessment of his position. If he fails to do this, the situation can become especially difficult; for, if his assessment is wrong, the auditor may in the long run, lose much more than the amount in controversy, including the time of the top people in the firm, enormous legal costs, and unfavorable publicity, and all in a losing cause.

How does the auditor assure himself of an objective assessment of his position when he is in difficulty? One way is to have the engagement reviewed in its entirety by one or two experienced people not associated with the engagement. Perhaps arrangements can be made for someone from another firm to make such a review in some cases, if the question of client confidences does not interfere.

Rationalization

Another point that should be mentioned is the very significant hazard in becoming overly defensive when we are challenged.

There is a danger that an auditor may get too committed to positions or conclusions that he has reached in the past. Upon reexamination a year or two later he may not be completely satisfied, but through rationalization he may convince himself that the prior position was proper.

The auditor must resist any inclination to rationalize a weak position. Rationalization may breed anxiety and drain off energies, leading to bad judgment. A mistake or error in judgment raises questions about financial liability; failure to correct such errors objectively when disclosed not only increases that liability but may raise more serious legal issues.

What should be the posture of the profession in the face of these problems? A few observations may provide some clues to possible positions for the future.

In 1897 there were only 37 industrial stocks listed on the New York Stock Exchange. This list has expanded tremendously in the last 70 years. The number of shareholders in American business corporations now totals in the neighborhood of 25 million, close to three times the number of stockholders just 13 years ago. The accounting profession now operates in a more public sphere, and old rules based on more or less private relationships between the auditor and his clients no longer have much significance. The widespread public interest demands reliable, understandable, unsophisticated financial information.

A primary function of the audit today is to provide an independent expert Opinion on financial statements that others can rely upon. In many publicly held companies, an independent audit might not be considered necessary if it were not needed to give assurance that management's financial presentations to outsiders are reliable. The profession must be shaped to serve the public accordingly. To evade this is to invite oblivion; the public's needs will be served—if not by CPAs, then by others.

Need to eliminate alternative accounting principles

The standard auditor's report expresses an Opinion concerning the fairness of financial statements in accordance with "generally accepted accounting principles." That phrase embraces alternative practices equally acceptable in many areas.

There is a real question whether many users of financial statements understand the auditor's intent in the phrase "fairly presents in conformity with generally accepted accounting principles" or are aware of the accounting alternatives that exist. Certainly there is the possibility that financial statement users attach as much significance to the words "fairly present" in the auditor's report as to the words "generally accepted accounting principles." A more important question is whether it is fair for users of financial statements to be put in a position of having to understand the nuances of the term "generally accepted accounting principles" in order to get meaning from a term such as "fairly presents." Even more perplexing is the fact that, in using the standard of general acceptance, the auditor does so with no clear understanding in his own mind, because the basic objectives of financial statements are unclear, having never been defined in an authoritative fashion. There is a cloud of uncertainty which obscures the auditor's responsibilities.

The use of "general acceptance" as a standard of accountability—a standard used for more than 30 years by the accounting profession—has led to a kind of accounting by consensus and a natural evolution toward an ever lower common denominator in practice. In addition, the range of alternatives in accounting may have created a general laxness in attitudes toward accountability on the part of managements and auditors. What difference does it make whether a particular write-off is made or a particular accounting recommendation is followed, if selection of another acceptable accounting method in another area would offset the accounting adjustment? Thus, loose accounting principles may tend to corrupt auditing standards as well.

It is crucial that the accounting profession work harder than ever to eliminate undesirable alternatives. There should be a better definition of what financial statements are supposed to show and a reexamination and redefinition of what the auditor's responsibilities are. These are very unclear. The auditor's responsibilities are defined in the AICPA literature in Chapter 1 of Statement on Auditing Procedure No. 33 almost entirely in negative terms—what we do not do. We must take a more positive approach.

Spirit and attitude of practice

Somehow the idea seems to have crept into the thinking of CPAs and others in the investment community that when it comes to financial presentation and footnote disclosures, one should think in terms of minimums. No one should be asked to do any more than others do, than the Securities and Exchange Commission demands, or than is precisely written into an APB Opinion.

In the long run, if auditors approach their work in the spirit that one does only what is absolutely necessary and takes advantage of every rule, public accounting as a true profession is certain of extinction. It would be impossible to write enough rules.

We must preserve a spirit in our profession which says that, in spite of what we might allow under the rules, we shall always recommend the very best in financial presentation and disclosure on the basis that the public deserves and is entitled to the best. This should not be from an attitude of pious self-righteousness, but because in the long run it is going to be best for the client, for his investors and creditors, and for the accounting profession. If a client gets into trouble, the auditor may also be in trouble. If the auditor hasn't followed the best standards, he may not be in a position to help defend the client—the auditor will be defending himself.

To operate on the fringes of the rules is to walk on the edge of a cliff. There is bound to be a misstep by someone sometime. The battles for better accounting and auditing should be fought on a much higher plane, away from the edges of disaster.

As disturbing as the unfortunate cases and incidents involving auditors may be in the short run, the long-run impact may be beneficial to the profession. From these cases should come some authoritative clarification of our responsibilities, underscoring their importance. If the accounting profession responds constructively to the issues and meets the needs of the public interest for more reliable financial information, these adversities should result in larger and more interesting opportunities for service on our part.

More than has ever been true in the past, attention is focused today on the public responsibilities of those who strive to serve the public, whether through the professions, through business, government, labor, or the courts. CPAs, bankers and other members of the investment community need to obtain a deeper understanding of their public responsibilities. The public in general, the SEC, the courts, and others are increasingly aware of these responsibilities. This is the consumer's day in court, and this includes the millions of consumers of financial information and auditor's reports.

Our profession needs the superior person who understands what is right rather than the inferior person who understands only what will sell. For we are really talking about the broad, moral issues of business.

Many in the world are challenging our way of free enterprise and asking, "Is it best for our people and for future generations?"

We can defend our position and demonstrate that it is the best way if everyone in the financial community, not just the auditor, recognizes his obligations to the public interest in business affairs, including the 25 million shareholders. One should not ask what he can get by with or what the SEC will allow. Each of us must recognize that stockholders are, in effect, depositors and that the publicly held company is like a bank, that it is not the management's, the director's or the auditor's company in any respect. The CPA's responsibility is to develop financial presentations that he honestly feels are the fairest.

The pressure on the profession to perform with independence and integrity has never been greater and, at the same time, the opportunity for the profession to grow in service and responsibility to the public has never been greater.

The role of the accounting profession in establishing principles

Before the First Annual Conference of the British Accounting and Finance Association, Edinburgh University, September 14, 1970
—Catlett

The future of the accounting profession is unlimited if we have the courage and resourcefulness to deal with our problems in an effective and constructive manner.

THE ACCOUNTING PROFESSION in the United States has been engaged in a tremendous effort to establish appropriate accounting principles for business enterprises. The total annual cost of this program, much of which is contributed time, is probably more than two million dollars. Serious questions have been raised from various sources as to whether the results are worth the effort and whether the program is sufficiently effective and timely to accomplish what needs to be done. The answers to such questions are clear: the accounting profession must have such a program, and; significant improvements in the program are essential if the necessary goals are to be attained.

As a member of the Accounting Principles Board (APB) and as chairman of my firm's policy committee on accounting principles, I have had an opportunity to observe the efforts to achieve progress in recent years. In this connection we should consider what needs to be done, including the obstacles that must be overcome, in the development and application of sound accounting principles. The difficulties involved are somewhat similar in many countries, even though the laws and customs are different. Hopefully, we can all learn by exchanging comments about our experiences.

Research

Adequate research is essential to achieving proper solutions to our accounting problems. The American Institute of Certified Public Accountants has published eleven research studies and several others are in process. The general quality of these studies has been quite good. The average time required to complete the studies has probably been about four or five years, with some taking longer. Since the need for a solution to many of these problems has been urgent, the delays in the completion of the studies have been a handicap. However, such delays have not been crucial in the work of the APB because of the huge backlog of work that has been on its agenda since it was established in 1959.

In addition to the formal studies, the American Institute staff and several accounting firms have done a wide variety of research of lesser magnitude. Also, the results of research done by other organizations, such as the Financial Executives Institute and the National Association of Accountants, have been made available.

While research is obviously necessary, there is a tendency at times to overemphasize its importance. Some accountants believe that a sufficient quantity of the right kind of research will solve most of our problems and overcome resistance to change by the sheer force of its volume and persuasiveness. However, such a conclusion is unwarranted in an area like accounting where practical effects are so pervasive and where the objectives are so undefined.

Research will never replace the need for the application of judgment and experience by a group of highly qualified and knowledgeable persons. The problems that exist in present-day business activities are so complex that unusual ingenuity and resourcefulness are necessary in dealing with them. The final authoritative decisions concerning the best accounting and reporting must be based on many factors, such as those involved in determining what represents the fairest presentation of the facts to the shareholders, potential investors, creditors, employees, customers and management. Accounting must have a sound and logical theory base, but the principles followed must be those that produce the most useful results in everyday life.

Many questions have been raised regarding the type of research that is best. At the present time only two of the eleven published research studies have been used effectively by the APB, even though pronouncements have been issued on several of the subjects. This lack of effective usage could be the fault of the APB as much as, or more than, that of the researchers. In the case of several APB Opinions, the conclusions drawn were probably the same as they would have been without any formal research study. The profession needs to give further consideration to ways and means of obtaining research that is of maximum usefulness and of improving the manner in which the research is used by the APB.

One of the questions frequently asked is —why have accountants in the academic field not made more of a contribution to research that would be of benefit to the accounting profession in solving its problems? With all due respect to Dr. Maurice Moonitz, who is a participant in this program and has made significant contributions to the accounting profession, the research by academicians as a group has not been as effective as it should have been and has not been as productive as in several other fields of learning. Efforts should be made by all concerned to correct this situation, because all available resources should be made available to, and used by, the profession.

In brief, research is important, but it is only the beginning of the task to be accomplished, and it is not the end by any means.

Responsibilities of various parties involved with the issuance of financial statements

One of the most difficult phases of the task of improving accounting principles relates to the responsibilities of the various parties involved with the issuance of financial statements. My comments in this regard should be considered in the light of the fact that many legal actions are being filed in courts in the United States against managements and independent auditors for damages incurred because of reliance on allegedly misleading financial statements. This trend has accelerated as a result of the sharp drop in the stock market over the past year and an increase in bankruptcies and other financial difficulties. When money is lost, investors and creditors have an incentive to try to blame their losses on someone with financial resources.

Managements—There seems to be general agreement that the primary responsibility for the preparation and content of financial statements rests with the management of the issuing company. Yet, the accounting profession, governmental agencies and stock exchanges are prescribing accounting and reporting rules that must be followed by managements. The alternative to not following such rules involves all sorts of dire consequences to the managements and their companies. Auditors threaten to qualify their reports. Governmental agencies have strong retaliatory powers. Stock exchanges have the right to remove securities from trading. What are the rights and responsibilities of managements when they honestly believe that rules imposed upon them do not result in the best presentation of the facts, but rather produce misleading results? Do managements have adequate defenses if they are required to follow accounting principles with which they do not agree, if they are subsequently attacked in court?

Independent auditors—The responsibility of independent auditors runs not only to their clients but also to third parties who rely on the financial statements upon which the auditors report. This third-party responsibility is unique among the professions, and the legal consequences of this responsibility may vary among different countries depending upon the laws and court decisions. Auditors in the United States have a significant potential legal liability to third parties, and their responsibility is being expanded by the courts. The reliance by third parties on the reporting of Certified Public Accountants on financial statements is one of the principal reasons why CPAs are licensed and regulated by the states.

Both under the Securities Act of 1933 and under common law, auditors issuing reports have a responsibility to base those reports on their own view of what represents a fair presentation of the facts. This responsibility cannot be avoided merely by blaming a host of other people. An opinion written in 1947 by a lawyer who was quite knowledgeable of the provisions of the Securities Act of 1933 stated as follows:

> "While the form and content of the financial statements are subject to the rules and regulations of the Securities and Exchange Commission, the opinions expressed in the certificate by the accountant are his alone and he is the person who will be held responsible therefor. The accountant is also responsible for the examination and review of those financial statements, used in the registration statement, as to which he undertakes to express his expert opinion, and his responsibility relates not only to the propriety of what is set forth in the financial statements, but also to the inclusion of such additional information as is necessary to make such statements not misleading."

What are the responsibilities of an auditor when he honestly believes that following a pronouncement of the APB or a regulation of the Securities and Exchange Commission (SEC) does not result in a fair presentation of the facts? Neither the APB nor a governmental agency has any specific responsibility, legally or otherwise, for the contents of a particular set of financial statements. This responsibility rests primarily with the management but the auditors also share in this responsibility. What position are the auditors in if they are forced, directly or indirectly, by professional organizations or governmental agencies to give an unqualified report on financial statements that they do not, in fact, believe are proper?

Governmental agencies—In addition to the SEC, which was established to protect investors, numerous Federal and state regulatory agencies in the United States have statutory powers to regulate particular industries, such as public utilities, transportation and communication companies, banks, savings and loan associations, and insurance companies. The rules and regulations of these agencies may or may not conform to what the accounting profession would consider to be "generally accepted accounting principles."

While the accounting profession has taken the position that rules published by a governmental agency with control over an industry do not necessarily establish generally accepted accounting principles for that industry, such rules frequently have the effect of law. Auditors can and do qualify their reports when companies follow required accounting that does not meet the standards of the accounting profession, but this situation is not desirable from the standpoint of the public, and efforts are being made to eliminate such differences.

In general, the SEC and the accounting profession have cooperated well enough to avoid significant differences in the accounting principles and practices followed by them. A similar level of cooperation has not yet been achieved between the accounting profession and the other Federal and state regulatory agencies.

Stock exchanges—The stock exchanges have certain requirements for listing purposes, and occasionally they have prescribed accounting rules. The exchanges have usually followed the lead of the accounting profession and the SEC. As a result, conflicts in policy between the profession and the stock exchanges have been rare.

Professional associations—Two types of pronouncements could be issued by a professional committee such as the APB: recommendations that are based only upon subsequent acceptance and do not have to be followed by members of the association, and; requirements that must be followed by members of the association in reporting on financial statements. A professional association cannot set forth absolute requirements for anyone but its members, unless there are laws giving the association, directly or indirectly, authority to do so. There are no such laws in the United States.

The Council of the American Institute (the governing body representing the members) stated by formal resolution in 1964 that its members should follow APB Opinions, as representing "generally accepted accounting principles," and there is to be no departure from such Opinions unless "substantial authoritative support" can be found for another approach. Departures from positions established in APB Opinions must then be disclosed in the auditor's report or in the footnotes to the financial statements. The burden of proof is placed upon the auditor who departs from the APB Opinion to support the alternative used. A recent attempt to incorporate this requirement in the code of professional ethics barely failed to obtain the necessary affirmative vote. Thus, the support of the APB Opinions is dependent upon voluntary cooperation of the accounting firms and the members of the Institute. This support has been almost complete during the last six years, but there is no assurance that such support will continue indefinitely.

I know of no case in which any member of the American Institute has relied upon "substantial authoritative support" to defend a direct and significant departure from an APB Opinion. Auditors have been qualifying their reports for such departures. However, the alternative of relying on "substantial authoritative support" is always available and is a potential weakness in establishing effective standards. This alternative was established by the Council as a compromise when there was a heated controversy in 1964 concerning whether American Institute members should be required to follow APB Opinions as representing the only acceptable accounting principles.

Only confusion results when "generally accepted accounting principles" are described officially as those principles that have "substantial authoritative support." An undefined term is used to define another undefined term. No one really knows what "general acceptance" means — by whom and to what extent. At one time, the accounting bulletins issued by the American Institute were based on subsequent "general acceptance" but the APB Opinions are now considered to be authoritative when issued and acceptance by the profession is assumed, whether the members of the American Institute approve of the conclusions or not. The members have delegated to the APB final authority, without review by any other group, to issue pronouncements on accounting principles. An APB subcommittee appointed to define or describe "substantial authoritative support" finally gave up in frustration after struggling with the problem for some time.

Relationship of responsibilities—The interrelationship of the various parties involved with the issuance of financial statements can be summarized briefly. A committee in a professional association can bind only the action of its members, and this may be done either by threat of expulsion from membership or by voluntary cooperation. The latter course is satisfactory as long as everyone sticks together, but such cooperation is tenuous and subject to breakdown at any time. In fact, if one major accounting firm refused to follow an APB Opinion, the whole structure might fall apart.

Managements cannot be required by auditors to follow the pronouncements of professional committees, but the auditors, as members of the professional association, can use the threat of qualification of their reports as a weapon. A governmental agency, such as the SEC, can refuse to accept an auditor's qualified report and can require companies subject to its jurisdiction to follow the professional pronouncements. Some managements are claiming that the SEC is using the APB as an unofficial regulatory arm and is enforcing APB Opinions as though they were SEC regulations, but without going through the rule-making procedures for a governmental agency as required by law.

While managements have a responsibility of their own, they have other organizations and agencies telling them what they must do. Yet those organizations and agencies do not assume any direct responsibility for the resulting financial statements.

The APB and the SEC obviously should work together. However, the APB needs the cooperation and support of the SEC, not its domination. While the SEC has generally supported the APB, and the SEC has frequently acknowledged its reliance on the accounting profession, there is no requirement for it to do so. The SEC has extensive statutory powers to prescribe accounting principles and practices to any extent it chooses. Also, the regulatory function of the SEC under the laws should not be mixed up and confused with the professional function of the APB in establishing accounting principles.

With respect to auditors, it is unlikely that the courts will permit the self-established standards of the accounting profession to be a successful defense for a member of that profession unless the results in the particular case represent a fair presentation of the facts and are not misleading in any significant respect. The courts are likely to hold to a standard of fairness in financial reporting that will not necessarily be limited to "fair presentation in conformity with generally accepted accounting principles."

Thus, the foundation of existing relationships is on somewhat shaky ground with respect to who is really responsible for what. Perhaps only the legislative bodies and the courts, which represent the public broadly, can make the final determinations.

Obstacles to progress

The APB has been involved in some very controversial and bitter debates in recent years. The most recent one, which has just been completed, relates to the accounting for business combinations and for intangible assets, including purchased goodwill. The wounds from this battle are still open, and the ultimate repercussions are as yet unknown.

The eighteen members of the APB are as sincere and hardworking a group of men as I have ever known in connection with a volunteer professional committee. The time and effort expended have been far more than most people can imagine and more than anyone has a right to expect. The APB has been meeting for three or four days about every six weeks. More than 25 subcommittees are in operation. Each member of the APB is on several of these subcommittees, and these meet frequently. One subcommittee, of which I was a member, met about twenty times within a year. Vast quantities of all kinds of information, including numerous drafts and letters, are sent constantly to all APB members. Each member was furnished with copies of the 860 letters received on the last exposure draft of an Opinion submitted for public comment. Any deficiencies in this program cannot be traced to a lack of effort. Yet lessons are still to be learned and obstacles to be overcome.

The pressures against change, when the changes are on a mandatory basis and are significant in effect, are very strong. These pressures are a natural result of a quasi-legislative process in a democratic society. Such pressures are not to be deplored but should be dealt with for what they are, as a part of our system. It is naive, however, to assume that the various viewpoints vigorously expressed in a variety of ways do not have an effect on the total process. These pressures come from within the profession as well as from outside.

A quasi-legislative body such as the APB can reach agreement only by compromise. With eighteen members on the APB and a two-thirds vote required to issue a pronouncement, solutions to highly controversial subjects are almost certain to end up in compromise. While rules and regulations can be arrived at by compromise, this process strains the logic and reasoning that are so necessary in establishing a reasonable set of accounting principles. One proposed principle in a particular area may be as logical as an alternative principle, but halfway in between is no principle at all. Such compromises are very vulnerable to attack, and subsequent deterioration in practice is likely.

One form of compromise is the temptation, when dealing with difficult problems, to "patch up" the situation rather than to be more decisive and constructive. This approach ends up with patches that do not stick. The result usually is a deterioration in practice which ultimately requires another and delayed effort to achieve the improvement that was needed in the first place.

There is a tendency on the part of the APB to want to stop alleged "abuses" in practice and to restrict certain business activities that are perfectly legal and appropriate. Such an attitude is viewed by some persons as an attempt to regulate business. The APB and the profession are on questionable ground to the extent that the pronouncements are of this type. The APB should deal with accounting principles and the accounting for transactions as they occur and not try to influence the occurrence of the transactions.

With the APB dominated by auditors, there is an unconscious inclination to adopt the viewpoint of auditors. Practices that might create auditing problems tend to be deferred or avoided. Such a bias is not necessarily in the best interests of the public.

One of the most frustrating aspects of my service on the APB is the constant presence of a formidable roadblock. This barrier, which frequently prevents the right kind of progress, is the argument that one change in current practice cannot be made unless many other related changes are also made. Since many changes cannot be made at once, it follows from this argument that no change, or little change, should be made. As an illustration, the APB is considering whether investments in marketable securities should be carried at quoted market prices rather than at cost. The predictable opposition states that such a change cannot be made until other assets are also carried at current or fair value.

The solutions to our problems cannot successfully be arrived at on an isolated and uncoordinated basis. When a group of individuals such as the members of the APB try to deal with a controversial problem, the determination of a solution is made much more difficult when each member formulates his reasoning from his own basic concepts. The solution would be difficult enough to agree upon if there were some agreement about concepts and base points. In the absence of such agreement, the various views on concepts and base points get mixed up and confused with solutions to particular problems.

As an example, how can anyone decide whether lessors should reflect lease rights and obligations in their balance sheets until some decisions are made concerning basic concepts affecting a balance sheet, its contents in general, and the nature of assets and liabilities. The purposes and objectives of financial statements should be established, and then agreement should be reached on certain basic concepts and principles that will accomplish those purposes and objectives. Otherwise, nothing but a group of unrelated rules exist, not supported by any logical framework of theory and not based on any defensible reasoning. Until these objectives can be established on an authoritative and sound basis, controversy and disorder will prevail. Such an approach is the only way to overcome the previously mentioned argument that piecemeal changes should not be made. If the pieces all fit into an overall plan, it is easier to demonstrate that each of the pieces is an organized step in an evolutionary development, that will all fit together when completed.

As I have asked many times—can we decide how to do something before we decide what it is that we are trying to do?

The APB has made an effort to improve its relationship with organizations representing business enterprises, including several industry associations, as well as organizations representing bankers, lawyers, financial analysts, and other groups. While these organizations tend to represent what might be considered to be the biased viewpoints of their members, improved cooperation would result in a better understanding of the problems involved by everyone concerned and a better acceptance of the solutions when they are determined. Dealing with a large number of these organizations presents some practical difficulties. However, such cooperation is essential to the long-range success of the program.

The future

In the United States, about thirty million persons own shares, directly or indirectly, in publicly held companies. The uses to which financial statements are being put are expanding in all directions in a dramatic manner. The needs of all of these users of financial statements can be met if the necessary goals are attained by the accounting profession. The profession can and should play a decisive part in establishing sound principles and in improving financial reporting.

The problems and obstacles, that I have reviewed briefly, must be overcome if the accounting profession is to carry out the role our society has given to it. The profession must take the lead, but the cooperation and assistance of managements, governmental agencies, and other interested parties are needed. Ways and means must be found to achieve what is necessary for the common good.

The work of professional committees, such as the APB, involves the public interest in such a significant way that their work must be conducted more like a public body than a private group deliberating in secret. Public hearings and more responsiveness to the views and needs of the public are necessary. Exposure processes must be improved, while at the same time the final decision must be based fairly on all pertinent facts and without any improper influence.

The future of the accounting profession is unlimited, if only we have the courage, ability, resourcefulness, and independence to deal with our problems in an effective and constructive manner. Our success will be judged by only one test—do the accomplishments meet the needs of the public and do the results best serve the public?

Protest over accounting principles

Before the Financial Executives Institute, Dallas, Texas, January 12, 1971—Olson

The current unprecedented reliance on financial statements presents a challenge to the accounting profession and management to establish the highest standards of fairness, competence, and independence in financial reporting.

IT IS A REAL PLEASURE to be in Dallas to discuss current developments in the accounting profession and the problems that face the financial executive and the independent accountant today.

1970 — year of protest, violence and economic difficulty

Most of us, I suppose, breathed a sigh of relief when the year 1970 was over. It was a year of Kent State and Cambodia. Business had its problems too; the high leverage and technologically escalated fixed costs of the soaring sixties produced a severe crunch on earnings and cash flow as business volume leveled off and declined in 1970. There were spectacular bankruptcies and near-bankruptcies, which scared the daylights out of all of us.

Protest and near violence also confronted the accounting profession. At the same time the merger movement was leveling off, reflecting the depressed market conditions and other factors, the profession attempted to deal with the difficult problem of accounting for mergers. There were deep divisions on this issue within the accounting profession and sharp conflict developed between the profession and industry.

It is fair to say, I believe, that the year ended with a general disenchantment on the part of industry and members of the accounting profession with the Accounting Principles Board and the methods by which accounting principles are established in this country.

APB Opinions No. 16 and No. 17

Controversy and compromise

The new merger accounting requirements are spelled out in APB Opinions No. 16 (Business Combinations) and No. 17 (Intangible Assets). The Opinions include a long list of criteria designed to restrict the application of pooling-of-interests accounting, and introduce a mandatory requirement to amortize goodwill by charges to earnings in mergers accounted for as purchases. The new rules became effective on October 31, 1970. The fact that the new rules went into effect on Halloween evening may be more than coincidence and may be a portent of things to come.

The arguments over the proper accounting for business combinations and goodwill have existed for generations in the accounting profession, but reached a crescendo in the months following distribution in February 1970 of the APB's exposure draft of a proposed Opinion. The exposure draft produced an unprecedented confrontation between the accounting profession and the business community. The controversy centered around a restrictive size test for pooling and the mandatory amortization of goodwill when pooling is not available. The size test required that the parties to a merger be of some reasonably comparable size in order for pooling accounting to be followed.

When the APB met in June 1970 to consider the flood of comments which had been received as a result of the exposure process, it relaxed the initial 3-to-1 size test to 9 to 1. When the Board met again in late July to consider final wording preparatory to issuance of the Opinion, the size test was scuttled completely. The requirement to capitalize and amortize goodwill under purchase accounting, avoided under pooling, survived. The intensity of disagreement and the wide divergence in viewpoints are vividly demonstrated by the composition of the members' dissents. The subject was divided into two Opinions, one covering pooling of interests and one the question of goodwill, in order to get the necessary two-thirds vote for approval.

Summary of new requirements

The new Opinions provide for the retention of both purchase and pooling-of-interests accounting, but not as alternatives in any given business combination. Detailed conditions or criteria have been established that must be met if the business combination is to be accorded pooling accounting. A business combination that meets all of these prescribed conditions must be accounted for as a pooling and all others as purchases, but managements who have a preference for purchase accounting should have little difficulty in drafting a merger plan that fails to meet one or more of the conditions for pooling.

Under the prescribed purchase accounting procedures, goodwill must be capitalized as an asset in the balance sheet and must be amortized by charges to earnings over a period not to exceed forty years. Since the amortization of goodwill is not deductible for income tax purposes, the net effect on earnings of a 40-year amortization period is comparable to that of a 20-year period of depreciation for plant and equipment.

Pooling vs. purchase accounting

With a few exceptions, once the merger meets the qualifying conditions for pooling of interests, the procedures to be followed in pooling accounting under Opinion No. 16 are substantially the same as those that have existed for some time. Pooling-of-interests accounting views certain business combinations not as the purchase of one company by another but as a transaction occurring outside the corporate entities being accounted for — a mere pooling or sharing of risks among the shareholders. Thus, the reasoning runs, no new basis of accountability is established, and the amounts at which assets and liabilities are recorded in the accounts of the predecessor companies should simply be carried forward to the accounts of the combined enterprise. There is no accounting in the financial statements of the continuing enterprise for the fair value at the time of the transaction of the separable resources and identifiable property rights of the absorbed business, nor is there any recognition of goodwill.

From the time of the combination, the constituents of a pooling are viewed as though they had always been together; and financial statements issued by the combined enterprise, earnings of all constituent companies for the entire current year and for all previous years, are combined.

Those business combinations that do not meet the pooling criteria must be accounted for as purchases. Under the purchase accounting procedures, the tangible assets, identifiable intangible assets, and liabilities are to be recorded at their fair value at the date of the merger. The excess of the consideration given above the net amount of such fair values is considered goodwill.

Under purchase accounting, earnings of the acquired company are to be reported only from the date of acquisition in the financial statements of the buying company. However, the Opinion requires the presentation as supplemental pro forma information of the combined earnings of the companies for the year in which the merger occurs and for the immediately preceding year where comparative statements are presented.

The general requirement of the new Opinions for amortization of all intangibles under purchase accounting will reduce future reported earnings. For example, the cost of acquiring unlimited-life rights, such as sports franchises, broadcasting licenses, and highway trucking routes, must be amortized against the earnings they produce, even when the values of these properties may be rising, a little-known sleeper in the Opinions.

But the most difficult problem in business combinations remains as before. The difference between the fair values assigned to the net separable resources and identifiable intangibles and the consideration given—goodwill, merely a stock market speculative value — must be recorded as an asset and amortized by charges to earnings over a period not to exceed forty years. Thus the application of the new rules is likely to result in strenuous efforts to structure merger plans to meet the necessary pooling criteria and to avoid the undesirable and, to many of us, improper requirements of accounting for goodwill. And these efforts have already started, as I will touch on later.

Pooling criteria

Let's look for a moment at the criteria that must be met for a business combination to be accounted for as a pooling.

Opinion No. 16 limits pooling-of-interests accounting to those combinations effected by voting common stock and lays down an intricate set of rules in an attempt to prohibit gimmicks or merger terms that would tend to negate, even though common stock is used, the fragile sharing-of-risks concept upon which pooling accounting is based.

1. In order to qualify for pooling accounting, a business combination must be effected by the issuance of voting common stock in exchange for at least 90% of the voting common stock interest of another company or for all of its net assets. The remaining 10% may either continue outstanding as a minority interest or be obtained for cash or other considerations.

   The issuance of a voting preferred stock would disqualify the combination from pooling even though the APB considers many such securities as the equivalent of common stock for purposes of computing earnings per share. This prohibition, together with the requirement that the rights of the voting common stock issued in the combination must be identical to those of the majority of the corporation's outstanding voting stock, is very significant. The historical dividend patterns of combining companies often differ. The effect of these rules is that disparate dividend rates cannot be continued for the shareholders of combining companies if a merger is to be accounted for as a pooling.

2. A number of detailed criteria, which we do not need to get into here, are provided in an attempt to assure that no part of the plan disturbs the essential stock-for-stock nature of the transaction. Thus, criteria are established to prohibit bailouts of common stock ownership interests before the transaction is consummated and to prohibit prearranged bailouts after the combination is consummated.

   The Opinion does not prohibit the use of treasury shares in a business combination. However, if a company is to use its shares in mergers to be accounted for as poolings, the company must not acquire shares for use in business combinations or unusually large amounts of treasury shares, or make acquisitions which do not follow a consistent pattern. Thus, a company cannot issue shares in a business combination accounted for as a pooling and simultaneously purchase an equivalent number of shares in the market for cash.

   The effect of this rule can be catastrophic. For example, if a company sells off a division or a subsidiary to large stockholding interests in return for its own shares of stock—and this is happening, as you know — presumably it would appear to be prohibited from any pooling transactions for two subsequent years. This seems grossly unfair, but this is what happens when arbitrary rules are issued.

It is interesting to note that no longer is there a restriction on what selling stockholders can do with stock received in a pooling. The old holding periods are no longer applicable, so selling stockholders may immediately dispose of the stock they receive. The combination agreement itself, however, must not provide that the combined corporation undertake to retire or acquire stock issued to effect a merger, nor may it contain any financial arrangements for the benefit of former stockholders of the combining companies.

3. Another criterion for pooling is that each of the combining companies must be autonomous and independent and must not have been a subsidiary or a division of another corporation within two years before the combination is initiated unless the new company was created to acquire assets disposed of by another company in compliance with a governmental or judicial order. Also, the combination must be completed within a year.

   These conditions will make it difficult to obtain the advantages of poolings in business combinations resulting from takeovers, since all shareholders must get the same number of shares, and you must get, in effect, 90% of the stock at one price within one year.

   The criterion that each combining company must be autonomous and independent and must not have been a subsidiary or division of another corporation within two years before the plan of combination is initiated is completely irrelevant. It was introduced in the draft at the time the draft included a size test, the thought being that companies would circumvent the size test requirement by fracturing businesses to meet the necessary size test. When the size test was removed from the final Opinion, this "autonomous" criterion was not. This is creating havoc now as companies attempt to sell subsidiaries or divisions to raise capital, since the acquiring companies cannot use pooling even though voting common stock is used. This can affect significantly the price at which subsidiaries can be sold, since acquiring companies must set up and amortize goodwill.

4. Another important criterion to be met for a merger to qualify for pooling is that the merger plan must not provide for any future issue of additional shares or payment of other consideration on the basis of some contingency. Thus, the popular earn-out provisions under which the terms of mergers are tied to successful future earnings performance for a given number of years disqualify a merger from being treated as a pooling. Similarly, selling stockholders cannot be given any protection by provisions to issue additional shares in the event there is a subsequent decline in the market price of the issuing company's stock. The theory underlying this criterion presumably is that the sharing of risks would be negated during the period of contingency, but it borders on the absurd that contingency arrangements should drastically affect the whole approach to the valuation of assets and the determination of earnings in a business combination.

Other matters

There are a number of other provisions in the new Opinions that are interesting and of potential significance. In poolings, merger acquisition costs such as finder's fees, costs of preparing and publishing proxy statements, registration, legal and accounting fees, and other merger expenses must be charged to earnings of the combined company in the year that the merger takes place and cannot be capitalized as an asset or charged to stockholders' equity. However, direct costs of acquisition in a merger accounted for as a purchase are considered as a part of the cost of acquisition, and the direct cost of registering securities issued is accounted for as a reduction of the fair value of securities issued.

Two years of study, new rules, and emerging problems

The procedures adopted for accounting for business combinations and goodwill are diametrically opposed to the conclusions of two extensive Research Studies published by the AICPA before the Board commenced its deliberations. Those studies had concluded that pooling of interests was not a valid concept of accounting and that business combinations should be accounted for as the purchase of one business by another. However, the second study, which concentrated on the problem of goodwill, and in which I participated, concluded that it was improper to include a fluctuating value such as goodwill as an asset in determination of financial position or to amortize it by charges against earnings; rather, goodwill should be eliminated from stockholders' equity at the date of combination. Adoption of the treatment for goodwill recommended by the second study would have reduced the urgency to continue pooling accounting and could have led to adoption of only one concept in accounting for business combinations.

After the years of research, the APB deliberated for approximately two years, departed completely from the conclusions of the studies, and eventually issued the set of detailed rules I have summarized. These represented a compromise of sincere but widely differing views, with little demonstration of how the rules would serve the needs of the investor. There appears to be little real conviction in the profession that the new Opinions are truly right in their conclusions. Without the energy that flows from conviction, application of the new rules is likely to run into difficulty and bring the whole subject to the boiling point again.

In fact, problems are already arising. One of my partners and I have received probably a dozen calls everyday since November 1. Most of these calls are inquiries from our partners having discussions with clients involving the structuring of mergers in such a way as to avoid the goodwill problem by obtaining pooling accounting. This necessarily gives the professional man some discomfort.

The no-bailout provision is being circumvented by having buying stockholders bail out the selling stockholders outside of the business combination agreement. The no-contingency provisions are being circumvented to some extent by entering into options to buy stock with formulas based on, say, a three or four-year profit performance rather than initiating a business combination. Furthermore, the contingency provisions can be circumvented for a year as long as the business combination is finally consummated in 364 days. Some imaginative people have avoided the charge to earnings of finders' fees and acquisition costs by arranging to have sellers pay those fees; undoubtedly such arrangements are borne in mind when the exchange-of-shares terms are negotiated. There are many other ideas being generated, and a serious question is raised as to the future effectiveness of these Opinions.

Current agenda of APB

Having disposed of the business combination and goodwill problem, at least temporarily, the Board is currently involved in a host of other accounting principles and financial reporting matters. It might be interesting to you for me to run through a few of these briefly; some of them you are well aware of, I'm sure.

1. *Long-term investments*—The APB has recently issued an exposure draft on a proposed Opinion on accounting for long-term investments. This Opinion relates primarily to substantial investments in other corporations in which the investor owns less than a majority interest.

As you know, such investments must now generally be accounted for on a cost basis and income is recorded only as dividends are received. The proposed Opinion requires an investor who has effective control (defined as 20% or more) of another company to recognize his proportionate share of each year's earnings or losses of that company. Deadline for comments on this exposure draft is March 1. There is broad support for the Opinion in the Board and, I believe, in industry also. However I understand that the SEC has expressed some reservations about it.

2. *Funds statement*—The APB has also issued an exposure draft of a proposed Opinion on statements of funds. This Opinion would require that a funds statement be presented as one of the regular financial statements of a company. The APB's action is rather late, since the new SEC rules will now require the presentation of funds statements in all financial statements filed with the Commission.

3. *Accounting changes*—In early 1970, the Board released an exposure draft on accounting for changes in accounting principles. The Board had second thoughts on that exposure draft, however. There has been lively debate on the question of how much restatement of prior years' financial statements should be required. The present

draft, which is not yet in exposure form, suggests a solution that would preserve the original historical amounts of earnings per share as previously stated but would disclose the restated amounts for prior years on a pro forma basis. The so-called catch-up adjustment would be reported as an extraordinary item in the year of change.

This is interesting. I worked out an example where a company had extraordinary items and primary and fully diluted earnings per share. By the time one gets through presenting all the official historical data as well as the pro forma restated data, you have ten per-share figures for the year.

The draft states that there is a presumption that there should be no accounting change except as the change improves financial reporting. The APB defends the dual treatment on the basis that changing the old figures might disturb public confidence and the pro forma ones are needed to show consistently computed earnings.

4. *Marketable securities* — The Board is also considering the question of carrying marketable securities in financial statements at market value.

5. *Income tax allocation* — Also, the Board is studying the applicability of deferred tax accounting to the five areas exempted in Opinion No. 11 on accounting for income taxes. These are the questions of whether deferred taxes should be provided on undistributed earnings of subsidiaries, IDC costs in the oil and gas industry, general reserves of stock savings and loan associations, policyholders surplus of stock life insurance companies, and statutory deposits of United States steamship companies.

6. *The issue of how to account for gain on early retirement of debt is also up for consideration* — This has become important because the rise in interest rates has given companies opportunities to retire debt at substantial discounts. In some cases the gain has been treated as an extraordinary item; in other cases the gain on conversion or retirement has been spread over some future period.

7. *Premium and discount on long-term receivables and long-term debt* — The question of imputing current market interest rates to debt obligations that are issued with unrealistically low interest rates is under consideration. As you know, in some purchase contracts the seller may obtain maximum benefits available from capital gains tax treatment by issuing notes with low interest rates. In these cases the actual market interest expense is understated by the borrower. The Board probably will conclude that the current interest rate should be imputed to these obligations in order to state the liability on a more realistic basis. The same would apply on the receivable side to the seller.

8. The Board is studying the accounting problems related to interim financial statements, and is reconsidering APB Opinions No. 5 and No. 7 on leases. It is also involved in a number of problems relating to individual industries, such as the extractive industries.

Thoughts on the Future

Need for statement of objectives

Based on its performance on the subject of business combinations and goodwill, a serious question can be raised whether the accounting profession is properly organized to establish accounting principles in a manner adequate to meet today's needs for reliable financial information. The processes involved should be reappraised in a search for more objectivity in the determination of accounting principles.

One of the first steps in this direction must be that of defining the purposes and objectives of financial statements, so that the solution to individual accounting problems can be achieved in the framework of an overall plan. The disagreement over objectives of financial statements surfaces every time the APB tackles a difficult question.

A statement of objectives need not be long nor should it be a dissertation of arbitrary rules. Rather, it would be in the nature of a constitution or charter. By way of comparison, the Constitution of the U.S., including the Bill of Rights, is less than 5,000 words and was written in approximately 120 days. It has been in effect for almost 200 years. It established the principles on which the laws of our country have been developed and provided a system whereby the voices of all interested parties can be heard. Decisions made can be appealed and can ultimately be tried through our legal system when a person feels that he is being damaged.

We need something like this in the accounting profession, and it can be done if we really put our minds to it. When a statement of objectives has been prepared, procedures from that point forward could be designed to insure complete independence and objectivity, and accounting principles could then be established on a sound basis. Our big mistake in the past has been that we have tried to establish principles and procedures before we have stated our objectives. We have been trying to erect a building without a blueprint.

The need for a blueprint was recognized when the APB was established in 1959, but we as a profession have never given it any real priority. The Board did issue in October 1970 its Statement No. 4 entitled "Basic Concepts and Accounting Principles Underlying Financial Statements of Business Enterprises." But this is not really a statement of objectives; rather, it is mainly a synthesis of existing practices.

Unfortunately, by issuing this Statement the Board established a new acceptability on behalf of the profession for many accounting practices that have not previously been covered by pronouncements of the Board and that have not been studied by the accounting profession in any organized way.

Structure of the Board

In addition to the matter of objectives, there is this question. Is the ad hoc accommodation and compromising of conflicting views of the eighteen voluntary Board members a good structure for establishing sound accounting? Isn't compromise guaranteed to provide wrong answers? Consideration should be given to establishing a high-level, full-time, paid Commission of, say, five men who could act with dispatch and decisiveness before serious problems develop. If such a permanent Commission were created, there would need to be two provisions:

1. All deliberations should be a matter of public record. Members of industry, the accounting profession and other segments should present briefs on their positions.
2. There should be a vehicle for appeal of decisions by such a Commission.

This is just one possible idea, but it certainly appears that the present structure must somehow be changed to obtain greater objectivity and efficiency.

Clarification of responsibilities

In addition to establishing objectives and restructuring the method by which accounting principles are developed, I also believe there is a need for clarification of responsibilities. We in the accounting profession like to say (and it's all over our literature) that the financial statements are management's responsibility and we auditors are only responsible for the quality of our opinions. I seriously question whether that assertion would ultimately stand up in a real test.

The APB issues Opinions that prescribe accounting to be followed if the CPA is not to qualify his report. Just exactly what is management's responsibility when it follows Opinions that, in effect, the profession and the SEC say they must follow? What is the individual auditor's responsibility when in fact he is forced to follow an APB Opinion even though he may not believe in its soundness, since unless he follows it his clients' financial statements will not be accepted by the SEC?

What about the responsibility of the SEC? The SEC issues deficiency letters requiring changes in financial statements in a registration statement and management often has little choice but to go along with the request. Yet the SEC insists that every prospectus have printed in bold letters on the cover, words stating, in effect, that the SEC takes no responsibility for the prospectus.

No wonder the respective parties, the SEC, the accounting profession and management, are at odds with one another. I sympathize deeply with your problem as financial executives. This is a new year and someone told me the other day that a good way to have a roaring fight with your wife is for you to write her New Year's resolutions and let her write yours. This describes part of our problem. The Accounting Principles Board is writing your New Year's resolutions.

I don't have the answers here, but we are in urgent need of clarification of responsibilities if this whole system is going to work.

Recent developments

There are some encouraging recent developments, however. The general disenchantment of many people in the profession over the performance of the Board on the matter of accounting for mergers and goodwill led the president of the American Institute of CPAs to call a "Conference on Accounting Principles." Invited to attend that meeting were representatives from twenty-one accounting firms.

The meeting was held last Thursday and Friday, January 7th and 8th. The net result of that meeting was encouraging. Subject to the approval of the Board of Directors, the president of the Institute will:

1. Set up a commission specifically to examine the question of objectives of financial statements, with the hope of coming up with a definitive constitution or statement of objectives; that takes the objectives project out of the Accounting Principles Board.
2. A separate commission will be appointed to study the whole subject of how best to establish accounting principles in this country. This commission will include not only members of the accounting profession but other persons as well.
3. It was agreed that all of the deliberations of these commissions will be a matter of public record and all interested parties will have an opportunity to file comments and views.

This is a most significant development. By bringing in people from outside the profession and by requiring that the deliberations be a matter of public record, it is hard to see how the commissions could possibly come up with a whitewash. These commissions will be getting into action soon. It is too early to state when they will report, but the pressure on the profession to perform is very great, and I believe that over the next few months we will have some significant developments.

That is one good and encouraging piece of news I have to report to you in what has been a rather bleak period indeed.

Impact of change

There is another aspect to the job facing accountants, both the independent auditor and the financial executive, and that is the impact of change on what we are doing. I have been impressed with the need to reexamine what we're doing, particularly as a result of reading Alvin Toffler's *Future Shock*. Many of you have read it, I am sure. The tremendous changes taking place in our society, in technology, in business methods, in markets, and in consumer tastes; and the accelerating rate of these changes challenge some of our basic concepts. They challenge in particular the validity of the concepts of permanence and stability which underlie many existing practices in accounting and finance.

The impact of some of these changes has been reflected in an unusually large number of extraordinary charges that have occurred as companies have abandoned product lines, closed down plants, reorganized, retooled, or relocated. While the extraordinary charge may correct the balance sheet with respect to the particular assets involved, it cannot eliminate the consequences of the failure to have spread the costs over the years of the actual use of the plant, equipment, or other assets. The extraordinary charge raises questions concerning the usefulness of earnings previously reported.

Equally important, where there is a large extraordinary charge, it means that certain costs were probably not considered in determining product costs used in establishing selling prices, in assessing product-line profitability, and in many other production and operating decisions. Neither were they considered in making decisions on distributions to shareholders or in evaluating management performance. The fact of the matter is that the failure to spread the costs of assets over their productive lives results in charging capital with the unamortized costs. Thus the costs of technological and other changes in our society may become a drain on capital, since they have not been considered in the prices charged for goods and services rendered.

People in business are creative and innovative but, as one businessman has said, they have sacrificed their flexibility to respond to change on the altar of capital investment. The underpinnings for that altar have been provided by accountants employing concepts of permanence and stability. There are no easy answers, but there are exciting things to be done. There is at least a need to maintain flexibility in everything we do.

Conclusion

In conclusion, let me say that as accountants and financial executives we must create in this whole area of financial reporting a greater spirit of public-mindedness. It is not our company, it does not belong to management, to the auditors, to the directors, to the employees; it belongs to the shareholders, and all of us are their agents. We should not seek the minimums in financial reporting standards and ask only what the APB or SEC will allow. Shareholders deserve the best in financial presentation and, if we will all assume our proper responsibilities, the solution to the problem will be easier. The consequences of acting otherwise will be more and more detailed rules that will lead to an erosion of our freedom in business.

The direct public stake in business in the United States today is enormous, including that of 31 million shareholders. The resulting unprecedented public reliance on financial statements presents a challenge to the accounting profession and to management to establish standards of fairness, competence, and independence in financial reporting of the very highest order. This is absolutely vital if we are to meet the needs created by the magnitude of the direct public interest in business today.

The need for a new approach in improving financial reporting

Before the Southern Florida Chapter,
Financial Executives Institute,
Miami, Florida, April 13, 1972—Catlett

If the new Financial Accounting Standards Board is to be successful, it must avoid the mistakes of the past.

THE ACCOUNTING PROFESSION is now going through another period of transition. The time for a new approach in improving financial reporting has arrived.

Two major efforts to develop accounting principles under the general sponsorship of the American Institute of Certified Public Accountants have occurred: by the Committee on Accounting Procedure (1939-1959) and by the Accounting Principles Board (1959-1972). The next effort will be the Financial Accounting Standards Board that recently has been recommended by the Study Group on Establishment of Accounting Principles. This new Board will likely be approved by the AICPA Council in May and commence operations early in 1973.

This third effort, if not sufficiently successful, could well be "strike three—you're out" insofar as the accounting profession is concerned. Therefore, consideration should now be given to what has been learned from our experiences in recent years, and what may be necessary for the new approach to be successful.

The report of the Study Group is well written, and it includes a careful analysis of the APB. I would agree with many of the comments and conclusions in that report. However, I would like to discuss with you this evening my personal observations and views of:

1. The operations of the APB as a result of my experience as a member for six years (1965-1971).
2. What will be necessary in the operations of the new FASB if that organization is to do what is required.

The Accounting Principles Board

The results achieved by the APB have not

been commensurate with the effort. In the light of what has been needed, the accomplishments can properly be characterized as "too little and too late." Why has this situation occurred when so much time and money have been put into this activity?

The members of the APB have probably been one of the most conscientious and hard-working volunteer groups that have ever existed in a professional or business association. Yet, increasing concern has been expressed about the quality and rate of progress in developing and implementing accounting principles and reporting practices to meet the current needs of investors and others in our society.

One of my impressions, which stands out above most others, is the great difficulty of making improvements of some consequence in a democracy such as we have. All of the many pressures against change and the vast number of reasons put forward for why changes should not be made are extremely difficult to overcome. This probably occurs in different degrees in all walks of life, but it is certainly true in the case of the APB. The frustrations arising in trying to accomplish improvements on a timely basis seem to be almost endless. Yet, ways and means must be found to avoid the many obstacles that constantly are put in the way of progress.

Since we should be able to learn from our experiences, I will summarize briefly what to me are the significant reasons why the APB has not been more successful.

Objectives of financial statements—The greatest deficiency in the operations of the APB has been the absence of agreement on the objectives of financial statements. Such objectives could serve as base points and furnish criteria for judging the best solutions to accounting problems. With no overall philosophy or theoretical framework, the Opinions of the APB have represented arbitrary and uncoordinated conclusions based only on the views (and individual premises) of each of the APB members at a particular time.

The discussions in APB meetings have been time-consuming, repetitive, confusing and misdirected, and one of the principal reasons for this condition is that absolutely no agreement on any base points has existed. The APB was doomed when it fell into the trap of trying to deal with several very controversial problems without any agreement on what the objectives and basic concepts should be. Statement No. 4,* issued eleven years after the APB was established, furnishes no real guidelines for progress because it represents an elaborate rationalization of existing customs and practices. As I said in my dissent to that document, the APB was "looking backward to what has occurred rather than forward to what is needed." Also, I indicated that this Statement "creates a significant roadblock which will seriously impede the efforts of the business community and the accounting profession to establish sound principles for financial accounting and reporting."

Organization—The APB has not been organized in an effective manner, and too much inefficiency has existed. The size of the APB, which has varied from 18 to 21 members, and the fact that the members have had responsible positions in various firms and organizations, have contributed to its lack of effectiveness.

The last two chairmen have been the managing partners of large accounting firms and, without any criticism of them, the fact is that they have not had adequate time to properly manage this major undertaking in addition to their other responsibilities. Better management could have overcome some of the deficiencies, but this was not possible with the part-time nature of the endeavor. The AICPA staff has not done a very good job in filling this void.

*APB Statement No. 4, "Basic Concepts and Accounting Principles Underlying Financial Statements of Business Enterprises," published in October 1970.

Regulatory attitude—In some respects, the greatest deterioration in recent years has been the increasing tendency to issue arbitrary and inconsistent rules. Some of the members seem to have become obsessed with a self-appointed role of trying to plug up "loopholes" and stop alleged "abuses." With no objectives or basic premises of any kind, compromises of personal viewpoints have replaced principles, and regulations have replaced reason.

This trend toward filling Opinions with arbitrary rules actually has resulted in the creation of additional "loopholes." The more precise the rules, the more questions that arise and the more interpretations that are needed. Arbitrary requirements encourage "corner cutting" and create an atmosphere of "gamesmanship." Such rules do not have the respect that would result from sound concepts and principles based on sensible objectives and logical reasons.

My comments in this regard are not intended to indicate that pronouncements should contain only generalizations and that no rules are necessary. Some rules are required in order to furnish reasonable guidelines for implementation. However, the point is that the APB has gone in the direction of using rules as an objective, with no underlying concepts or philosophy and with no coordinated plan. Thus, the arbitrary rules have become regulatory in nature, with no real objectives in mind at all.

Research—The new research program, which held such high promise when the APB was established, has fallen far short of what was expected of it. Why has this occurred?

The research program has suffered from the same major deficiency as the APB itself—no objectives. Each person performing research and writing a study has of necessity based his work on his own objectives and concepts. Thus, there were no common objectives among the APB members and the researchers.

No effort of any consequence has been made to determine what type of research would be most helpful to the APB. Even though some of the individual research studies have been quite good, considering the lack of any overall plan, the research has not been very useful to the APB—and this may well be as much the fault of the APB members as the researchers or the administrative head of the research program.

It is quite likely the Opinions that have been issued by the APB would have been about the same if there had not been any AICPA research studies published or any research done by the AICPA staff*. To the extent that research had any bearing on the conclusions in the Opinions, it resulted more from that furnished by the APB members and their organizations. The APB has not been particularly oriented to the use of the results of research, and the members have tended to rely more on their own experiences.

Independence—Much has been said about the degree of independence that has existed with respect to the pronouncements issued by the APB. While pressures of various sorts on APB members have occurred, in my view, the members have been as independent as could be expected for a professional group of this type working on a volunteer basis.

It is probably fair to say that a group with no business affiliations of any kind could be somewhat more independent than the APB has been. Also, and perhaps more important, the APB has not had the appearance of independence to a degree that would be desirable.

Public record—The APB in its earlier days did almost all of its work in complete secrecy. Very little liaison existed with other business and professional organizations. Almost no public record of any kind was available.

---

*The AICPA research staff did make major contributions to APB Statements No. 3 and No. 4

For several years, I contended that public hearings should be held by the APB on every major subject. The first such hearing was held in May 1971, and then everyone thought it was a great idea.

The availability of the record has improved gradually, but the realization that the APB was a body with important responsibilities to the public came slowly. Nevertheless, the "secrecy complex" resulted in the APB getting off on the wrong foot originally.

Financial Accounting Standards Board

The Study Group has recommended that a Financial Accounting Standards Board be established and that it have seven full-time members who have disassociated themselves from all business connections. This Board would be established by a Financial Accounting Foundation. The governing body of the Foundation would be a Board of Trustees, who would select the members of the Financial Accounting Standards Board (FASB) and would make the necessary financial arrangements.

We might consider for a few minutes what will be necessary for the FASB to be successful. Some of the deficiencies that have existed with respect to the APB could continue to occur in the case of the FASB if care is not taken to make the necessary corrections.

Objectives of financial statements—A separate AICPA Study Group is considering the objectives of financial statements. How the recommendations of that group will fit into the work of the FASB is not clear. There is considerable danger that the FASB will make the same serious error as the APB (and the previous Committee on Accounting Procedure)—jump directly into consideration of various problem areas and never get around to establishing objectives. If this mistake is made again, the result will be the same—failure.

Appeals—One of the subjects that has always lurked in the background and that was not really dealt with by the Study Group was the right of appeal from pronouncements of the FASB. A person does not have to be a lawyer to realize that in a democracy a private organization cannot issue pronouncements that have a great effect on the business community and the public without anyone having the right to appeal the decisions of such an organization.

Certain rights of citizens do not have to be granted—they exist. Companies and independent accountants subject to the jurisdiction of the Securities and Exchange Commission can appeal to that agency. The right of appeal to a court of proper jurisdiction certainly is present. Whether the court would accept such a case may depend upon the facts and circumstances.

The Board of Trustees of the Financial Accounting Foundation and the FASB will make a serious mistake if they continue to ignore the subject of appeals and merely hope that the problem will go away; this problem will not disappear.

Dissents—An influential group within the AICPA has been trying for several years to eliminate the publication of votes and dissents in connection with APB Opinions issued. Others, including myself, have successfully resisted this change. However, the report of the Study Group recommends that the pronouncements of the FASB not disclose the vote or permit any dissent to be published with the pronouncement.

To me, the suppression of dissents in this fashion is inconsistent with our democratic process. Such an approach is a great disservice to the business community and the accounting profession, and is a sign of weakness that could crumble the foundations of the FASB.

Unless each member of the FASB considers himself to have an important, individual responsibility and believes that it is necessary for him to state clearly his own views—either affirmative or negative—the FASB will become some sort of "club" where the views of individuals are submerged for the alleged benefit of the group. I cannot imagine anyone agreeing to serve on the FASB with dissents suppressed in this manner.

Relationship to SEC—Where the SEC will fit into this picture in the future may be subject to some question. The SEC has generally supported the APB and has had an official position of preferring to have the AICPA take the lead in establishing accounting principles. Whether this same support will continue for the FASB remains to be seen. My guess would be that the SEC will be more aggressive in encouraging the FASB to act promptly. Also, the SEC may gradually assume more of this function, depending upon how well the FASB accomplishes its mission.

General—My earlier comments concerning the APB that related to organization, regulatory attitude, research, independence and public record are all matters that could be corrected by the FASB if proper attention is given to them.

The FASB can be a major step forward if it really does the kind of job that is now required. This new Board undoubtedly will start with everyone's best wishes for success.

* * *

The integrity of financial reporting by business enterprises is essential to the free enterprise system. Many millions of people use financial statements for important decisions. We should all hope that on a collective basis we have the judgment, intelligence and perception to learn from the past and to make the progress that is needed for the future.

Testimony of George R. Catlett and Norman O. Olson at public hearing

Before the AICPA Accounting Objectives Study Group, New York City, May 16, 1972

Arthur Andersen & Co. in July 1972 published a book entitled "Objectives of Financial Statements for Business Enterprises." Messrs. Catlett and Olson at this hearing discussed the views to be presented in that book.

CHAIRMAN TRUEBLOOD: Next is Arthur Andersen & Co. George will you introduce yourself?

Mr. George R. Catlett: My name is George Catlett and I am accompanied by Norman Olson. We are partners in Arthur Andersen & Co.

Norm and I appreciate having this opportunity to present the views of our firm to your Study Group. The time available will not permit us to do anything other than give you some very brief comments. We do have in preparation in our firm a comprehensive document setting forth our conclusions and our reasoning in more detail and we plan to submit this to your Study Group as soon as it is completed.

Norm will now give you a brief summary of our views and then we can answer your questions.

Mr. Norman O. Olson: It seems to us that perhaps the difficulty we have encountered in searching for an agreement on objectives may be due in part to trying to cut through the layers of networks of concepts, postulates, principles, conventions, and methods; but if we can get underneath all of that, the basic idea is a simple one, even though its implementation may be very difficult.

Without defining our terms for the present, are not financial statements intended to provide some information on two fundamental questions? And those are: How much wealth does the company have and how successful is it likely to be in producing additional wealth in the future?

There are a number of general considerations and factors that we feel were helpful in leading us to our particular conclusions regarding the objectives. There is not time to run through all of these but I would like to mention just two that I think are particularly significant.

First of all, financial statements should aid the investor and others in appraising the future. The statements are intended to present a picture that is true of the present and information about what has happened in the past concerning business enterprises. Yet almost all economic decisions made from that information are oriented to the future. Therefore, financial statements should present information that is as useful as possible to investors, creditors, and others in assessing the future prospects of a business—the basis for all economic decisions.

And second, we believe that it is important for the accounting function to be segregated from the investor or user function. The evaluations and interpretations made by investors, based in part on information provided by financial statements, should not be allowed to affect or to be introduced directly into those statements. Failure to observe this segregation of functions in the past may have introduced a circularity that has reduced the usefulness of financial information at times and has resulted in confusion in the resolution of individual problems, and perhaps even in a growing confusion, for example, over the responsibility for financial forecasts.

Segregation of these functions demands that a careful distinction be made between presenting financial information and predicting the future and, as you all know, that is not always a clear line. While financial statements should be presented in a manner that will assist as much as possible in assessing the future and its risks, the role of accounting or financial statements is not to predict or to interpret the future. That is the function of the investor.

The statement user has the responsibility for predictions and reaching decisions. Accountants should not attempt to relieve the statement user of this responsibility. Otherwise, accountants and not the investor should be entitled to the rewards of risk taking.

Auditors are almost being charged or considered responsible for the quality of investments, as compared to the quality of financial reports.

Well, we believe those are two basic considerations to bear in mind, not only in reaching agreement on objectives, but perhaps also in individual decisions regarding the selection of accounting practices and presentation of information.

In our view, the overall purpose of financial statements is to communicate information concerning the nature and the value of the economic resources of a business enterprise and the interests of creditors and the rights of the owners in those resources and the changes in the nature and value of those resources from period to period.

We recognize that the term "economic resources" has been defined in various ways and we might ultimately settle on a different term for that reason. But for our purpose, we have defined "economic resources" —and this definition has been used by others—as those elements of wealth which possess three basic characteristics; namely, utility, scarcity, and exchangeability.

The term "exchangeability" as used here is not intended to suggest that an economic resource is necessarily immediately marketable nor that it is being held for immediate sale by a business. It does mean, however, that an economic resource is separable from the business as a whole and that it has value in and of itself. This will be a difficult distinction to make for the identification of economic resources from other elements of wealth, but we believe that it would provide a useful thrust and a desirable emphasis. This identification, of course, would become a major concern in the accounting process.

This definition of economic resources would tend to exclude from the balance sheet a myriad of unidentifiable intangibles or attributes of a business that may give it an advantage over others in a competitive system and hence enable the business to achieve profits beyond the pure cost of money. These intangibles and attributes include a whole range of elements from the quality of management to the quality of product and human resources, but these attributes lack the basic characteristics of exchangeability or separability from the business as a whole. And these attributes or unidentifiable intangibles, may be extremely valuable—much more valuable than the economic resources in many cases; they may arise through deliberate effort or fortuitous accident; but information about their quality and potential value is conveyed primarily by information on earnings rather than through direct measurement in the balance sheet. And in this view, at least, the conversion of the intangible wealth or intangible attributes of a business into economic resources is what constitutes the earnings process.

Under this definition the balance sheet would also generally exclude categories of deferred charges not directly identified with economic resources, particularly when deferment is based solely on the expectation of matching such deferred amounts against future revenues. Economic resources may arise in the future from such expenditures and this fact also will be reflected in earnings.

We have talked about value of economic resources. We feel that it is important to distinguish those values from the value of the business as a whole. Our view of the objectives of financial statements does not embrace reporting market value information about the equity of owners in the business. To attempt to present the current value of the equities of owners would be to attempt to value the business as a whole; to repeat, that is an investor function. To reflect in the financial statements the investors' decisions would introduce this hopeless circularity of which I spoke earlier.

I believe that agreement on this point, one way or another, is crucial to a meaningful statement of objectives.

You have noticed, I am sure, that we used the term "value" of economic resources—a fighting word, as we have observed. Let me emphasize that it is not our purpose to encourage a radical and sudden departure from existing practice in the area of financial reports. Rather, we would like to encourage a redirection of attitudes and to establish goals, even though those goals may never be completely attainable. In this way solutions to accounting problems can be sought in a cohesive manner directed toward common goals.

Our statement of purpose does not contemplate a wholesale abandonment of the transaction-oriented cost approach. Transactions translate values into costs that under many circumstances will be a continuing, dependable, and reliable means of conveying value information about economic resources. I doubt, for example, that the value approach would justify extensive, frequent write-ups of plant and equipment. In fact, under the value approach we might have more write-downs than under the cost-matching emphasis. And, actually, the value approach, when combined with a hard economic resource test for the admission of assets to the balance sheet, may result in more prudent financial information in many cases than that which flows from our present concepts.

We also believe that the value objective is sensible and not really a radical one because this objective is intuitively held now by a wide range of users of financial statements, including business managements. Many of us, as accountants who prepare statements, intuitively feel that value is what this game is all about. Much of our literature, of course, has denied value as an objective. We speak of depreciation as a process of allocation and not valuation. But the resolution of day-to-day problems in accounting belies the literature. There is, for example, a continuous concern among auditors in practice today with one aspect of value, and that is: Is the asset at least worth its carrying value? Is its carrying value recoverable from future operations?

Businessmen, accountants, and knowledgeable users consider many balance sheets to be almost worthless in the sense of conveying useful information. And why is this true? Because they do not regard the information as indicative of the value of the assets.

Now isn't this attitude really a subtle acknowledgement of what our objectives are, or should be?

The value of an economic resource at any time is the price it commands in exchange. It may be indicated by an initial cost, by a cost to reproduce, by a market price, or by reference to value of other economic resources that provide comparable services, and so on. And the question of the most appropriate value to use in various circumstances will involve very difficult areas of judgment, but we feel these difficulties must be faced eventually if financial statements are to be made more relevant and useful.

Under this concept, earnings should be considered a result of the measurement of economic resources, and periodic earnings would be determined by the change in the owner's equity shown by comparative balance sheets, other than changes, of course, that result from distributions to or additional investments from owners.

Perhaps more than any other statement, the statement of income is used in assessing the future prospects of a business. Thus, we believe it is important to highlight, for example, the impact of fixed expenses as an aid in evaluating the future with respect to volume fluctuations, and to point out major gains or losses of an unusual nature, whether from regular operations or not, and which may not occur frequently. Emphasis should also be given to major expenditures made strictly for the purpose of creating future income benefits, such as for general research and development and major advertising, and designed to create intangibles, which in our view should be charged off as incurred. In addition, major holding gains or losses should be segregated from operating results.

The approach we are advocating and an evaluation of how it might lead to greater progress in improving financial reports may be better understood by a very brief review of two key issues that may be the source of some of our difficulties.

There is, we believe, a confusion of cost as an objective rather than a method. And in looking back over the literature, it seemed that in the early part of this century cost was becoming regarded as a means by which information on value was conveyed. Cost was simply a dependable, objective method to provide information on value. But the thinking gradually changed so that as accountants, in ever-increasing numbers, we proclaimed that we had nothing to do with values. Thus, while cost was originally considered as a means of conveying value information, it has now tended to become an objective or an end in itself. In the evolution, utility regulation, Supreme Court decisions that defined income under the separability concept, and the implementation of the Securities Acts, have all tended to elevate cost to the level of an objective as opposed to a method of conveying value information.

And coincident with this solidifying of cost as an objective rather than a method of providing value information was the introduction of a sort of reverse approach to accounting measurement. The profession in the United States, as you recall, in the early 1930's began to suggest that balance sheets were not very useful and that asset valuations were not practicable. The income account was emphasized as all important. This approach seemed to assume that earnings could be measured in a vacuum; that increases in wealth could be measured without measuring the wealth itself.

This emphasis and subsequent developments in the profession led to this broad and intricate network of methods and rules, all designed, in effect, to enforce the basic concept of allocation or matching of costs with revenues. Thus, a major thrust of accounting in the last 35 years has been to measure earnings and plug the balance sheet with debits and credits as a result of the matching process, rather than to measure the assets or the economic resources and obligations and designate the net change as earnings. There are a number of examples of this that we could go into.

But this combination of cost as an objective and reverse measurement is loading balance sheets to where they are little more than fluffy dreams of the future—preoperating costs, development costs, advertising costs, and general R&D, etc. On this basis these expenditures will be matched against future revenues even though they attach to no economic resource in which there can be a viable equity and they certainly can have little meaning in any computation, for example, of debt-equity ratios.

Also, as a result—and I think this is important—of a too rigid attachment to the cost-matching approach, accountants have often resisted write-downs, for example, in plant and equipment for loss in value so long as they are in use. The major criticism, for example, as I recall, of Penn Central's accounting on the part of the ICC is that they had written down some railroad property and thereby relieved future income statements of depreciation charges.

The value approach actually is likely to result in more prudent financial statements in many cases than the cost approach, and I think that it is important to remember that when we talk about current costs, current values, fair values, and so on, it isn't exclusively a write-up process.

The objectives of financial statements, as we see them and which we have summarized briefly here, should lead accountants to address themselves to current problems in a different fashion. Agreement on objectives will not necessarily make accounting any easier; it may make it more difficult but it should help assure meaningful and coordinated solutions.

Any useful objective should provide us, as accountants, with a basis for making choices. Whenever alternative accounting principles or procedures are being evaluated, there is a need to refer to the purpose of the accounting process. If value is selected as the goal, the basis for making choices exists. The accounting alternative believed to have the capability of producing the closest approximation of the best indicator of value should be preferred even if based essentially on cost data, given, of course, compliance with supplementary tests of feasibility and objectivity.

If there were agreement that the goal of accounting is to provide information on values and that even the cost approach is intended to do this, more meaningful solutions would be reached and perhaps some of the inadequacies in present financial reports would begin to disappear. The focus of the measurement process would be clarified and earnings would again come to be regarded as the result of the measurement of assets and liabilities and not vice versa. And whether many adjustments to cost are made or not, we really need a simple acknowledgement of the goal that is even now intuitively felt, probably, by the majority of us.

If agreement can be reached that the assets presented in the balance sheet should be limited to economic resources, as we have defined them, and should be presented on the basis of the most reasonably relevant value information available, progress could be achieved in dealing with many subjects, such as those relating to intangibles and deferred charges, even though the distinctions would be extremely difficult.

But whether you agree with our view on those types of assets or not, we are sure that you will acknowledge that agreement on this issue—the criterion of asset admission—is essential.

The delineation of the accounting and investor function, we think, can also eliminate much confusion.

Regardless of the difficulties of measurement which may be encountered, mere acceptance of the objectives and goals could result in all of us working toward a common goal. Then we would have less rhetoric over uniformity and detailed rules, and the exaggerated emphasis on the elimination of alternatives would be avoided.

Mr. Catlett: I might make one general comment. Part of the problem is what we are thinking about when we talk about objectives. To me, what is so badly needed by the accounting profession is a compass and a North Pole to serve as a guide. The accounting profession has constantly been running up blind alleys. We have been reaching ad hoc decisions on problems without any general guidelines. And the way I like to think about it is that, in establishing objectives, we are trying to find a North Pole; we are trying to set our compass on that Pole, which is our objective. We may never get to the North Pole, but that may be irrelevant.

The key question is: Where are we heading, on a consistent, coordinated basis? This can change from time to time but at any one point in time we ought to know where we are going. The accounting profession, in my view, has not known this, and that is why we need objectives and that, of course, is why your Study Group is in existence.

Chairman Trueblood: Thank you very much, George and Norm. I'm going to break in just a minute before we start the questioning.

Dick Cyert was unable to be with us yesterday because of commencement at his university. Dick is an economist and presently Dean of the Graduate School of Industrial Administration at Carnegie. He is the incoming President of Carnegie-Mellon University in Pittsburgh and we're happy that he is going to have two full days with us even though we missed him yesterday.

Now, for a first question, Norm or George, I perhaps missed some refinements as you went along but you state that income should be predictive or income should be stated in such a way that it can be a predictive tool.

My question is: If you indeed advocate that all expenditures made for noneconomic resource assets—and I presume that to be the intangibles such as human capital, R&D, and so on—if you advocate that they should be expensed, then aren't you impeding or impairing in some way the predictive qualities of the residual income?

Mr. Olson: Well, I suppose you could argue it both ways, Bob. I don't believe so because the accountant can't predict the values of expenditures for intangibles; it is solely dependent on earnings. And I do not see how any kind of capitalization can possibly help the investor or the user in predicting the future. I also think that all of the amortization techniques on that type of asset are completely arbitrary. They are not tied to any life at all.

In this kind of an approach to intangibles, and with the heavy emphasis on expenditures for intangibles in these days of high technology, further disclosure than the mere segregation in the income statement is necessary. We are suggesting, for example —I did not get into this in our presentation —that perhaps there should be a statement of intangibles, particularly with companies heavily oriented in that direction, which could show not only expenditures on an annual basis but on a cumulative basis. And perhaps some information could be provided for the user on the amount of earnings being dedicated to the creation of future economic resources.

Chairman Trueblood: I have a second question also, this one from the floor, which relates to the same general subject. But I guess you did say, apart from a listing of intangibles as a supplemental statement, that there should be a further clarification within reported results of the nature of expenditures so that the residual income would be, in a sense, explained with the ups and downs of that kind of expenditure. Is that right?

Mr. Olson: That's right.

Chairman Trueblood: I think that's an answer to this question.

Mr. Catlett: I think we could say, Bob, that in this area the objective would be to disclose in the most meaningful fashion what is being spent in the whole intangible area. Of course, there may be many different ways of doing that and more study and consideration should be given to that; but there should be maximum disclosure in a manner that would be as useful as possible.

Mr. Gellein: I am sure I will have to read your paper to fully understand all of its implications, and I look forward to doing that, but I wonder if we could take a simple situation and see what it entails, using your notion of economic resources, finding this North Star, and heading toward it.

Let's take a simple case of a manufacturing concern that puts direct materials into the manufacturing process, applies some direct labor to it, and the product is part way down toward being finished. Now, how would you see the application of your notion to the determination of the value of that product, that inventory—work in process or finished goods, whichever it may be?

This of course, gets at the question of: What is income?

Mr. Olson: I want to emphasize again that our major point on value is to regard our cost process as a value informant. We have a section in the area of inventories. There are some difficult questions there. Basically, in most situations of goods manufactured to stock or goods held for resale, the present practice of FIFO or average cost conveys meaningful information. The risks of sale in that the part of the earnings process that's involved in the selling effort are so great that valuing it at selling price is not justified.

I think that this approach, however, might give us a different answer on goods custom-manufactured under specific order where the selling risks and the credit risks have been evaluated before the earnings process. There should be no reason under those circumstances to delay profit recognition or to value finished custom-made goods at cost; those ought to be valued at realizable values.

LIFO valuation would disappear, for example, and this is where we feel that adopting the value attitude would tend to point us toward coordinated solutions.

Mr. Gellein: It seems to me that you are just redefining the realization concept.

Mr. Catlett: Exactly.

Mr. Parker: Would an example of this be a DC-10 aeroplane which has been ordered? Is that a custom type of manufacturing?

Mr. Catlett: When you get over into big items and long construction contracts essentially made to order—either specifically to order or generally to order—you probably go to percentage of completion. That is what is being done now in some cases, of course.

Mr. Parker: Could I ask Norman a question in terms of the factory that makes the widgets that you were talking about? How does your value approach work there?

Mr. Olson: As we mentioned briefly, and which we discuss quite extensively in our study, the concerns in the area of fixed assets or plant and equipment and buildings these days should not be, or probably should not be, with undervaluation. I think that we need to be far more concerned, perhaps, as accountants than we have been with whether or not our depreciation formulas are adequate. Someone asked a question this morning about a 50-year life asset. The kind of technological changes that are occurring today and the kind of changes that are occurring socially and in markets makes you wonder whether anything should be depreciated over 50 years.

The depreciation of hotels or buildings over 40 years may be hard to justify. We may be living in plastic bubbles in ten years. I think the emphasis in plant and equipment should be on whether or not the assets are overstated and I think that's what the result could be from a solid value approach to accounting.

Mr. Parker: Suppose we take a steel company today. There it is with all its assets in place, some of them old, some of them new —more of them new than old. How do you, then, as the accountant or auditor, go at tackling the question of what kind of depreciation charge should be made?

Mr. Catlett: I agree with you that we should not generalize on matters like that. You would have to study that subject.

We are suggesting a change in approach. Norm and I suspect that we might have about as many write-downs as write-ups if you really did what ought to be done today in a lot of cases. When you look at all the special charges that have been running through the income statement in the last two or three years, you note that a lot of that is underdepreciation in the past.

Mr. Parker: What kind of tests or what kind of rationale would you run through in trying to decide, either in general or using the steel plant as an example, if that's helpful?

Mr. Olson: Of course, in auditing we make a lot of these tests now. We all intuitively worry about whether the assets are there. You look at the profitability, whether the plant is generating a profit. You ask questions about innovations, about plans for replacement, to determine, first of all, whether the assets are worth what they are now carried at.

I think if you get into a situation where you have a healthy plant, turning out a good product and resulting in profits, that is fully depreciated we ought to stop and establish some reasonable value on it so we can get a legitimate depreciation charge. That's the kind of an effort that now is generally not made, on the basis that the costs have been matched and allocated against profits. The value attitude would in those extreme cases restore the plant and equipment under some formula and it probably would be under some depreciated replacement cost basis.

Mr. Catlett: Let me give you a concrete example; some people in the room will recognize it.

Several years ago our firm was auditing a meat packing company. It had a large plant that was not very successful in its current operation. There was a labor contract with very high termination pay and the termination pay requirements were so large that they couldn't afford to shut down the plant. The management offered to give the plant to the city, or anybody else who would take it, provided they would take over the labor contract. Nobody would take it.

This company then wrote down the plant substantially. We certified this and several prominent accountants jumped all over us under the reasoning that, as long as the plant was in operation, the company should not write the plant down because this would relieve future income statements of the depreciation charge, even though the plant really wasn't worth anything.

That is what we are talking about, changing the emphasis away from matching depreciation with revenues just because you are using an asset. They offered to give the asset away to anybody who would take it and there wasn't a single taker; under those conditions the value was zero and it should have been written down. I don't care whether they were operating it or not.

Chairman Trueblood: Let me pick up Reed's question about the steel plant in a different context. I rather think I know what your answer will be. Given this steel plant, such as we have all over the place, in the South Side of Chicago, whether it be new or old, it is a polluter. This is presently illegal or prospectively illegal. That plant is not going to be operable within our time span in the same manner as your glass bubble.

I presume your theory would be that, with or without the present statute, even though the plant is presently operational, the required rejection of the facility should be presently recognized.

Mr. Olson: Yes, it should be a consideration in the valuation and depreciation practices applied to that plant. I'm not familiar with the steel industry at all there, with that particular problem or how imminent it is, but given those facts, this is true.

I gather the auto industry faces the same problem in meeting the pollution standards of a number of states. Certainly it's a consideration that managements and accountants should take into account in depreciation practice.

Dean Cyert: Do you think that your theory holds equally well in a period of falling prices? One thing that worries me is that current conditions are influencing thought in this area to the point where we are sort of deluding ourselves and thinking we are getting at the truth, and what we are really doing is reacting to the situation.

For example, suppose in a period of falling prices the firm has positive earnings, as we would now define it, but not great enough to make up for the loss of current value. Would you say that it could be accurate to say that that firm is making a loss or has zero earnings?

In other words, think through your position under opposite conditions.

Mr. Olson: There's no question that the value approach cuts both ways, up and down, and I would reemphasize again that I think the value approach, if administered with integrity, may produce more write-downs than it will write-ups, even under today's conditions.

Dean Cyert: Don't you think that's misleading? I mean that, in a sense, one of the things we are trying to measure is the performance of a particular system of machines and managers, and those machines and managers may be performing well, but something else is happening in the society which is affecting the particular values.

What is it that we are really trying to measure? Are we really trying just to reflect what society is saying in general or are we trying to measure the particular enterprise?

Mr. Catlett: To me, we are trying to reflect the facts and, of course, there's a great deal of judgment in this area you're talking about. You have short-range trends and long-range trends. I think you have to analyze each case and use your judgment.

There may be areas such as a series of computers that are going to be obsoleted by another series of computers. You can have things like steel mills that may get to the point where you can't even operate them anymore. It just seems to me that you have to evaluate all these factors; you are not going to be writing plants up and down every month and that sort of thing. You have to take more long-range factors into consideration.

But if you have a high degree of evidence that in five years it's not going to be worth anything, you have to take this into account; that's more in line with what we are talking about than the value of plants going up and down.

And when you get over into marketable securities, such as a thousand shares of General Motors, and you go to market value, that's a lot different than a steel mill. Securities would tend to go up and down more.

Dean Cyert: It seems to me there you are contradicting one of the points that you made earlier, when argued that it wasn't the accountant's function to begin to predict the future, because now you are predicting the future in terms of trying to value this particular asset.

Mr. Olson: Let me go back to your earlier question. I'm not sure that I grasped the thrust of it, but, basically, the income statement would separate holding gains and losses. And I would envision that if you did have a write-up for example, in plant and equipment, you would then have a higher charge against operations for depreciation. Similarly, if you should have a write-down, you would have a lower charge against operations. The operating results would still be carved out separately albeit they would reflect from a depreciation standpoint any changes in value.

I think this touches a little bit on the question that someone asked Larry Vance earlier, and maybe this is also partially what you are driving at. As far as accountability is concerned, it is difficult for me to say how you can establish any real accountability insofar as management is concerned unless you charge them with some reasonable measure of value of the resources they take over. A management, for example, that takes over a company that has a $200 million unrecorded profit in marketable securities can show profits of $100 million on sales and yet actually be losing $100 million. There is no real accountability without value recognition.

Chairman Trueblood: Aren't you really asking the question, Dick, as to whether the change in value resulting from falling price levels would be reflected as a holding loss in this valuation process?

Dean Cyert: Yes.

Mr. Catlett: You would have such a segregation but changes in some items would be reflected faster than others by the nature of them.

Chairman Trueblood: So you would tend to hold operating results separate and therefore you would have a continuing thing.

Sid Davidson is next, I believe, if you still wish to ask a question.

Dean Davidson: Yes. Well you know, it's all right for you practitioners to be visionary in this regard but we academics have to be concerned with the problems of implementation.

I am kind of worried about whether this system would envisage the continuation of unit property records and what would be the clues. If the answer to that is yes, what would be the clue for change in the valuation attached to units of property and who would make this revaluation?

I think I'm wholeheartedly in accord with your objectives but I'm not quite clear how we'd move in that direction.

Mr. Catlett: I think there are two aspects of this. One is, we have to first decide whether it's desirable to move in this direction. That's the first question. We are concerned about implementation also but you do have to first decide whether you want to go in a certain direction; if it isn't desirable, it doesn't make any difference about the implementation. We, at least, have concluded that it's desirable to go in this direction where there are significant departures from cost.

In many areas of plants, equipment and inventories, the departure wouldn't be sufficient to recognize; but you are talking about the cases where it would be. And wherever there are significant departures, either up or down, based on all the facts, adjustments would be made.

We are not going to be able, as you well know, to sit here this morning and say exactly how we're going to accomplish all of this vast array of changes. You have thousands of companies, hundreds of industries, and a great variety of circumstances, and we believe that it's feasible to approach the facts in each case and use judgment as long as we know what we're trying to accomplish.

At times you might use price-level indexes; at other times you might use other approaches. I don't think that it's possible to have any one approach to valuation when you have such a huge variety of circumstances. If we know what we are trying to accomplish, we might end up using eight or ten different approaches. Overriding the whole matter is the evaluation of the facts anyhow.

Whether a computer that's now in use is going to be obsolete three or four years from now becomes a highly judgmental matter. But you do have to use judgment, and managements must do this all the time; auditors are also forced to do so, and that it is why we have a profession. If it was easy, only bookkeepers would be needed.

Dean Davidson: Yes, but I guess you might run into the attitude that the use of values of economic resources as a means of controlling our recordkeeping is desirable, if attainable.

Mr. Catlett: Right, and we should do it to the extent it is attainable.

Dean Davidson: Sure.

Mr. Catlett: We are establishing objectives and we are trying to take steps in that direction on a controlled basis to the extent feasible and practicable, and if we can figure out where we want to go, then we can address ourselves more to arriving at techniques and ways and means of getting there.

The trouble with most discussions on this subject so far is that many persons have not really decided in what direction they want to go; therefore, they haven't even seriously considered the problem. I just will not accept as a fact that it is impossible to establish objectives—assuming that it is a good idea to do so.

Mr. Parker: I just want to follow Sidney's question a little bit; I think it's a good one.

You said a little while ago that if you had a plant that was all written off and was still obviously humming along, producing fine profit at good margins, there ought to be some way to write that plant back up and start depreciating again and, I suppose, there would be the converse.

But just at about what point do you think you begin to cut in? Would you say somewhere between minus two percent rate of return and a plus ten percent rate of return we leave the valuation alone and flow on the depreciation like we used to; get outside those parameters, and we think it's enough to trigger valuation. Would you apply that kind of a technique?

Mr. Olson: Well, I really think, Reed, it's impossible to generalize in that kind of an area. We're making those kinds of judgments now, everyday. There's some instinct involved; there's a lot that goes with knowing the company, knowing its product, and knowing its plans. I have sensed from years of experience in this field that if you know your client, you get a pretty good feel of whether they are being too short or too long on their depreciation lives.

It's a very judgmental area and I don't think it's possible to reduce it to any precise formula.

Mr. Gellein: I was going to ask a little different sort of question of George and Norm. It will take a long time to get to the North Star, I suspect.

Mr. Catlett: You may never get there.

Mr. Gellein: My question really is this, George, that this becomes a very long-range goal and, of course, generations of investors and other users may come and go before we attain those long-range goals. Do you have any views that you could express now that would help us set the midrange goals and the short-range goals within that framework?

Mr. Catlett: Your question raises an important point. I want to comment on it and perhaps Norm will too.

We aren't talking about shortrange, middlerange, or longrange. When you put a compass on the North Star, you do not have degrees of direction. What we need to decide is where we want to go and this goal may never be reached in all respects, but we need a guide for tomorrow, next week, and next month, on every decision we make.

And the point is, as we take our steps, with tomorrow being the first step, this guide would be applied as the accounting profession addresses itself to problems. If we've decided where we want to go, then the question is which of the alternative solutions to problems best goes in the right direction. This will apply everyday and to every decision.

That is the point. It is not a question of goals with various ranges.

As far as I am concerned, the main justification for the equity method of accounting, which is not what APB Opinion 18 says, is that it is a step closer to value accounting. We have taken that step because it's on a controlled basis. You can audit the numbers fairly well; but the answer is closer to value than cost is. And you can say the same about a lot of other possible changes.

If you can agree on goals of this type—whether it is the goal we suggest or some other goal—then guides are available for every single decision. We don't mean a big framework of accounting theory; there may be only four or five objectives. If you have established those and agreed on them, then you say: Which one of the four alternatives in solving an accounting problem best meets the objectives? That will not be so difficult to decide. That settles it, and you don't spend two or three years arguing about it.

Chairman Trueblood: So the short-range, long-range dichotomy comes more on the implementation side than on the statement of goals or objectives.

Mr. Catlett: That is correct, and the objectives guide every step.

Mr. Olson: I think it could affect the individual decisions, and I would be opposed to designating any period of transition. I think when you are talking goals and objectives, the profession, in particular, is always in a state of transition.

Mr. Weston: I was interested in your exclusion, basically, from your definition of economic resources of many intangibles. If your goal is to measure wealth of entities and your three criteria are utility, scarcity, and exchangeability, I guess it's the latter one which causes the problem. Did you eliminate things like trade names and goodwill and some of the things that make some of our large corporations very valuable in the sense of economic wealth these days? Did you eliminate those because of the difficulty of measurement?

Mr. Olson: Yes, in general, Frank. The concept of exchangeability and separability is a difficult one and the distinctions will be difficult; I don't know that you can say that R&D should all be treated alike. There are various types, and I think there could be different answers under different circumstances if we want to get into that.

Basically, as I said or tried to say, the intangible attributes about which you really cannot provide information regarding value in the balance sheet may be more valuable than the economic resources in which there can be viable equity, and which are more or less bankable and have some meaning in the balance sheet.

The point is that we believe the only information we can provide the investor and other users about the elements of wealth that do not meet our standards of the economic resource is to provide him the best possible information about earnings. Earnings and profits are what indicate the existence of those attributes.

Then it becomes the investor's function to place a value on those when he values the business as a whole in the marketplace. This is why we feel it's important not to interject those into the balance sheet because we don't believe you can really convey any meaningful information on the cost basis, or any other basis, regarding their value.

Now, that may also be true of some economic resources too, at times.

Mr. Catlett: Another way of saying that, Frank, is that the cost of many of these things has nothing to do with the value, as you know. There's no relationship between cost and value when you get into the intangible area. You might spend a thousand dollars and find something worth a million dollars.

As you know, the marketing organization, the research division, the management ability, and that type of thing, may be most valuable aspects of a company, but you can't put dollar signs on them.

Mr. Weston: Well, I'm a little disturbed, I guess, conceptually. Reed's plant which is turning out widgets at a great profit rate may be a terrible plant, overvalued and very inefficient, and the reason they are making money is because they have some very valuable intangibles which aren't on the balance sheet; your financial statements, therefore, not only don't show the proper wealth of the entity, they are misleading in at least two major areas.

Mr. Olson: We feel that the profits speak for themselves with the investor, Frank, and tell the investor about the existence of the intangibles.

Mr. Weston: I know, but your articulated statement, the balance sheet, shows assets that aren't contributing to those earnings and does not show the principal assets which contribute to them.

Mr. Catlett: Yes, but I would ask you what you would do, because the cost has absolutely nothing to do with the value of what you are talking about. Are you considering capitalizing the market value of the stock and putting that amount on the balance sheet?

Mr. Weston: Oh, no. I'm saying that each of the economic resources of an entity, if you go to the value route, should be in the balance sheet. To pick out the ones that are exchangeable or separable, as your idea does, may get an entirely misleading and wrong answer which supports earnings with values that aren't there and doesn't show the real values that are there.

Mr. Catlett: Yes, but the value, Frank, of goodwill, management research, marketing, and such items, has nothing to do with the cost.

Mr. Weston: Exactly!

Mr. Catlett: . . . and the only way you could record such value would be to capitalize the earnings and put the market value of the stock on the balance sheet and everybody would show a normal rate of return; that's the circular reasoning that Norm talked about, which couldn't serve anybody.

Mr. Weston: But that is, in fact, showing the wealth of that entity which I thought was your primary goal.

Mr. Catlett: No, it is not our goal, because we are not trying to equate the balance sheet with the market value of the stock.

Mr. Weston: No. I know.

Mr. Catlett: And otherwise, there's no way of getting it in the balance sheet unless you put the market value of the stock in.

Mr. Weston: The market value of the stock is something else. That's in the marketplace. But the assets and the wealth of the entity do include these intangibles which you are excluding from the balance sheet.

Mr. Catlett: We think they have no place there.

Mr. Weston: The trade name, the proprietary drug abilities, the contracts with executives, and so on, are, in fact, resources; they are wealth. But they wouldn't be in the balance sheet, as I gather your value proposal.

Mr. Catlett: Right. We don't think they have any place there. They are valuable. In fact, in a company like IBM they may be more valuable than what is in the balance sheet; but we don't think it's the purpose of financial statements to capitalize that.

Mr. Weston: I'm troubled by the approach that you have selected—relatively speaking, to value the resources is easy. You say those will be in the balance sheet; the difficult ones won't. And my point is that you end up with a hodgepodge, which maybe is really meaningless.

Chairman Trueblood: I think this exchange pretty largely takes care of one of the questions from the floor and we must finish up and have a short break here. The same point was made from the floor, that if cost is a reasonable proxy or an initial indication of value in the case of fixed assets, why is it not in the case of intangibles?

But it seems to me from your earlier presentation that this leads into another question from the floor, which in effect says: Are you stating that where the degree of subjectivity and uncertainty is large, we must rely on extended disclosure as in the manner of listing of intangibles, and so on? Is that your suggestion?

Mr. Olson: I think that's partly right. More precisely, I would say we have tried to define assets, using the term "economic resources," as those which do possess some value not completely dependent on the fortunes of the particular company involved. But we would add that there may be some items that meet the test of an economic resource—and we discuss this some in our study—for which just out of sheer immeasurability, no useful information as to value, whether on cost or any other basis, can be conveyed in the balance sheet. I think with those elements of wealth, all accountants can do is provide information on profits and then the investor places a value on them.

Getting back to your point just briefly, Frank, take the illustration of a public accounting firm; many of us are familiar with them. I suppose that, certainly, the real wealth of Arthur Young or Arthur Andersen has to be in the competence of its people. But isn't it the translation of the competence of its people into assets that constitutes the earnings process? And could you really help a banker or a partner in a firm by trying to reflect what the costs of recruiting and training are in the balance sheet and then amortize this over some personnel turnover figure?

I think partners in the firm and bankers would take it off the balance sheet to get at the facts. The profits, or the success, or the growth of the firm speaks for the wealth of its people, and I don't think there is any other way for accountants to convey that information.

Chairman Trueblood: Thank you very much, Norm and George. We do look forward very much to your presentation in the next several weeks, and I know it will be extremely helpful.

Trustees: Stewards of a commitment and guardians of the mission

An article published by
Lutheran General Hospital,
Park Ridge, Illinois, August 1972—Olson

A philosophy of the Chairman of the Board of Trustees relating to human ecology. "The magnitude of our obligation to deliver the type of healing to which we are committed is awesome."

THE MANDATED RESPONSIBILITY from the church to the Board of Trustees is to serve people on behalf of the church. In line with this responsibility, the trustees were the originators of a commitment—a personal, collective dedication. That commitment is to a more profound type of healing contemplated by what we have chosen to call "Human Ecology"—a term adopted 10 years before the word "ecology" became popularized in today's concern over environmental disruptions.

As stewards of this commitment, the trustees have responsibilities for its adequate implementation. In simplest terms, they do this through policy decisions and through responsible delegation of executive authority to the Office of the President.

Selection of trustees

The American Lutheran Church exercises ultimate control of the hospital through its Lutheran Institute of Human Ecology, which has final authority in the selection of trustees. The selection is made from the recommendations of others, including those of the Board of Trustees of the hospital implemented through its nominating committee. Recommendations for, and selection of, trustees are made strictly without prejudice or bias by reason of sex, ethnic origin, financial circumstances or other such considerations. Nor does religious affiliation enter into the selection process except as necessary to satisfy charter requirements for a minimum number of Lutheran members.

In making recommendations for members on its Board, the trustees have adopted three criteria. First, the potential Board member should have an area of competence with which he or she can make a specific contribution to the hospital. It is only in this way that the tasks associated with our commitment can be performed effectively.

Second, there must be a genuine interest on the part of the person considered for Board membership in what the hospital is doing and in its approach to healing. If a trustee is truly interested, his contribution is potentially immeasurable. If he is not, it is simply another assignment for him that becomes a big chore that often creates a burden on others.

Third, without regard to particular religious affiliation, a person must have a deep, underlying religious philosophy and a concern over the issues of ethics, justice, human well-being and human suffering.

Board members are individually responsible to the church and to the total community that the hospital serves. Each must bring a special competence but should not consider himself as representing a particular group or the views of a special constituency.

Board members contribute of their time and competence without pay. They must jealously guard against becoming involved in any potential conflict-of-interest situation and refrain from voting where conflicts obviously exist.

Others serve to provide invaluable guidance to the deliberations and decision-making of the trustees. The president of the Medical Staff, as well as the presidents of the Service League and Men's Association, together with the members of the Office of the President, all serve as advisory trustees and participate in deliberations of the Board.

In addition, most Board committees include as full voting members representatives from the medical staff in order to achieve maximum benefit from their specialized knowledge and competence as well as to provide a vehicle for more effective communication between the Board and the physicians.

Restructuring and reorganization

Lutheran General has become a very large and complex institution. It has almost 300 physicians on its medical staff, over 2,200 employees and an average census of almost 600 patients each day. In addition, there are a large number of other persons with whom the Board and management of the hospital deal, including 950 members of the Service League, 345 members of the Men's Association and up to 150 young Candystripers. By adding the fact that each patient will have the deep personal concern of family and friends while in the hospital, the magnitude and depth of the problems and opportunities in personal relationships can be appreciated.

Management of an organization involving this number of people, together with the growing sophistication and complexity of facilities resulting from the advancement of medical technology and the complex financing involving a variety of governmental and private third-party payers, requires executive ability and organizational strength equal to that required in the most complex of corporate business enterprises.

About two years ago, in recognition of this growth in size and complexity, the Board of Trustees undertook a restructuring and reorganization of its own activities as well as a strengthening of the executive organization of the hospital. A principal thrust of this effort was to create stronger and broader on-the-spot executive capability through the creation of an Office of the President, consisting of the president as the chief executive officer and two executive vice presidents. This reorganization also included a culmination of the effort started earlier of appointment of paid medical department heads with designated time to discharge this responsibility—a responsibility that it would be unrealistic to expect from a strictly voluntary staff at this stage of the hospital's development.

At the same time an attempt was made to elevate the Board's own operations to that of policy determination and to channel its implementary responsibilities strictly through the Office of the President. It is no longer realistic to expect that the function of a hospital can be discharged with executive responsibilities residing in the officers of the Board who may have full-time jobs as bakers or bankers, household or business executives, pastors or professors, or in other vocations.

The terms of Board members were changed from six-year terms to three-year terms with a maximum limit of four consecutive terms. The terms of the chairman and vice chairman of the Board were limited to three consecutive one-year terms in order to assure a continuing introduction of fresh philosophy to the leadership of the Board. Such limitations are practical when the continuity of executive management is with paid employees rather than volunteer Board members.

Results of restructuring and reorganization

It is my view that the reorganization and restructuring have given us the basis for solid progress in the future. The hospital corporation is financially sound. The working relationship and the communication between Board, management and medical staff have been greatly improved. Overall room rates and other hospital charges have been stabilized with no increases over a period of more than 18 months of significant general inflation going back to February of 1971. A department has been created that is concerned strictly with efficiency and productivity. A new and thorough-going budgeting procedure has been installed that embraces a responsibility-type of accounting so that all levels of management and administration throughout the hospital participate in the budgeting process.

While the effort may have temporarily delayed the institution of new programs, including those of brick and mortar, I believe that the restructuring and reorganization were absolutely essential. It is only as these basic management and operational matters are taken care of and are in good order that the hospital can fulfill its goals. The Board makes no apology for doing its utmost to maximize the productivity and efficiency of all its operations and to create a sound financial picture. This is a stewardship responsibility not only to the church but to the community and every patient of the hospital, all of whom are concerned with the effectiveness and the rising costs of health care. The trustees do not intend to lessen the intensity of their efforts in this direction. The personal discipline that is required on the part of everyone to make optimum use of hospital facilities and of each person's time surely will not lessen the quality of patient care—rather, that discipline will tend to permeate and enhance the quality of care.

The hospital's mission and opportunity

In a sense we have "put it all together" these first 12 years. Someone has asked: "Will success spoil Lutheran General Hospital?" In an eloquent statement, Dr. Norstad, vice president of the hospital, has described our condition as a "crisis in opportunity."

The trustees are continuously reminded that every action on the part of a department head or an employee, be he or she a medical professional, dietary worker or maintenance engineer; every implementary decision by the Office of the President; every medical procedure by a physician; every action by a volunteer; every policy decision by the Board must focus on one central objective—the best interests of the patient, whether he be hospitalized or served on an outpatient basis. No decision, no action on the part of anyone connected with the hospital, be he employee, member of the Medical Staff, Service League, Men's Association or Board of Trustees, can ever be tolerated unless it serves this objective.

But ours is a more profound concept of healing. We are performers of a revised theology. The philosophy at Lutheran General is that we treat individual human beings—not individual diseases or individual broken bones—but the total person. This is the concept we have labeled Human Ecology.

We believe there is an essential unity about a healthy, happy man. He respects himself; he loves and has a sense of oneness with his fellowmen; he feels as one with his God and is in tune with the rhythm of nature; he adopts one central philosophy of living for all his actions whether at home, at work or at play. He is not three persons, body, mind and soul; he is all three of these in one integrated unit.

This philosophy views much illness as a disruption of this essential unity—as brokenness, reflecting man's personal fragmentation or his disassociation from others, from his family or from nature. It is within this basic belief that at Lutheran General we feel a major emphasis in healing must be in curing the brokenness and fragmentation of life. While the specialty of those serving the patient may cause them to concentrate on differing aspects of illness—the surgeon on the physical aspects; the psychiatrist on the emotional; the clergyman on the spirtual; and the social worker on social maladjustments—there is and should be an indivisibility to these disciplines. The know-how in all fields must blend and be brought to bear in the interests of individual persons.

Everyone in the hospital, regardless of his field of activity, who is involved or comes in contact with the patient or his family in any manner, must continuously remember this aspect. The careless remark of a trustee in an elevator or of a cleaning lady in a patient's room may undo weeks of effort of physician and pastor. Contrarily, a demonstration of sincere concern and interest on the part of a receptionist in the problems of a family visiting a loved one who is ill in the hospital can greatly augment the healing process. The reassuring smile of a nurse, Candystriper, or Service League volunteer may restore much-needed hope, but an indifferent attitude on the part of someone else may heighten anxiety with its undesirable effects.

Yesterday's cardiac victim in Room 901 and yesterday's gall bladder case in Room 602 are not the same as today's—regardless of the similarity of the physical manifestations of their illnesses. Each illness is a highly personal phenomenon. Emotional and spirtual circumstances, problems of family relationships and reactions to illness and many other factors all combine to make every illness unique when viewed under our concept as affecting the total person and his environment. Thus, attention to patients must never become routine or calloused regardless of the repetitive nature of certain types of medical diagnoses. There is more to the nightly back rub than cleanliness. Each illness must be treated in an intensely human way under our concept of healing, and all of us who are involved with the hospital must constantly remind ourselves of this fact. Nor are efficiency and productivity incompatible with this humanness.

A look toward the future

The trustees must exert every effort to assure that the concept of Human Ecology saturates every activity in the hospital. But the concept must become an even more constructive and positive one. Our mission extends beyond the treatment of illness and the healing of brokenness. It must become an instrument for keeping people healthy and keeping them out of the hospital. Under a much earlier social scheme the medicine man got paid as long as his patient stayed well. While I do not propose an impractical reinstitution of such a system, it nevertheless is a sobering reminder of what our primary mission should be.

Thus, in plans for the future, the hospital must not be regarded as simply an institution where people come to be healed when they are sick, or as a place to die. Services in these areas will always be important, but our emphasis must be increasingly turned in the direction of reducing the need for hospital care and toward providing services that will help people stay healthy and, when they become sick, to maximize care without hospitalization. In this connection, the $6 million program currently under way in expansion of the hospital's facilities will add only a handful of hospital beds. The thrust of the program is to create additional space and capability of serving people on an outpatient basis.

More importantly, the trustees must encourage and open the door to a greater involvement of the church, its pastors and its congregations in the preservation of health and in the care of the sick. While the funding of hospital institutions these days may come in large measure from outside the church, and while paid professional personnel may, to some extent, have displaced some services previously provided by certain religious orders, the church should not regard itself as having no significant place in health care. In the profound type of healing and health care that is envisaged at Lutheran General, the church should be deeply involved.

In all too many cases, the spiritual and moral problems that concern the church come to focus in the mangled bodies resulting from drunken driving, in the horror and agony of the drug addict, and in the terrible anguish of severe mental depression. The service and competence that physicians, nurses, pastors, social workers and others bring to the alleviation of such suffering are miraculous. Yet the church itself must get intimately involved with the persons in these professions, since their effectiveness in dealing with the human weaknesses and frailties that underlie so much disease and illness can be enhanced by the counsel and guidance of the church.

The church's guidance is also needed in wrestling with the baffling ethical questions that pervade health care from birth to death, including such crucial modern-day problems as those of abortion, "death with dignity" and transplants. The problems of ethics in health care are further escalated as medical know-how and technology search ever deeper into the mysteries of life's processes.

But the biggest search is the one in which the church is involved and where progress is probably agonizingly slow for the majority of us. And it is this search, the search for meaning in life, that will contribute in more than any other way to healing and to the maintenance of good health. For as a person finds meaning and purpose in his life, he acquires the essential unity of which I spoke earlier. The result is a deep desire and zest for life from which flow the energies for recovery from much illness and for the maintenance of good health. This is the church's domain and nowhere is the question of life's meaning asked more clearly and poignantly than in the hospital room, and in no place is there a greater opportunity to present satisfying answers.

In all of these matters I speak as neither physician nor theologian but strictly as a layman. Yet the experiences of life, including that of serious and distressing personal and family illness, convince me beyond all doubt that we have the right idea. Its implementation may be extraordinarily difficult at times and can never be perfect. But progress will be made toward the goal as the concept of Human Ecology becomes a pervasive attitude or state of mind in all our contacts and relationships with patients and their families and with one another.

We have the resources. We have a medical staff second to none. We have the organization. We have the competence. We have been blessed beyond our biggest dreams. The magnitude of our obligation to deliver the type of healing to which we are committed is awesome. Our God is waiting.

Postscript

Some observations about developments in the accounting profession, November 1972—Catlett

The accounting profession has a tremendous opportunity to serve the business community and the public if it has the determination, ability and foresight to meet the challenges of the future.

THE LAST TWENTY-FIVE years have been a dynamic and revolutionary period in all walks of life. During these years, atomic power, missiles, electronic computers, jet airplanes, color television and other scientific marvels have become commonplace. A vast expansion of public ownership has accompanied the rapid growth of business enterprises, and many far-reaching social and economic developments have occurred.

The accounting profession has been in an excellent position to play an important role not only in reporting independently upon the financial statements of business enterprises but also in improving the techniques and systems for the accumulation of financial and accounting data. These requirements, along with the increasing complexity of the income tax laws and regulations, have created an unprecedented demand for the services of accountants.

This has been a most interesting time in the accounting profession. I have tried to sort out a few matters that seem to be of some significance, and my observations and impressions on those matters are summarized in the comments that follow.

Standards for financial accounting and reporting

AICPA committees and boards — The subject that has had the most publicity and has created the greatest controversy is standards for financial accounting and reporting. The AICPA's Committee on Accounting Procedure was superseded in 1959 by the Accounting Principles Board, which in turn is now being superseded by the Financial Accounting Standards Board (located in the Financial Accounting Foundation). Each change has represented a new type of organization with a considerable increase in expenditures. Yet, the success of such ventures is dependent upon much more than organization or funds. A change in scenery does not necessarily change the characters.

Committees have limitations on what they can do effectively, and the accomplishments usually are in inverse proportion to the size of the committee. If the future of the accounting profession were to be dependent upon the work of committees, we would indeed be in a deplorable situation. Part of the difficulties that have been encountered may have arisen because the profession has left too many important matters to committees.

One of the questions relating to the future is—from where is the leadership in the profession going to come? I have been a member of the AICPA Council and of various boards and committees, and I have observed the operations of many others of which my partners have been members. The results are generally disappointing. The AICPA, because of its size and the lack of cohesiveness of its membership, will follow much more than it will lead—and thus it will generally continue to be in the position of "too little and too late."

Leadership will come principally from individuals (and perhaps from accounting firms in some instances) and not from professional groups or committees. The foresight to see what is needed, and the ability to do something about it, results in timely progress. Sensitivity to changes in public attitudes on matters such as independence and conflicts of interest is required. Acting in a decisive and responsible manner to anticipate how services can be improved is obviously much more desirable than reacting to criticism and conditions of crisis. Yet, a leadership role is always a difficult one; in this respect the accounting profession is not unique.

Who is responsible for standards?—The confusion that exists concerning the responsibility for standards is monumental. The accounting profession has tried, with only mediocre success, to take the lead. Managements have emphasized their responsibility for the preparation of financial statements and have objected to the AICPA appointing itself as the sole group to promulgate standards. Independent public accountants have considered that they have personal responsibilities when issuing their reports. The New York Stock Exchange has been showing an increasing interest. The SEC has always been influential in this area, either directly or behind the scenes. Many other Federal and state regulatory agencies have statutory authority relating to financial accounting and reporting of certain industries.

These responsibilities have not been sorted out very well on an authoritative basis. The Report of the Study on Establishment of Accounting Principles (March 1972) does analyze this situation to some extent. That report seems to contain a vague hope that everyone in the accounting profession, the business community and governmental agencies will cooperate and support the recommended mechanism because of the possibility that an alternative approach might be worse. Whether this hope will become a reality remains to be seen.

Relationship between the AICPA and SEC—A curious relationship has existed for the last forty years between the AICPA and the SEC. The SEC, since its inception, has consistently maintained a public posture of supporting the efforts of AICPA committees and boards to establish standards for financial accounting and reporting. The SEC has probably adopted this position for two reasons: first, the belief that the accounting profession is better equipped to handle this task; and second, and perhaps more important, the SEC can exert considerable influence on a group such as the APB and still avoid much of the "pressure" and "heat," as well as political overtones, that might be generated by pronouncements on controversial subjects.

In practice, the AICPA and the SEC have had an informal alliance and each has needed the other. The accounting profession has not been strong enough in its own right to enforce controversial pronouncements without the statutory enforcement powers of the SEC. In other words, a requirement issued by the APB would be difficult for CPAs to enforce if the SEC did not support the requirement, as in the case of the investment credit. The SEC has been in a position of having a veto power over the Opinions of the APB, and this veto power has been used from time to time. As an example, the SEC sent word to the APB when accounting for business combinations was under consideration that any Opinion relating to goodwill that did not contain a requirement for the mandatory amortization of goodwill would not be acceptable to the SEC. On the other hand, the SEC has accepted some APB Opinions without any serious questions.

Whether this relationship, which generally has been supported by the Chief Accountant of the SEC over the years, can be continued indefinitely is not known. The trend toward more governmental control of business may inevitably be extended in this area. Much may depend upon the philosophy of the Chairman of the Commission and the Chief Accountant, both of whom are new appointments from time to time. Also, how well the new FASB performs its functions will be a factor.

Legal basis for establishment of standards—The Report of the Study on Establishment of Accounting Principles intentionally deemphasized the legal basis for establishing standards. A basic question exists concerning whether any organization in a private association or foundation has a right to establish accounting standards that have such a significant impact on the business community and the public. The question, of course, that goes along with this is the right of appeal with respect to such standards.

Some lawyers have believed that the courts might look favorably upon the right of a professional organization to establish accounting standards if this is done by competent persons, under reasonable procedures, and in good faith. The new FASB is not directly oriented to a professional organization as much as was the APB, and the additional influence given to organizations other than the AICPA with respect to the FASB could weaken the professional nature of the endeavor.

On the other hand, the AICPA undoubtedly has a clear right to establish standards relating to auditing procedures.

Objectives of financial statements—Since the subject of objectives of financial statements is covered elsewhere in this book, that discussion will not be duplicated here. However, I would like to review briefly my experiences on this matter in the APB.

Shortly after I became a member of the APB in 1965, I stated that: The APB had let six years go by without establishing any objectives; Accounting Research Studies Nos. 1 and 3 relating to basic postulates and broad accounting principles had been ignored by the APB; Accounting Research Study No. 7, "Inventory of Generally Accepted Accounting Principles for Business Enterprises," had been completed; and objectives should be given a high priority to furnish much needed guidelines for the APB. A subcommittee of the APB was then appointed to consider this matter.

Insofar as this project was concerned, the next five years represented a most frustrating experience for me. The APB, as a whole, absolutely refused to deal with objectives and insisted on rehashing the past; the reason given was that it was necessary to record "what is" before considering "what ought to be." I contended that everyone knew what was going on, and this had been well documented in Accounting Research Study No. 7. I emphasized that the time of the APB members could much better be spent on trying to agree on a few objectives. About one hundred hours were devoted to this project in full APB meetings, and thousands of hours were spent by APB members and AICPA staff. The result was the issuance in 1970 of Statement No. 4, "Basic Concepts and Accounting Principles Underlying Financial Statements of Business Enterprises." This document is nothing but a rationalization of existing customs and an attempt to establish concepts to support present practices. When I announced in an APB meeting my formal dissent to this document, several of the APB members looked on me as some sort of traitor to the cause.*

A question could be raised about why there was so little real enthusiasm in the APB to deal with objectives, and why, at at least in my view, five years of vital time were wasted. Some accountants apparently believe that the task is too difficult to undertake. My answer to that always has been: "If we cannot establish what it is that we are trying to do in the issuance of financial statements, then we should all quit and go home."

The view apparently is held by some people that progress in accounting can be made only by solving each individual problem with a utilitarian approach and that these solutions will form a basis for concepts that will then evolve. All of my experience indicates that the right kind of progress in accounting will never be made by trying to solve problems within an existing framework of customs that caused the problems in the first place. I firmly believe it is necessary to decide what we are trying to accomplish, and then determine how best to achieve that goal.

One of the real reasons that some accountants do not want effective objectives is that such objectives might lead to conclusions that those accountants have already decided (for one reason or another) they do not want.

In any event, the lack of objectives is one of the most important reasons for the demise of the APB. I certainly hope that the Accounting Objectives Study Group is productive in its work and that the FASB does not make the same mistake as the APB in this regard.

The uniformity issue—While uniformity in accounting has been discussed and written about for many years, it was a particularly controversial subject in the 1960's. The debate was characterized by such words as "uniformity versus flexibility" and "rules versus judgment." This debate became so heated that most people forgot what the argument was all about, and the real issues almost became lost in the barrage of accusations and innuendos.

---

*The wording of my dissent to Statement No. 4 is quoted below because it describes in more detail my belief that the APB had failed to do what was so much needed:

> George R. Catlett dissents to this Statement because in his view it fails to provide what purports to be "a basis for guiding the future development of financial accounting." He believes that guidelines for the future are urgently required, but the Accounting Principles Board is looking backward to what has occurred rather than forward to what is needed. As a result, the concepts and principles set forth in this Statement are based upon ineffective foundations, along the lines of the following: (1) vague generalizations which are noncontroversial but serve no useful purpose; (2) circular reasoning, with undefined terms being defined by other undefined terms, such as the description of assets and liabilities as those items "recognized and measured in conformity with generally accepted accounting principles"; and (3) reverse logic, by summarizing a wide variety of customs and practices, many of which need to be changed and improved, and then rationalizing back to principles that presumably support what now exists. The Board in this Statement is establishing a new acceptability on behalf of the accounting profession for many accounting practices which have not previously been covered by pronouncements of the Board and which have not been studied or even seriously considered by the Board. Mr. Catlett also believes that this Statement—by providing a conceptual basis for, and by giving authoritative status to, current accounting practices—will represent an unfortunate deterrent to the achievement of improvements in practice. Thus, rather than setting forth effective guidelines for progress, this Statement creates a significant roadblock which will seriously impede the efforts of the business community and the accounting profession to establish sound principles for financial accounting and reporting.

Those who supported uniformity really did not want a detailed rule book or a mandatory chart of accounts, as alleged by their opponents. On the other hand, those who preferred flexibility did not want complete freedom for everyone to do as he might choose. This entire debate was diversionary and accomplished little in achieving progress.

What is obviously required are uniform objectives and basic concepts oriented to what is needed, and room for judgment in applying the resulting standards and criteria to the vast variety of circumstances. Here again, the time wasted in the debate about uniformity could better have been spent in establishing objectives.

Accounting for business combinations and goodwill

Several of the articles and addresses in this book discuss the accounting for business combinations and goodwill. Norman Olson and I spent a great deal of time in studying this particular area of accounting during the years 1964-1968 when we were preparing Accounting Research Study No. 10, "Accounting for Goodwill," and when we were involved from a policy standpoint in hundreds of actual cases of business combinations among the clients of our firm. Also, I was a member of the APB during the entire time that this matter was under consideration by the APB.

Events that occurred both inside and outside the APB which led up to Opinions No. 16 and No. 17 are unbelievable in many respects and are hardly a credit to the accounting profession. However, I will comment only briefly in this regard. Much of the discussion in the APB preceding the issuance of earlier Opinions had indicated to me a great need for agreement on objectives; and, I was almost certain that the APB could not deal successfully with the accounting for business combinations and goodwill without first reaching agreement on some objectives and basic concepts relating to financial statements. I had a feeling that the APB, by avoiding the matter of basic concepts, was going to commit suicide, and in my view that is exactly what it proceeded to do.

Not only are Opinions No. 16 and No. 17 proving to be a failure as could easily be predicted, but the events leading up to their adoption have resulted in the demise of the APB.

I dissented to Opinion No. 17 and approved Opinion No. 16, because only by this approval (which permitted a two-thirds vote on that Opinion) would either Opinion have been issued. The APB had agreed that since the two Opinions were so closely related and had resulted from one proposed Opinion being divided into two Opinions, neither Opinion would be issued unless both were issued. The SEC was threatening, in the absence of these Opinions, to move in and issue regulations in this area. The dilemma for me was a particularly difficult one, because I believed that the APB was doomed either way. It had failed to deal with this problem in an effective manner. Whether my decision to vote for Opinion No. 16, with all of its deficiencies, benefited the accounting profession, the business community and the public in the long run is difficult to evaluate even now, because we do not know what the alternative would have been. What has occurred can now be considered in retrospect, and the lessons to be learned, at least to me, seem to be clear.

Earnings per share

Many investors and analysts appear to view earnings per share as the ultimate in judging corporate performance. "EPS" has become the name of the game in the view of many persons. During the 1960's, with increasing price levels, with rising stock market prices, and with the rapid expansion of so-called "conglomerate" companies by means of business combinations, the primary score-keeping was done on the basis of earnings per share.

The accounting profession for many years had taken the position that earnings per share represented an oversimplification of the operating results of a company. Therefore, any particular responsibility for the manner in which earnings per share were computed was generally avoided insofar as possible by most independent public accountants.

However, in the 1960's, a major merger movement was fueled by various types of securities (convertible and participating preferred stocks of all kinds, with unusual and imaginative provisions, and convertible debentures and warrants) being issued in the acquisition of other companies. The post-merger earnings per share—when pooling-of-interests accounting was used and only outstanding common shares were related to earnings to compute earnings per share—increased dramatically and constantly in many companies, and stock market prices followed.

The APB dabbled with a new concept of "residual securities" in Opinion No. 9 when the SEC was insistent that the "problem" which was obviously developing be dealt with. That Opinion was generally ineffective in this regard. The SEC threatened to take direct action and put pressure on the APB to reconsider the matter. The result was APB Opinion No. 15, which represented a mass of detailed rules and regulations to attempt to control the computation of earnings per share. A complex capitalization situation, as existed in many companies, could not successfully be converted into a few simple amounts. In any event, no recognizable accounting principles were involved, particularly when the APB reached the curious conclusion that the statistical rules for earnings per share did not apply to the accounting and the financial statements.

Thus, the APB, with no objectives and basic concepts to relate to, dug a deeper hole with Opinion No. 15 and then proceeded to fall into the hole with Opinions No. 16 and No. 17.

Cost Accounting Standards Board

The establishment of the Cost Accounting Standards Board under a Federal law enacted in 1970 was somewhat of a shock to the accounting profession. However, the AICPA and other professional organizations had done little on an authoritative basis to determine standards as they might relate to cost accounting, and the APB had given primary attention to other aspects of accounting.

The CASB could prove to be significant in two respects. Its pronouncements may have far-reaching effects on accounting generally and it could be the forerunner of a similar type of board in the Federal government relating to financial accounting.

This is a good example of the AICPA and other organizations leaving a void in an important area while spending their resources in part on less important matters.

Rules of professional conduct

The accounting profession has essentially been ineffective in the area of rules of professional conduct—both in the determination of the rules and in their enforcement. Fortunately, the importance of this area has not been great enough for the profession as a whole to have been adversely affected. However, the importance is now increasing.

With the need for true independence on the part of public accountants and the greater emphasis on avoidance of conflicts of interest on the part of everyone with a responsibility to the public, these subjects are now becoming much more important. In my view, independence is the most important issue facing the accounting profession. Independence pervades all aspects of public practice and is also involved in actions of professional committees dealing with matters affecting the public. The attest function, as we now know it, will not endure without public confidence in the independence of the persons performing this function.

Independent public accountants are in a unique position, because they are expected to be independent of the managements and boards of directors that hire and fire them and pay for their services. Such a position requires very special consideration, and accountants should deal with it in an honest and forthright manner. The real issues must be determined and faced squarely.

The AICPA, in behalf of the accounting profession, has not chosen to deal effectively with the problem of the scope of practice of public accounting firms as it might affect the question of independence. Some accounting firms appear to be adopting the attitude that they can perform any service that people can be hired to perform. This might involve executive recruiting, market surveys, and actuarial work as well as giving opinions on financial forecasts. The lack of foresight of some of the leaders of the profession in this regard, when viewed in the light of the possible jeopardy to the future of the profession, can only be characterized as appalling.

The AICPA has appeared to deal with the rules of professional conduct as a means of protecting practicing members. Perhaps this occurs because any other approach would not receive the necessary two-thirds vote for adoption of the rules. However, until these rules are oriented to the public welfare and the rights of others outside the profession, the rules will continue to be misdirected and largely ineffective.

Quality of auditing and reporting by independent public accountants

The quality of the auditing of, and reporting on, financial statements is a significant matter to the profession. There have been enough cases in the public press and in the courts where questions have been raised about the quality of the work to cause concern. Accounting firms are giving increasing attention to ways and means of better controlling the quality of their work. If the profession is to attain a level of confidence that we all hope for, improvement in the quality of performance should be one of the primary goals.

The "lawsuit explosion" that has occurred in recent years has been an unfortunate experience for those accountants involved and a worrisome development for everyone. The result of all of this has been to put the accounting profession in a defensive frame of mind. More of these cases have involved questions of auditing and disclosure than accounting principles. While the lawsuits are troublesome and costly, the end result may be of some benefit to the profession, because this may be the only way that the responsibilities of accountants (as well as of managements, directors, lawyers and underwriters) can be properly determined so that everyone knows what is expected of him.

The accounting profession and the accounting firms must adopt a positive attitude to establish what their rightful responsibilities are and do everything possible to live up to them.

While a question may exist regarding how standards for financial accounting and reporting should be promulgated, responsibility for standards of auditing and reporting by independent public accountants, and the quality of their performance, rests primarily with the accountants themselves under standards set by professional organizations.

Auditing procedures must be reevaluated in the light of current circumstances. New techniques are needed with the increased usage of more complex electronic computers. Statistical sampling and other new approaches will undoubtedly be used to a greater extent.

International aspects of accounting and auditing

The international developments in accounting and auditing are certain to be of considerable interest over the next several years. With the rapid increase of international business and the expansion of multinational companies, a new dimension is added to accounting and auditing problems as well as to the opportunities for service.

The status of the accounting profession varies considerably in the countries around the world—from almost no recognition in some countries to considerable recognition in other countries. This variation and the many differences in laws, customs and business practices and "nationalistic attitudes" result in barriers to common understanding and mutual cooperation.

While an international congress of accountants is held every four years, and other groups of accountants from various countries meet from time to time, little of any consequence has been done to develop international standards. Certain countries have common interests or similar legal and cultural backgrounds, such as the United Kingdom, Canada and Australia. Also, new international relationships are being formed, such as the European Economic Community. Thus, groups of countries may, for one reason or another, attempt to develop standards on an international basis.

One of the important developments over the next decade will be the increasing awareness of the need for accounting and auditing standards that are international in nature so that financing and many other aspects of international business will be facilitated. Our firm is dedicated to establishing such standards for our practice insofar as it is possible for us to do so.

A look to the future

A great opportunity available — Pessimists, as usual, are taking a negative view of the future prospects of the accounting profession. To me, the problems of the profession, some of which are discussed in this book, represent a tremendous challenge for service to the public, not only in the United States but in many countries around the world.

History is full of examples where a positive and constructive approach to the solution of problems has resulted in substantial progress. The accounting profession can benefit a great deal from the past if it will only study the lessons to be learned and then do something about benefiting from those lessons.

The question is whether the profession will successfully overcome the pressures that always seem to favor moving toward the lowest common denominator. Only strong leadership can overcome those pressures. The road upward is much more difficult, but more rewarding, than the road downward.

Avoidance of regulatory attitude—The accounting profession does not have a responsibility to regulate the operations of business enterprises. To the extent that such regulation is necessary, it is a function of the appropriate governmental agencies. As an illustration, the professional services performed by accountants should not become so intertwined with the regulatory activities of governmental agencies, such as the SEC, that the two blend together.

The accounting profession should be a strong link in the free enterprise system and, as such, it should be independent and responsive to what is needed to make that system strong. The profession should avoid the temptation to be a regulator, and it should not permit itself to be used by governmental agencies for regulatory purposes.

Professional approach—Public accounting is a profession and not a business. This distinction is more than mere words. Many of the problems we face today, including some of those I have discussed above, arise because the underlying concepts are not being established on a professional basis. If we are to have a profession, we must conduct ourselves like one and measure our conclusions against what is best for the public.

Not only the accounting profession as a whole but also the members of the profession individually can represent a powerful force for the right kind of progress if a truly professional attitude is adopted. The excitement of the challenges that face us should serve to increase our desire to achieve the satisfaction of a professional job well done.